AN ELECTORAL ATLAS OF EUROPE 1968–1981

Butterworths European Studies is a series of monographs providing authoritative treatments of major issues in modern European political economy.

General Editor

François Duchêne   Director, Sussex European Research Centre, University of Sussex, England

Consultant Editors

David Allen   Department of European Studies, University of Loughborough, England

Hedley Bull   Montague Burton Professor of International Relations, University of Oxford, England

Wolfgang Hager   Visiting Professor, European University Institute, Florence, Italy

Stanley Hoffmann   Professor of Government and Director, Centre for European Studies, Harvard University, USA

Hanns Maull   Journalist, Bavarian Radio, Munich. Formerly European Secretary, Trilateral Commission, Paris, France

Roger Morgan   Head of European Centre for Political Studies, Policy Studies Institute, London, England

Donald Puchala   Professor of Government and Dean, School of International Affairs, Columbia University, USA

Susan Strange   Professor of International Relations, London School of Economics, England

William Wallace   Director of Studies, Royal Institute of International Affairs, London, England

Already Published

Europe and World Energy by Hanns Maull
European Environmental Policy: East and West by Josef Füllenbach
Monetary Integration in Western Europe: EMU, EMS and Beyond by
D. C. Kruse
Europe Under Stress by Yao-su Hu
Pay Inequalities in the European Community by Christopher Saunders and
David Marsden
The Defence of Western Europe by B. Burrows and G. Edwards

Forthcoming Titles

European Political Cooperation
The Mediterranean Basin: Its Political Economy and Changing International
Relations
The EEC and the Developing Countries
European Integration and the Common Fisheries Policy
Political Forces in Spain, Greece and Portugal
Britain in the European Community

An Electoral Atlas of Europe 1968–1981

A Political Geographic Compendium including 76 maps

John Sallnow

BA, DipRuss, CertEd

and

Anna John

Cartography by
Sarah K. Webber

DipCart

Butterworth Scientific

London Boston Sydney Wellington Durban Toronto

First published 1982

© John Sallnow and Anna John 1982

British Library Cataloguing in Publication Data

Sallnow, John
    An electoral atlas of Europe 1968–1981.–
    (Butterworths European Studies)
    1. Voting–Europe
    I. Title   II. John, Anna
    324.94   JN94
    ISBN 0-408-10800-2

Photoset by Butterworths Litho Preparation Department
Printed by Robert Hartnoll Ltd, Bodmin, Cornwall

Preface and Acknowledgements

This atlas and political geographic compendium developed from a series of articles published by the authors in the *Geographical Magazine* in 1977 and 1978. The primary interest at that time was focused on the increased electoral support for the communist parties in southern Europe: the analysis included cartographic representation of general elections at the macro scale. In particular the example of the French general election of March 1978 was used; this was appropriate as the production and study of electoral patterns and cleavages is well developed in that country and major French newspapers publish maps of electoral support at all national and presidential elections.

The study presented here is at the macro scale so that it attempts to show the degree of electoral support in major administrative divisions of European countries. In most cases this has meant a simplification of the complex pattern of voting totals: however, a complete set of electoral statistics has been produced in the hope that this will provide a valuable reference function. It would of course be possible to produce several plates for each election in every country but space does not permit.

It is right and proper to acknowledge the names of the people who have helped this project: at the same time any errors that remain are those of the authors and all persons mentioned below are absolved from any blame resulting from inaccuracies.

Derek Weber, former editor of the *Geographical Magazine*, encouraged the initial venture into political geography by agreeing to publish a series of articles on southern Europe under the broad concept of the emergence of Eurocommunism. We thank him for giving us the opportunity to explore this idea. Bob Seal of Dawsons Publishers was responsible for forging the initial concept of a European atlas, while Peter Richardson of Butterworths has carried it forward, cajoling at the correct moments, sympathizing in the troughs and being suitably euphoric at the peaks of the creative cycle that afflicts authors.

We wish to acknowledge the help of Mary Bugles who translated material on Swedish elections and advised extensively on the politics of the Federal Republic of Germany. My colleague at Plymouth, Mark Wise, proved to be a great source of inspiration and helpful advice at all stages of the project. Leslie A. Sallnow helped with the acquisition of data from embassy press offices: much of this was collated and filed by C. J. Oxford and D. J. Lee whose help is gratefully acknowledged. Audrey Sallnow undertook the bulk of the typing and re-typing, and Seana Doyle assisted in the later stages.

Acknowledgement with thanks is due for the assistance of Carpress Ltd in providing material incorporated in *Figures 2.7* and *2.11*; thanks are due to Iain Bain, Editor of the *Geographical Magazine* for permission to reproduce the map of the French general election, published in that journal in September 1978, and now part of *Figure 4.5*.

Embassy staff too numerous to mention responded to the request for data: in particular the staff of the Icelandic Statistical Bureau in Reykjavik were very helpful, as were Mrs Gerda Poulsen and Mr Flemming Andre Larsen of the Royal Danish Embassy in London. Staff at two British libraries have assisted in great measure and although they are not known by name to the authors it is appropriate to make due acknowledgement of their help. The institutions are the British Library, Newspaper division at Colindale, London and the Statistics and Market Intelligence Library in London. Without their help this atlas would not have come to fruition.

Since compilation recent electoral history has produced items of note: thus it was felt appropriate to include statistics relating to the French presidential election of 1981. The authors would of course be pleased to learn of any inaccuracies contained in the text so that the records can be corrected.

J. S.
Plymouth Polytechnic

Contents

List of Figures

List of Tables

Western and Southern Europe: A Political Overview 1968–1980

Introduction

Figures 1.1 to *1.4* represent the political geographic pattern of Europe on four different dates. In 1968 (*Figure 1.1*) Greece, Portugal and Spain were still ruled by fascist regimes and did not have democratically elected governments. Coalition administrations dominated the political scene, being present in seven of the 15 countries. By 1973 (*Figure 1.2*), left or left minority governments were in power in six countries, notably Scandinavia and Central Europe. This trend was followed by the United Kingdom in February 1974 and Denmark in February of the following year. Western Europe's voters appeared to have had more confidence in parties of the left in the face of the so-called energy crisis of the winter of 1973/74. By 1977 (*Figure 1.3*), a balance had developed between left and left minority governments and those of the right and centre-right. This was due to the inclusion of the three Mediterranean countries in the arena of elected European governments, combined with an instability among the voters of Nordic Europe who questioned the desirability of the social democrats continuing in power in their countries.

By the end of the decade (*Figure 1.4*), a trend towards governments of the right had become more apparent. Electorates of Europe had turned their backs on socialism and nine of the 18 countries had right-wing based administrations. It remains to be seen whether the political philosophy of socialism will regain its electoral support during the decade of the 1980s: at the end of 1979 only Austria, Federal Germany and Norway had left-wing governments.

Parties of the centre-right

In the period under consideration, Western and Southern Europe shows a variegated pattern of success for the parties of the right and centre-right. The terms themselves pose something of a problem for the political scientist and political geographer: how right is right? Some governments, of which the 1981 Conservative administration in Britain is the best example, are quite happy to adopt the label 'right'. In fact, Margaret Thatcher and the government she

leads, formed after the British general election of May 1979, is possibly the only one in Western Europe that is happy with the label 'right'; other parties prefer the terms 'centre-right', 'Christian Democrat', 'moderate'. During the decade of the 1970s it was not fashionable to term the allegiance or orientation of a political party as right-wing. Following the election of a right-wing, conservative administration in the United States in November 1980, it seems possible that the term may again become fashionable. To some degree it represents the electorate's desire for a government that is seen to govern; the question of the type of political policies included in a party programme and how far these will be acceptable to an electorate as the basis for re-election remains another matter.

The centre-right governments of Mediterranean Europe between 1968 and 1980 have been successful in continuing in office. At the beginning of the period only France and Italy had democratic governments. They have been joined by Greece and Portugal in 1974 and Spain in 1975. The record shows that, with the exception of Portugal from 1974 to December 1979, right-wing governments have maintained their hold on power and, in general, socialists or social democrats have been excluded from direct power. However, after the Italian general election of 1979, the Italian social democrats and later the socialists returned to coalition governments as minor partners. The return of Portugal to a parliamentary system in 1974 heralded a five-year period during which the Portuguese Socialist Party (PSP) under Mario Soares appeared initially as the party of government. The PSP were soon eclipsed by the well-organized, disciplined but anti-Eurocommunist Portuguese Communist Party (PCP), led by Stalinist Alvaro Cunhal. During 1975 it seemed possible that the PCP might seize power, but the skilful tactics and strategy of Colonel, later General Ramalho Eanes, managed to prevent a communist takeover in this founder member of NATO. From 1976 to December 1977 the PSP under Mario Soares as Prime Minister ruled Portugal in a majority administration and from December 1977 to December 1979 in a minority government.

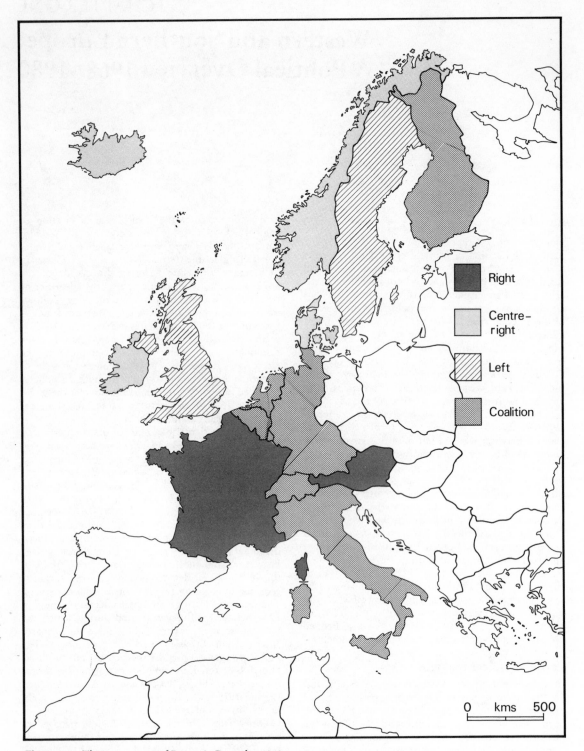

Figure 1.1 *The governments of Europe in December 1968*

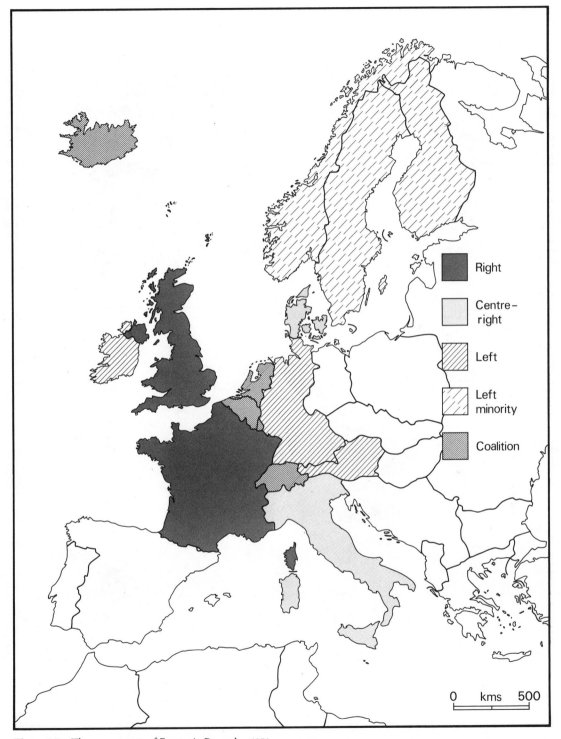

Figure 1.2 *The governments of Europe in December 1973*

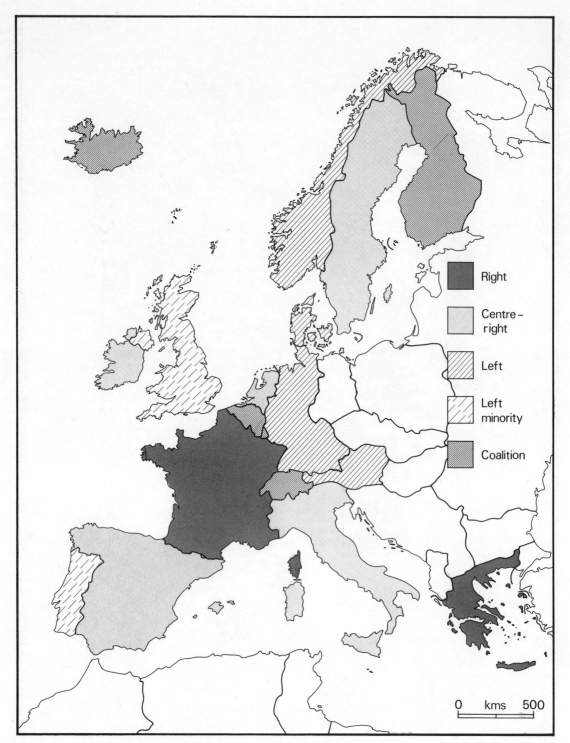

Figure 1.3 *The governments of Europe in December 1977*

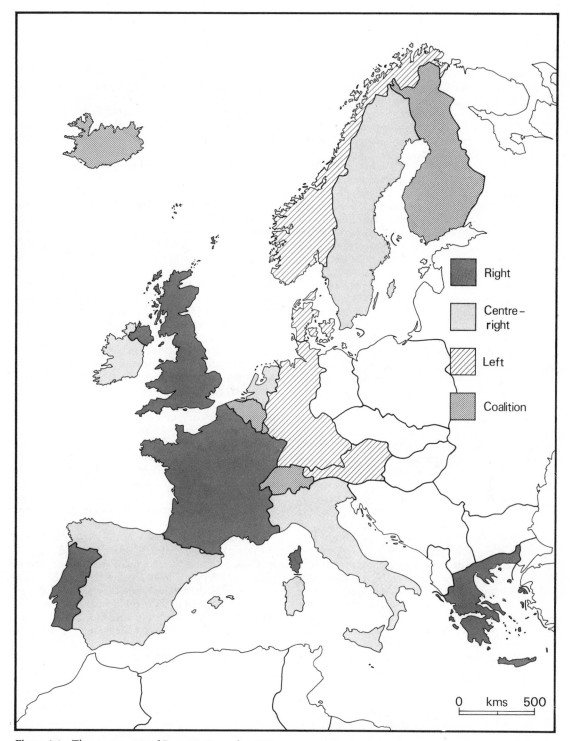

Figure 1.4 *The governments of Europe in December 1979*

However, at the December 1979 election, the centre-right Democratic Alliance (DA) consisting of the Centre Democrats, Social Democrats and Popular Monarchist Party, led by the late Francisco Sa Carneiro came to power and had its position confirmed by the October 1980 election increasing its share of the vote by 2.3% and raising its assembly total from 128 seats in 1979 to 136 seats in 1980.

For the other countries in Mediterranean Europe, the pattern is one of continued support for the centre-right in the old established democracies of France and Italy. In France the Gaullists, later transformed into the RPR (Rassemblement pour la République), and after the 1978 general election in association with the liberal centre, the UDF (Union pour la Démocratie Française) maintained their hold on the reins of power. This is indicative of the political nature of one of Europe's most traditional societies, where it is considered chic to be left-wing, but where few wish for radical change. In Italy the general elections are complemented by the addition of three regional elections of 1970, 1975 and 1980. The June 1975 elections provided the boost to the political phenomenon known as Eurocommunism, when the Italian Communist Party (PCI) dramatically increased its share of the vote. However, throughout the period under study, the Christian Democrats (DC) through 20 administrations in 13 years have remained the party of government, a tribute to their staying power. Although dipping to 35.3% in the June 1975 regional elections, the Christian Democrats have managed to maintain their 38% plus share of the ballot at general elections, while seeing the communist party vote fluctuate. For a period from June 1976 to January 1979, the abstention of the PCI on crucial votes was necessary for the DC to remain in government, but otherwise the DC have been the government of Italy. However, since April 1980 the Italian socialists (PSI) have again joined the DC to form a centre-left coalition, similar to those which existed in the period 1968 to 1974. In Greece and Spain the return to parliamentary democracy has seen the parties of the centre-right, New Democracy (ND) and the Union of the Democratic Centre (UCD) win the first and second elections in their respective countries following the end of fascist rule. New Democracy was led by Konstantinos Karamanlis until he became president of the Greek Republic in May 1980, and is now headed by former foreign minister George Rallis; the UCD has been led since its inception by Adolfo Suarez. The first elections took place in November 1974 in Greece and June 1977 in Spain and both parties have won subsequent elections. In the case of Greece, New Democracy is confronted with a formidable left-wing rival in the form of PASOK (Pan Hellenic Socialist Movement) which it must face in a general election by November 1981.

The pattern of Maritime Europe (Belgium, Ireland, Luxembourg, Netherlands and the United Kingdom) does not present itself as definitively as Mediterranean Europe. Observations which can be made are the success of left-wing parties in the mid 1970s, which contrast with the swing to the right by the late 1970s. The period 1973/1974 to 1978/1979 (with Belgium as the exception after March 1974) was a time of socialist and social-democratic success with the coming to power of a Socialist–Liberal coalition in Luxembourg (which stayed in power until May 1979), a Labour–Fine Gael coalition in Ireland from 1973 to 1977, Harold Wilson's third and fourth Labour governments in Britain (although after March 1977 under the premiership of James Callaghan the Labour Party required Liberal support in the so-called Lib–Lab pact) and the Labour Party (PvdA) with two confessional parties, the Catholic People's Party (KVP) and the Christian Historical Union (CHU), in the Netherlands. The electorates of Ireland, Luxembourg, the Netherlands and the United Kingdom shifted to nominally socialist governments for the period 1974 to 1977/78. They appear to have believed that socialist or socialist-dominated coalitions could deal better with the impact of the quintupling of crude oil prices in the winter of 1973/74 (and the subsequent boom in world commodity prices which resulted in rates of inflation unknown for generations), along with the need for monetary or real wages to keep pace to protect the living standards of the employed population. Failure to carry out such policies can result in extensive problems with the employed labour force, the scenario often referred to as the prices and incomes spiral. This dilemma is one which the voters of Maritime Europe, certainly in the years immediately following the increase in the price of oil, preferred to be solved or at least attempted by socialist or social democrat governments rather than those of the centre-right.

By the end of the decade of the 1970s the shift to the right of the political spectrum had become marked, so that governments of the right or centre-right were in power in all five countries of Maritime Europe. Only in Belgium were the socialists still part of the government in the form of a coalition administration; no other country of Maritime Europe at the beginning of the 1980s had a left-wing government in power.

In contrast to Maritime Europe, the electoral pattern of changing fortunes for the centre-right, in Central Europe (Mittal Europa) Austria, Federal Germany and Switzerland shows a process of defeat for the centre-right partners or parties at the beginning of the 1970s and their subsequent exclusion from power throughout the decade. In the case of the Federal Republic of Germany, the partnership of the Christian Democratic Union and the Christian Social Union in Bavaria (CDU–CSU) were in power in

1968 but were defeated in the general election of 1969. Willy Brandt, former burgomaster of West Berlin and leader of the Social Democrats (SPD) won power in a coalition with the Liberal Free Democrats (FDP). Through Brandt's abilities, and later when his finance minister Helmut Schmidt became Federal chancellor, the coalition of the SPD–FDP has stayed in power ever since, winning renewed mandates from the electorate in 1972, 1976 and 1980. It seems reasonable to suggest that by this process the SPD has itself become a centre party, if not a party of the centre-right. The SPD has made itself a party of the centre, hence its continued electoral success; the political fulcrum of Western Europe in the second half of the 1970s balanced on the amicable relationship between the SPD leader Helmut Schmidt and the charismatic President of the French Republic from 1974 to 1981, Valery Giscard d'Estaing. Austria parallels the experience of West Germany with the Socialist Party of Austria (SPÖ) under Bruno Kreisky coming to power as a minority in 1970, after defeating the conservative Austrian People's Party; the Socialist Party was confirmed in power as a majority administration a year later, and has been led since by Chancellor Kreisky. It has won renewed mandates at the elections of 1975 and 1979. Switzerland is in a category of its own; only half the electorate now bother to vote every four years at the ballot to the Nationalrat or Swiss parliament. A four-party coalition continues in power, as it has done throughout the late 1960s and 1970s. Consensus politics and what is known as an amicable coalition or amicable settlement of political issues appear to be the style of the federalist Swiss.

In Scandinavia the January 1968 election in Denmark constituted a resounding success for the centre-right coalition of Conservatives, Liberal Democrats and Radical Democrats. This coalition replaced the Social Democrats who had been in power either as a minority or as the leading member of a coalition since 1953. However, in September 1971, the Social Democrats were returned to power, only to be excluded again during the period December 1973 to January 1975. Arguably, it is in Scandinavia that the centre-right have achieved their greatest success in the 1970s. Despite the phases of centre-right rule in Denmark, the Social Democrats still dominate that country's political scene. This was also true for Sweden until 1973; after the dead heat of the 1973 Swedish election Prime Minister Olof Palme continued in office with a minority Social Democrat administration. The following general election to the unicameral assembly, the Riksdag, in September 1976 brought Thorbjorn Fälldin to power at the head of a moderate (Conservative), centre and liberal coalition, thus defeating the Social Democrats and forcing them into opposition after they had ruled Sweden, with only a short break in 1936, from 1932 to 1976. The

victory for the centre-right in Sweden may have influenced voters to support centre-right parties in other parts of Europe. For Finland the political norm is a four- or five-party coalition with the Finnish Social Democrats (SSDP) and the communist-oriented Democratic League (SKDL). It is a basic tenet of Finnish government formation to keep the Conservatives, known as the National Coalition (KK) out of government, although arguably even more important has been the avoidance of a division between socialists and non-socialists. Coalition government including the SSDP throughout the period of study has continued, with the exception of a short break from September 1976 to May 1977. The SKDL includes the Finnish Communist Party (SKP) which has been part of the government coalition except from March 1971 until June 1975, and again during the period from September 1976 to May 1977. Finland does not represent an electoral success from the centre-right point of view.

In Iceland the leftist coalition including the communist grouping, called the People's Alliance, which took power in July 1971 did not continue after the election of June 1974: this was at the time when the electorates of Maritime Europe. with the exception of Belgium, were turning to left-wing or socialist governments. Iceland reverted to the administration it had experienced during the 1960s, a centre-right coalition of the Independence and Progressive parties. This coalition continued in power for four years until June 1978: the two elections which followed in 1978 and 1979 have produced results leading to further coalition governments, both of which have included the communist-oriented People's Alliance. The administration following the June 1978 election had a more leftist outlook, which caused some observers to speculate that it might demand US withdrawal from its military bases in Iceland. The coalition formed after the December 1979 election can be termed centre-left, and appears to confirm that Iceland has its own political momentum which is not related to trends in the rest of Scandinavia.

Liberal parties

In the period from 1968 to 1980 the liberal and liberal democrat parties of Western and Southern Europe have shown a degree of electoral success which ranges from a liberal democrat government (Radikale Venstre) in Denmark from December 1973 to January 1975, albeit a minority administration, to the extreme of no political manifestation in different countries such as Austria, Ireland and Spain. There has also been the anomaly of the Liberal Party in the United Kingdom which, with 19.3% of the national vote at the February 1974 election, won only 14 seats in the 635 member House of Commons. These examples represent the variations in the political spectrum: the norm for European liberal parties, and one which the British Liberal Party aspires to, is that of coalition government with one or more partners. The majority of European countries have experienced liberal and socialist or liberal and right–centre-right coalition governments for varying periods since 1968. In the case of Switzerland, the Liberal Democrats (FDP) have been in the government coalition throughout the thirteen years; in the Federal Republic of Germany since September 1969 the Free Democrats (FDP) have been part of the ruling Social Democrats – Free Democrats (SPD–FDP) coalition; in Finland the Finnish Liberal Party (LKP) was part of the administration from 1966 to the general election of March 1979. These three countries represent the more substantial successes for liberal parties in terms of periods of continuous government office.

Mediterranean Europe as yet does not appear to be a fertile area for the nurture of liberal ideas or liberal parties. The legacy of fascism has not been conducive for the organization of liberal parties. In the case of Greece, the Centre Democratic Union (the party with liberal ideals) saw its electoral support decline from 20.5% to 11.9% between the elections of 1974 and 1977. Liberal politics make little impact on either Portugal or Spain where the electoral choice is centred on parties of the centre-right or democratic socialist parties, with the communists providing a third option. Currently both Iberian countries have governments of centre-right parties; the other political options are the Spanish Workers Socialist party (PSOE) led by Felipe Gonzalez and the Portuguese Socialist Party (PSP) under former Prime Minister Mario Soares. These two parties have between 28% and 30% of the national vote and contrast with the communist parties: the Spanish Communist Party, led by Santiago Carrillo, is Eurocommunist and still hopes for a breakthrough in electoral success. The Portuguese Communist Party (PCP) is at the other end of the communist political spectrum and under hardline Stalinist, but aging Alvaro Cunhal does not subscribe to the ideals of Eurocommunism. The PCP has consistently picked up more electoral support in Portuguese elections, averaging 16.5% to the 10% of the Spanish Eurocommunists (PCE).

The older established democracies of France and Italy have identifiable liberal parties or factions within larger party groupings. In Italy the Italian Liberal Party (PLI) obtained 5.8% of votes in the general election of 1968, and was in fourth place with 31 seats in the 630 seat assembly (compare the position of the Liberal Party in the United Kingdom with 19% of the vote). However, the PLI electoral support has declined to under 2% in both elections of 1976 and 1979 and the Italian Republican Party (PRI), which is part of the liberal grouping in the European Communities Parliament, now has more support. In 1979 the PRI with 3% of the national vote achieved 16 seats in the Italian assembly.

With France, one of the major problems in identifying liberal parties is the regular habit that political parties have of dissolving themselves, particularly those in the centre ground of politics, and then reforming under new political labels. 'On the right and centre it is rare for the same political designations to appear at consecutive general elections'[1]. Now part of the UDF (Union pour la Democratie Française), the Independent Republicans may be classed as a liberal party: this was the party from which Giscard d'Estaing developed his political experience and used as a political base in his successful bid for the French Presidency in 1974. In the general elections of March 1973 the Independent Republicans took 7.7% of the vote and obtained 55 seats in the 490 member assembly. By the election of 1978 they had become part of the UDF, which includes the former Centre Union. Consequently the UDF could not be described as a solely liberal grouping, but it is an important political party and nearest to the tradition of French liberalism.

In Maritime Europe only Ireland, with no identifiable liberal party, has not experienced direct or indirect involvement of liberals in government at some time since 1968. In Belgium the Liberal Parties (PVV, Flemish; PLP, Walloon) were part of the government coalition from 1971 to 1977; during this time, from August 1974, the Rassemblement Walloon Party was included in the administration, the first occasion that a federalist party had agreed to become part of a Belgian government. The two Liberal Parties were not part of the government coalition from March 1977 to May 1980, but helped to put together a new coalition in May 1980. The Dutch Liberal Party (VVD) has been part of its country's coalition government from 1968, through the 1971 election to December 1972, and again after the 1977 election in the government headed by Andreas van Agt, which is a coalition with the centre-right CDA–Christian Democratic Appeal. In Luxembourg the Democratic Party (PD) have been members of a coalition government with either the Christian Social Party, from 1968 to 1974 and since May 1979, or with the Luxembourg Socialist Party (LSAP) between 1974 and 1979. This type of political pattern tends to confirm the importance of the liberal contribution, and certain West European electorates seem to value it:

In their national party systems, where they (i.e. liberal parties) often function as the decisive weight in the balance of power, they have entered a variety of different coalitions and have therefore developed a comparatively greater flexibility and capacity for cooperation[2].

The United Kingdom had the indirect association of its Liberal Party in the minority Labour administration of James Callaghan from March 1977 to July

1978. This took the form for the Liberal Party leader, David Steel, of the 'right to be consulted' on the preparation of government business: it is hard to identify what the British Liberal Party actually achieved by the association in the so-called 'Lib–Lab' pact. The British Labour Party was able to survive votes of no-confidence in the House of Commons when it had lost its majority due to a series of by-election defeats and defections. The consultation process was a poor return for a party which obtained 6 000 000 votes in the British general election of February 1974. British Liberals may rightly claim they are victims of the British plurality system of electing its assembly, which neither the Conservative Party nor Labour Party show any inclination to reform.

The five countries of Scandinavian Europe have all at some time between 1968 and 1980 had liberal parties as part of government coalitions. Denmark provides the only example of a liberal minority government. This was the administration under the leadership of Poul Hartling of the Liberal Democratic Party who formed a government after the December 1973 election with only 22 seats of the 175 member assembly, known as the Folketing. From January 1968 to October 1971 the Danish Liberal Party (Venstre) and the Liberal Democratic Party (Radikale Venstre) were part of a coalition government, and from August 1978 to October 1979 Prime Minister Anker Jørgensen led a coalition of his Social Democratic Party and the Liberal Party. The results of the Danish elections (*figures 5.1 – 5.6 pages 000–000*) indicate the support that the Liberal Party (Venstre) has gathered at certain Danish general elections. In Sweden the Liberal Party (FP) has been part of the centre-right coalition which replaced 44 years of social democratic government in September 1976, while in Finland the Liberal Party (LKP) have been members of every government coalition from 1966 to March 1979. Iceland has had one period of liberal and leftist coalition government from June 1971 to June 1974, so that all Scandinavian liberal parties have had experience of sharing power during the 1970s.

References

1. Sallnow, J. and John, A. (1978). France Divided Right and Left. *Geographical Magazine*, **L** (No. XII), 792
2. Stammen, T. (1980). *Political Parties in Europe*, John Martin Publishing, London, pp 247–248

Social democratic parties in Europe

Social democratic parties in Europe came into existence with the extension of the franchise and, by virtue of their moderation, have had a strong influence on West European politics. While there is considerable divergence between these parties according to country, all can be broadly defined as left-of-centre, espousing some tenets of Marxism and committed to participatory politics and the welfare state.

Mediterranean Europe has provided a political laboratory for developing social democratic parties to try out their election strategies, but they have met with mixed fortunes between 1968 and 1980. Greece, Portugal and Spain emerged from right-wing dictatorships in the years 1974 and 1975 and should have been prime targets for the committed democratic liberalism which the social democratic parties had to offer. From 1975 to December 1979, Portugal accepted the socialist administration headed initially by Mario Soares, first as a majority, later under other leaders as a minority. Two general elections in less than twelve months have confirmed the Portuguese electorate's preference for a centre-right government. Both Greece and Spain have opted for administrations of the centre-right since their return to democracy based on a parliamentary system. Mediterranean social democrats have been confronted with the dilemma that, while they command a significant proportion of the vote, they never win enough to govern and have to choose between supporting centre-right parties or, in the case of France, Italy and Portugal, a powerful communist party with mass appeal to the electorate. At the time of writing France's Socialist Party (PS) and the Greek Panhellenic Socialist Movement (PASOK) both face general elections in 1981 and, following the success of Francois Mitterrand in capturing the office of the French Presidency, both the PS and PASOK must be hoping for electoral success that will enable them to form a government. However, both PS and PASOK may have to turn to their respective communist parties (or two in the case of Greece) for support if they fail to secure enough votes for a majority in the respective assemblies.

In Maritime Europe between 1973 and 1979 all five countries experienced socialist or social democratic governments either by individual parties or in coalition. In January 1968 only Luxembourg with a Christian Social and Luxembourg Socialist Party (LSAP) coalition, and the United Kingdom Labour Party were in office, although they were followed during 1968 by a Christian Social and socialist coalition in Belgium. As mentioned above, under centre-right administrations by 1974 voters of Maritime Europe had opted for socialist governments. In part this may be due to the electorates preference for socialist or social democratic governments to face and deal with the quintupling of crude oil prices and the world commodity boom. The welfare umbrella seemed more preferable in the uncertain years of 1974 and 1975. Only Belgium went against this trend; when the Belgian Socialist Party was returned to office in a coalition under Leo Tindemans in 1977 the Fine Gael–Labour coalition in Ireland and the coalition dominated by the Dutch Labour Party (PvdA) under Joop Den Uyl were both in their last three months of office. By the end of 1980, Maritime Europe, again with the exception of Belgium, had moved to the right of the political spectrum.

The social democratic parties' greatest success has undoubtedly been in central Europe. The record is quite clear: coalition of four parties including the Social Democrats remain in power in Switzerland throughout the period. Swiss politics, however, has a unique nature. Switzerland is Western Europe's only country with a genuinely federal history and tradition, and the existence of political parties which cut across cantonal, ethnic and religious boundaries is a crucial stabilizing factor. In both Austria and the Federal Republic of Germany centre-right governments were in power in 1968. The German Social Democrats (SPD) under Willy Brandt had their first electoral success, in association with the Liberal Free Democrats (FDP) in 1969. This was followed by the Austrian Socialist Party (SPÖ), remodelled during the 1960s on Scandinavian social democratic model/ lines by its leader Bruno Kreisky. It took office as a minority administration in 1970, but turned this into a majority the following year. The SPÖ led by Kreisky has repeated its success in 1975 and 1979. As Austrian Chancellor and government leader, Kreisky has the distinction of being the longest serving political leader after President Urho Kekkonen of Finland who was elected in 1966. The SPD–FDP coalition under Brandt, and since May 1974 under Helmut Schmidt, has repeated its electoral success in elections of 1972, 1976 and 1980. Along with Austria and Switzerland, Federal Germany constitutes the greatest success for the social democrats, with a solid social democratic bloc in central Europe. Perhaps in part this is due to the policies of the Austrian and German socialist parties, which are more centrist than social democrats in the rest of Europe.

In Nordic Europe mixed fortunes have prevailed for social democrats. The centre-right scored its most noted and outstanding success in Sweden in 1976 ending a 44 year period dominated by social-democratic administrations. Iceland's social democrats have been in leftist coalition governments between 1971 and 1974 and again from 1978 to December 1979, while in Finland every coalition has included the Finnish Social Democrats (SSDP) except for 15 months during 1977 and 1978.

The pattern is thus: social democratic rule in Sweden for many years since the 1930s until 1976; replacement by centre-right coalition. Finland and Norway, apart from brief intervals, have their social democrat party, or in the case of Norway the Labour Party, continuing in office; in Finland this is in

coalition with two or more parties (designed to keep the right-wing conservatives out of office). Iceland has two periods of left coalition rule which include the country's social democrats. Denmark from October 1971 is dominated by social-democrat administration apart from a period from December 1973 to January/February 1975 when a Liberal minority administration was in power. In general, the social democrats still dominate the welfare-orientated politics of Denmark, and since October 1972 the Danish political scene has been focused on the personality of the Social Democrat's leader Anker Jørgensen. The prospects for social democracy remain moderate in Nordic Europe; if Sweden moved left again this would be a great boost. The high degree of proportionality employed in the Swedish electoral system means that the balance between social democrats and centre-right is very fine. It remains to be seen whether the rightward shift of electorates which was observed in late 1978 and 1979 will now be reversed during 1981.

Women in European elections

Virtually all countries in non-communist Europe either had anti-discrimination laws in 1968 or have subsequently adopted such legislation. This study has tried to establish whether women's change in social status has had an effect on voting patterns: has their increasing awareness of themselves given them more political power as women, or is it more the case that a few women have taken advantage of prevalent official attitudes only to be sublimated into what continues to be a 'man's world'? Is the political woman a conundrum or a real force continuing to gain power?

While much has been written on women in general during the past decade, little data and few statistics have been produced on their specific voting patterns. It cannot be stated categorically whether they vote along with their male counterparts according to age, geographic location and social class, or whether other issues and factors determine how they vote.

Two reasons exist for this: the first is logistic. In Europe, the ballot is secret and therefore no way exists of proving which sex voted for which candidate without introducing sexually-segregated polls. A second way of establishing whether a 'sexual vote' exists would be in the numerous surveys produced at each election. Based on questionnaires, these surveys give statistics breaking down the vote according to age, socio-economic group, race and so on, but the most clearly visible difference, namely gender, is rarely if ever included in such classifications. However, the Swedish election for the Riksdag in 1979 did produce a percentage breakdown of male–female votes for the major political parties.

Such a problem must not always be considered the questioner's fault. In the summer of 1974, following the political revolution in Portugal, the then socialist-oriented Lisbon newspaper *Republica* published 'instant' interviews on the political situation in the country.

Women frequently refused to answer, especially in the presence of their husbands, or replied that politics was not a woman's business. And this in Lisbon itself which is much more politically active than other parts of the country[1].

What can be looked at with a greater degree of accuracy is how women active in party politics have fared since 1968. The women's movement has been strong on pushing for specific issues, but it is unclear how much real power and equality women have gained in the 1970s.

In 1968 women in Switzerland still did not have the vote: men in Mediterranean countries were officially the head of the household, giving them the legal right to decide all issues regarding the daily life of the family. Since then the position has altered to a legal right to equality virtually throughout Western Europe and the enfranchisement of Swiss women in 1971. However, discrimination or the lack of it exists not because of legislation but because of social attitude and cultural climate. Legislation does not ensure equality, but serves only to force members of society to examine their own attitudes. For example, no one would confuse the social status of women in Sweden and in Italy, yet both countries have the most comprehensive equality laws.

In politics itself, women would seem to be discriminated against, albeit subconsciously. In the British general election of May 1979, Shirley Williams, education minister in the previous Labour government and tipped at the time as a future Labour Party leader, lost her seat. British newspapers, seeking to answer why, pointed out that women in both major British political parties were inevitably given marginal seats. This is 60 years after first winning the vote. Such unsafe seats is another reason why so few women make it to the top in British politics: it is difficult to make long-term plans while attempting to defend a marginal seat.

A brief look at national legislative assemblies should confirm that this problem is common throughout Europe. In the national assemblies of 1975, women accounted for 16% of deputies in Denmark, 6% in West Germany, 4.6% in Italy, 3.3% in Britain and 1.5% in France[2].

Women find themselves in a dilemma in choosing to stand on the feminist issue. A unified Feminist Party campaigned in Belgium at the 1977 election and won 2481 votes in two house constituencies[3]. However, when Margaret Thatcher became Britain's first woman Prime Minister, she stressed she had never espoused the feminist cause and had won both the Conservative party leadership in 1975 and the premiership in 1979 without any help from women's groups.

West Europe's only other woman Prime Minister until 1981, Maria de Lurdes Pintassilgo, was given Portugal's premiership in July 1979 on the strict understanding the job was that of caretaker, preparing for December elections rather than leading the country. Pintassilgo herself said in an interview in 1975 that she had not been included in Portugal's cabinet at that time 'because she was a woman'[4]. Portugal's party make-up confirmed that such views on political equality of the sexes was battling against the prejudices of both men and women. The Central Committee of the PCP (Portuguese Communist Party) elected in November 1974 comprised 21 men and two women. The Socialist Party in the same year said it had 10 000 active male members and 100 women activists[5].

It is also true that at least in newly democratic countries, women enter politics specifically to fight for or to preserve women's rights. In the Spanish general election of March 1979, there were 1409 women candidates, more than twice the number in the 1977 elections, and most of them were quoted in contemporary newspapers as saying they were standing to prevent women's issues being side-stepped in the Congress of Deputies.

This attitude of women entering politics specifically for women's rights instead of simply as candidates who also happen to be women could prove self-defeatist, as it groups women as minorities, even though in all countries under study they make up at least half the population. Even those women who reach cabinet positions are given 'social' posts such as education, welfare, or, more blatantly in the case of France, women's issues. Pintassilgo conforms as she was given caretakership rather than winning the premiership. Margaret Thatcher is the single exception in actually leading her party, but it should be noted that she appointed not one woman to her cabinet. The appointment of Gro Harlem Brundtland in February 1981 as Prime Minister of Norway means that Margaret Thatcher is not the sole female leader, although she still has the distinction of winning her premiership by a successful general election rather than being appointed to it.

While it is possible to point to specific areas of discrimination and developing equality, it is impossible to claim that a 'woman's vote' exists.

Studies in the United States have shown women are more likely to vote for the liberal candidate[6] but it is maintained that French women vote along the same lines as their male counterparts[7]. The only country where it might have been able to discern whether women's votes influence the general electoral pattern is Switzerland, where women have been allowed to vote in national elections since 1971. In fact, although women in that country accounted for more than half the population in the first universal suffrage vote in November 1971, the only difference in the national assembly was that a dozen women were elected members and women's votes did not alter the country's general voting pattern.

The Swedish election of 1979 showed little variation in the percentage vote between men and women for the major parties[8]. While 45% of the female electorate voted for the social democrats, the figure was 44% of men; 18% of women voted for the Moderate Party (Conservatives) compared to 22% of men; 19% women to 15% men voted for the Centre Party. Even when such figures are available there appears not to be a marked division of the 'sexual vote'.

References

1. Vallelly-Fischer, L. and Fischer, G. (Fall 1975). Women and the Revolution in Portugal. *Antlantis* (US Women's Studies Journal), 1 (No. 1), 46
2. Makward, C. P. (June 1975). French Women in Politics 1975. *University of Michigan Papers in Women's Studies*, 1 (No. 4), 123
3. Henig, S. (ed.) (1979). *Political Parties in the European Community*, p. 13, Allen & Unwin/Policy Studies Institute; London
4. *Antlantis*, op. cit., p. 58
5. Ibid., p. 62
6. Steinham, G. (July 1972). Women Voters Can't be Trusted. *Ms Magazine*, p. 47
7. *University of Michigan Papers in Women's Studies*, op. cit., p. 123
8. *Statistical Yearbook of Sweden 1980*, (1980). Stockholm, p. 420

Central Europe

Austria

Austria in terms of its electoral geography presents something of a model of electoral stability in Central Europe, with the Socialist Party of Austria (Sozialistiches Partei Österreichs, SPÖ) being in power since it won the 1970 election with a narrow majority.

Post-war Austria emerged as a result of the Austrian State Treaty of 1955 committed to a foreign policy of permanent neutrality. Two parties have dominated its political structure: the SPÖ and the Austrian Peoples Party (Österreichs Volkspartei, ÖVP). At the beginning of the period under study

Political parties	
SPÖ	Socialist Party of Austria
ÖVP	People's Party of Austria
FPÖ	Freedom Party of Austria
KPÖ	Communist Party of Austria
CSA	Christian Social Workers Movement (Arbeitsgemeinschaft)
NDP	National Democratic Party

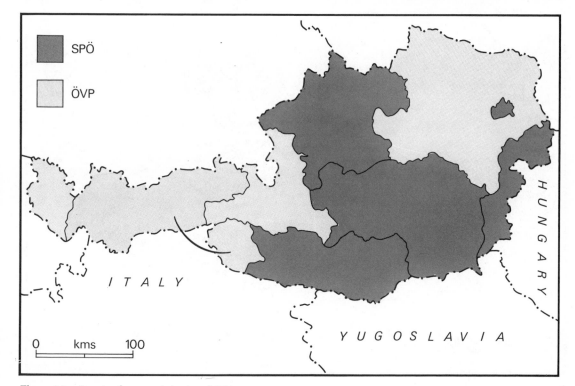

Figure 2.1 *Austria: the general election of 1970*

the ÖVP were in power, led by Josef Klaus, but were dislodged by the SPÖ in 1970. In the subsequent elections of 1971, 1975 and 1979 the SPÖ has remained in power and its leader Bruno Kreisky has now been the Austrian Chancellor for a decade. The electoral pattern has remained virtually the same and the election of 1975 produced no change in the seats won by parties in the Nationalrat compared to the election four years earlier.

The success of the Socialist Party (SPÖ) in 1970 was due primarily to the leadership of Bruno Kreisky. After its defeat in the 1966 elections he had reformed the party by changing its policies and abandoning traditional Austrian Marxism and replacing it by a modern image and policies similar to those of the social democratic parties of Scandinavia. This new outlook was successful and overcame the fear of a 'red peril' or 'red Austria' among the more conservative elements of the farmers and the urban lower-middle classes. The older voters in these social groups could recall the occupation of Vienna by the Soviet Army in 1945; to their change of support was added the votes of the 19 and 20 year olds, who were enfranchised as a result of the lowering of the voting age.

Kreisky formed a minority socialist government in April 1970. The election produced a controversy over

three of the seven Vienna constituencies. The cause was a complaint by the Freedom Party (FPÖ) that the electoral lists contained forged signatures in favour of the extreme right-wing National Democratic Part (NDP). The Austrian Supreme Court declared the results in the three constituencies invalid and ordered new elections which resulted in the FPÖ winning an additional seat.

In November 1970 electoral reform took place which reduced the number of constituencies from 25 to nine and increased the number of deputies from 165 to 183. The minority socialist administration increased its representation in October 1971 elections with 93 seats compared to 81 in 1970. This was sufficient for it to hold a majority in the Nationalrat. The ÖVP gained one seat to have a total of 80, and the FPÖ increased from five to ten. There was no representation for the Communist Party of Austria (KPÖ) despite an increased share of the poll. The issues of the 1971 electoral campaign were concerned with internal matters: principally inflation and the cost of living, the Army reform and the question of nationalization. The Army-reform question related to the reduction of compulsory military service from nine months to six; this was supported by the SPÖ and FPÖ but opposed by the ÖVP.

Following the SPÖ success, Kreisky became

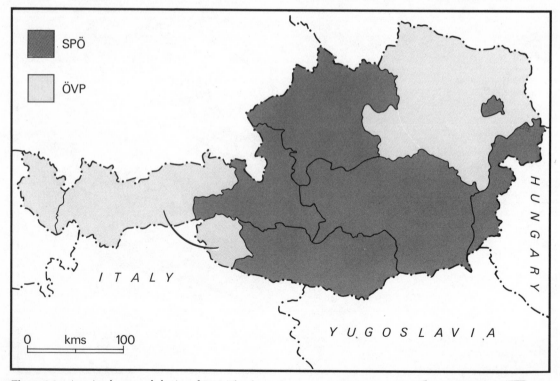

Figure 2.2 *Austria: the general election of 1971. The electoral pattern remained the same in the general election of 1975*

Chancellor for the second time and formed a majority socialist cabinet on 21 October 1971. He stated his policy and objective was the creation of a welfare state for all and the realization of modern social policy; this was to include a general plan for all branches of social security, improvement of pensions and health insurance and the codification of industrial law. Protection of the environment was also mentioned in the new government's programme, reflecting the general interest in such matters throughout Europe at the beginning of the 1970s. In foreign policy Kreisky stated the Austrian government would support the concept of *détente* and continue to advocate the calling of a European security conference.

For the elections of 1975 and again in 1979 the SPÖ campaigned on its record as a successful administration. In 1975 the allocation of seats among the parties remained unchanged (*Figure 2.2*); the election campaign focused mainly on the economy. The SPÖ went to the country on the slogans of 'Four more good years for Austria' and 'Kreisky, who else?'[1]. These slogans proved successful, allowing the party to 'have secured an absolute majority in two successive elections . . . in a country used to coalitions'[2]. Other issues in the country's politics between 1971 and 1975 were reform of the abortion law, foreign

policy, radio and television reform. However, in 1975 the economic issues predominated; the ÖVP accused the SPÖ of excessive government spending but unemployment was at a low figure of 1.3% and inflation was at a tolerable level of 8.4%. The electorate registered satisfaction with the government's record by returning them with the same number of seats. In terms of geographical distribution, the SPÖ took 60% of the vote in Vienna, which elects 39 of the 183 deputies; for the first time the SPÖ equalled the proportion of votes for the ÖVP in Lower Austria (Nieder Österreich), which had been regarded as a traditional stronghold of the ÖVP (Peoples Party).

The ÖVP also lost support in Styria; only in Vorarlberg did it increase its share of votes.

In 1979 the SPÖ again campaigned on its record in office and won its third consecutive election, increasing its number of deputies by two to 95. It made gains in all the provinces except the most westerly region of Vorarlberg. In Vienna the SPÖ took 61% of the vote.

Kreisky has remained at the head of the SPÖ and as Austrian Chancellor, giving him the distinction of being one of the few European leaders to remain throughout the decade of the 1970s. President Urho Kekkonen of Finland is the only other leader to have

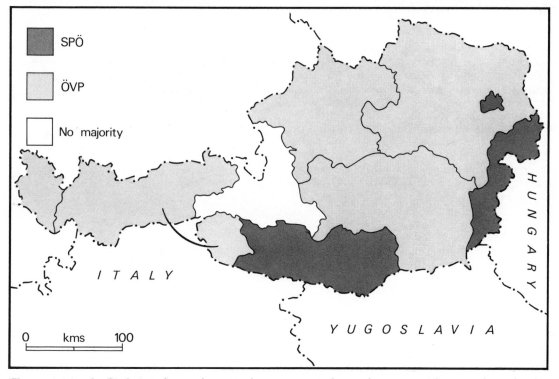

Figure 2.3 *Austria: the election of regional (provincial) governments in the period 1977–1979. (The regions do not elect their governments during the same year)*

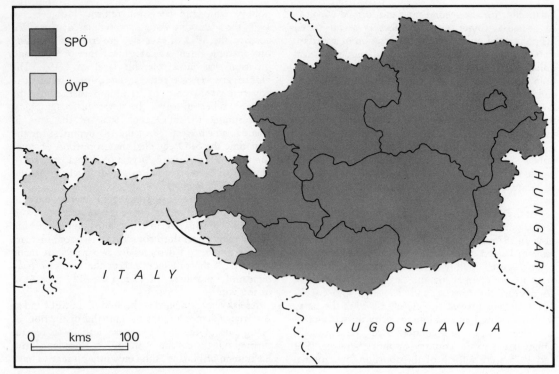

Figure 2.4   *Austria: the general election of 1979*

remained during this uncertain decade. The continued success of the SPÖ gave hope to the Social Democrats (SPD) in Federal Germany; with neighbouring Switzerland, Austria has been part of a bloc of electoral stability since 1970. In contrast to Switzerland, where voter turnout has fallen below half those entitled to vote, Austrian voters continue to record a oter participation level of more than 90%.

It remains to be seen whether the ÖVP can regain a majority in the Nationalrat and form a government, although this would appear to be unlikely.

The Communist Party (KPÖ), which has failed to gain a seat at any of the four elections, remains insignificant in Austrian politics, recording only 1.0% of the vote in 1979.

References

1. Sully, M. (November 1975). Austria's General Election. *The World Today*, p. 437
2. Ibid., p. 436

Table 2.1 *The Austrian electoral system 1970–1979*

Assembly	Nationalrat
Members	165 seats, increased to 183 on 1 January 1971
Dates of elections	1 March 1970 for all constituencies 25 June 1970 (16 seats in three Viennese constituencies declared invalid) 4 October 1970 election for 16 seats 10 October 1971 5 October 1975 6 May 1979
Method	Proportional representation (PR); Hagenbach–Bischoff system
Voting age	20, reduced to 19 in 1968
Voter participation (turnout)	1970 91.8% 1971 92.4% 1975 90.3% 1979 92.2%

Sources: Statistisches Handbuch für die Republik Österreich, Vienna, 1979, p. 517 and 1980, p. 505

Table 2.2 *Number of seats won in Austrian elections 1970–1979*

Party	Number of seats				
	1970 March	1970 October	1971	1975	1979
SPÖ	81	81	93	93	95
ÖVP	79	78	80	80	77
FPÖ	5	6	10	10	11
KPÖ	0	0	0	0	0
Other	0	0	0	0	0
Total	165	165	183	183	183

Table 2.3 *Percentage of votes cast in Austrian elections 1970–1979*

Party	Percentage of votes			
	1970	1971	1975	1979
SPÖ	48.4	50.0	50.4	51.0
ÖVP	44.7	43.1	43.0	41.9
FPÖ	5.5	5.5	5.4	6.1
KPÖ	1.0	1.4	1.2	1.0
Other	0.4	0.0	0.0	0.0
Total	100.0	100.0	100.0	100.0

Table 2.4 *Number of votes cast in Austrian elections 1970–1979*

Party	Number of votes			
	1970	1971	1975	1979
SPÖ	2 221 981	2 280 168	2 326 201	2 413 226
ÖVP	2 051 012	1 964 713	1 981 291	1 981 739
FPÖ	253 425	248 473	249 444	286 743
KPÖ	44 750	61 762	55 032	45 280
Other	17 793	1 874	1 464	2 263
Valid votes	4 588 961	4 556 990	4 613 432	4 729 251
Invalid votes	41 890	50 626	49 252	54 922
Total	4 630 851	4 607 616	4 663 684	4 784 173
Electorate	5 045 841	4 984 448	5 019 277	5 186 735

The Federal Republic of Germany

Political parties	
AUD	Action Association of Independent Germans
AVP	Action Association Fourth Party
BP	Citizens' Party
CBV	Christian Bavarian People's Party
CDU	Christian Democratic Union
CSU	Christian Social Union (Bavaria only)
Die Grünen	Green (Ecologist) Party
DKP	German Communist Party
EAP	European Workers Party
FDP	Free Democratic Party
5%	5 Per Cent Block Party (Bavaria only)
GIM	Group of International Marxists
KBW	Communist Union of West Germany
KPD	Communist Party of Germany
NPD	National Democratic Party
SPD	Social Democratic Party
UAP	Independent Workers Party (German Socialists)
VL	United Left
Volksfront	Popular Front

The electoral pattern of the Federal Republic of Germany is illustrated by *Figures 2.5* to *2.8*. These show the level of support for the Social Democratic Party (SPD) and the Christian Democratic Union (CDU), with the Christian Social Union (CSU) in Bavaria allied to the CDU in the Federal parliament (Bundestag). The Free Democrats (FDP) have, for the most part, supplied the needed coalition partner for the major party in power. *Machtwechsel,* that is change in power, has come about as the result of the switching of coalition partners, the SPD taking the place of the FDP as the CDU–CSU's partner in 1966, and the FDP taking the CDU–CSU's place as the SPD's partner three years later[1].

The support for the SPD in the industrial cities of Hamburg and Bremen remains strong throughout the period under study. In the other *Länder* or provinces the advances of the SPD in the 1972 election can be seen, although in the following 1976 election there was a reduced majority for the Social Democratic-Free Democratic coalition (SPD–FDP) which is shown in the extent of electoral support on *Figure 2.7* for 1976. The strength of the SPD lies in the industrial areas of the Federal Republic: it is consistently the dominant party in the most populous *Land* or province, North Rhine-Westphalia.

Four elections have taken place between 1968 and 1980; these were in September 1969, November 1972, October 1976 and October 1980. The 1969 election saw the dissolution of the Grand Coalition between the Christian Democrats and the Social Democrats: the Social Democrats (SPD) for the first time gained the highest number of constituency seats with a total of 127 compared with 121 for the CDU–CSU. The shift in favour of the SPD was expressed by its winning 34 constituencies previously held by the CDU–CSU, while the CDU gained only one seat from the SPD. The shift towards the SPD is shown by its re-emergence as the leading party in North Rhine-Westphalia. The 1969 election showed two major features for the political geographic pattern of Federal Germany: the trend towards polarization of Federal Republic politics in a two-party contest or system between the CDU and the SPD; and the failure of any extreme political movements to gain any significant response from the electorate. No party obtained an overall majority in the 1969 election, so there were three effective options open for the formation of a federal government:

(1) A continuation of the Grand Coalition between the CDU and the SPD;
(2) Coalition between the CDU and the Free Democratic Party (FDP);
(3) A coalition between the SPD and the FDP.

The result was agreement between Willy Brandt, leader of the SPD, and Walter Scheel, leader of the FDP, on an SPD–FDP coalition which meant the CDU went into opposition for the first time in 20 years. From 1969 to 1980 the SPD–FDP have ruled Federal Germany in coalition, creating with neighbouring Austria a bloc of stable socialist government in Central Europe. The continued success of the SPÖ (Socialist Party of Austria), especially in the 1979 election when it increased its number of seats, gave comfort to the SPD as it faced the federal election in the autumn of 1980. The SPD in 1980 campaigned on its record of a decade in office and on the lack of a viable alternative chancellor to Helmut Schmidt.

Willy Brandt became the first socialist Chancellor of the Federal Republic on 21 October 1969, winning 251 votes to 235 with 5 abstentions and four invalid votes; in fact he was the first social-democratic Chancellor for 39 years. He had been Vice-Chancellor and Foreign Minister in the CDU–SPD Grand Coalition formed in December 1967, previously having become known in the European political arena as an energetic mayor of West Berlin.

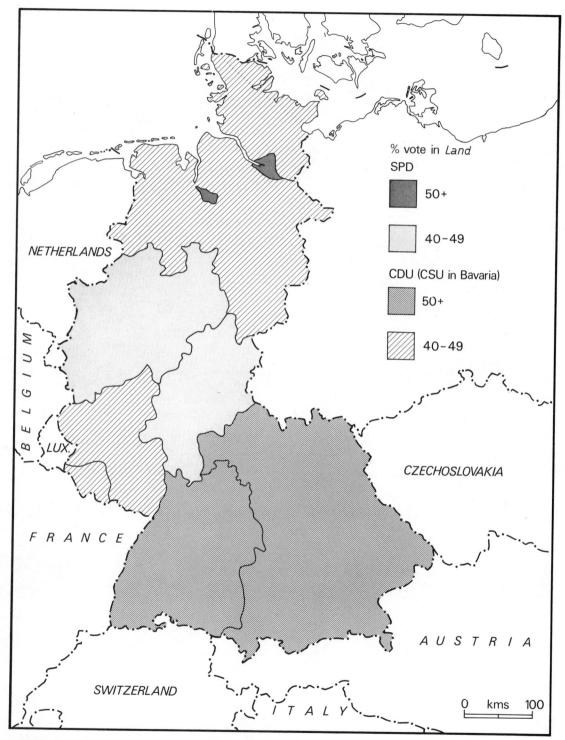

Figure 2.5 *Federal Republic of Germany: the general election of 1969*

Legend text within figure:

% vote in *Land*

SPD
50+
40–49

CDU (CSU in Bavaria)
50+
40–49

NETHERLANDS

BELGIUM

LUX.

FRANCE

CZECHOSLOVAKIA

AUSTRIA

SWITZERLAND

ITALY

0   kms   100

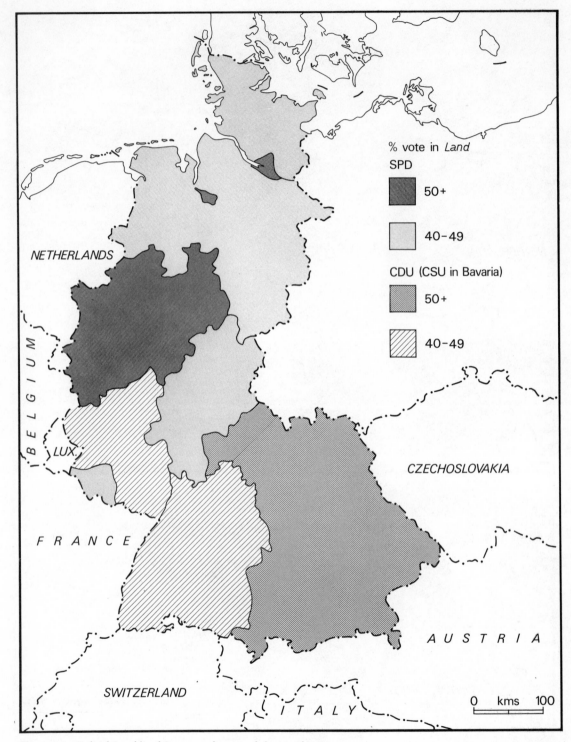

Figure 2.6 *Federal Republic of Germany: the general election of 1972*

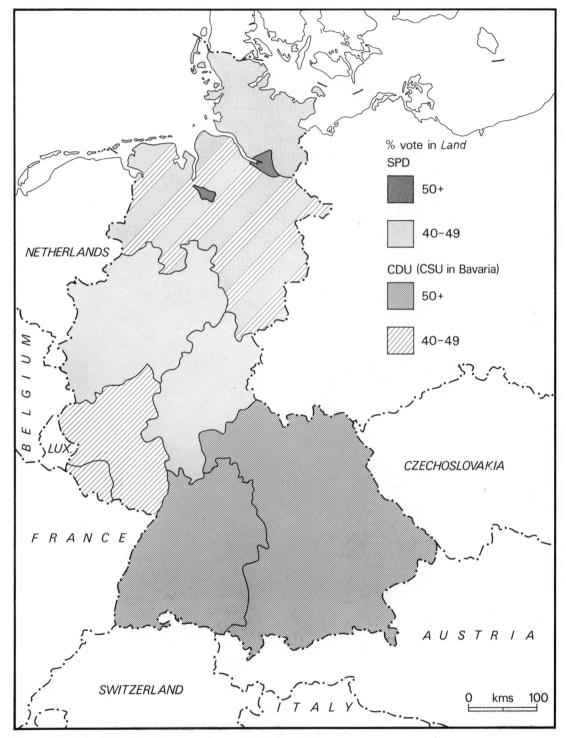

Figure 2.7 *Federal Republic of Germany: the general election of 1976*

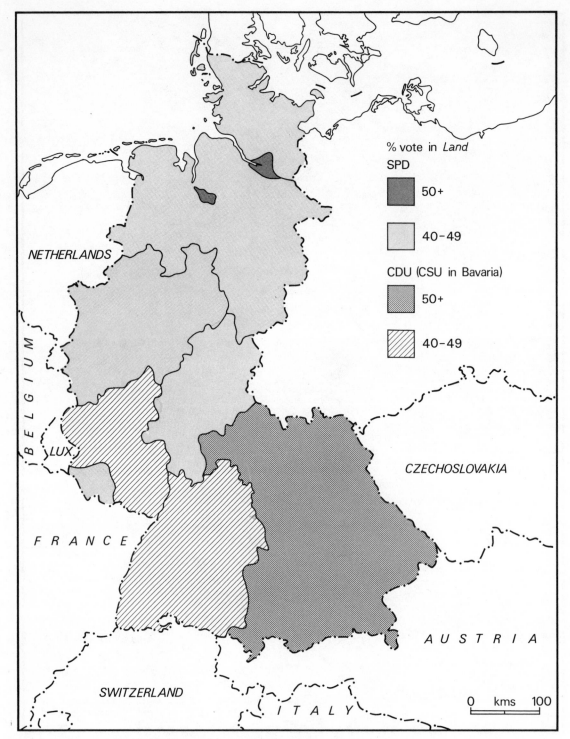

Figure 2.8 *Federal Republic of Germany: the general election of 1980*

In 1972 the election was held before the end of the four-year term, because the SPD–FDP coalition had lost its working majority in the Bundestag as a result of several defections. The deputies who left the coalition were not satisfied with the treaties signed with the Soviet Union and Poland, which formed the major part of Chancellor Brandt's *Ostpolitik* or new foreign policy towards East Europe. There were also disagreements over the government's monetary and economic policy and Professor Karl Schiller, minister of economic affairs since the 1969 election and minister of finance since May 1971, resigned in July 1972. Despite these signs of disarray within the government, the electorate showed its approval of Brandt's policies and both the Social Democrats and the Free Democrats made substantial gains.

The SPD became the largest party in the Bundestag for the first time in the history of the Federal Republic, with an increase of 3 000 000 votes over 1969 and gained six more deputies. The FDP also increased its vote total by over 1 000 000 and gained a further 11 deputies. The CDU lost 16 deputies compared to 1969; the CSU in Bavaria had a slightly increased percentage poll but had one fewer deputy. The CDU vote declined in Schleswig-Holstein and Lower Saxony as *Figure 2.6* shows, with the SPD obtaining a higher percentage poll than the CDU. Previously the CDU had always been the strongest party in Schleswig-Holstein and Lower Saxony. In North Rhine-Westphalia the SPD achieved more than 50% of the vote and obtained an absolute majority. The SPD also overtook the CDU in its percentage vote in the province of Saarland; it improved its percentage vote by 3.2% to 37.8% in Bavaria but the Christian Social Union, led by Josef Strauss, still took more than 50% of the vote.

The result in 1972 was a renewal of the coalition of the SDP and FDP with their leaders Willy Brandt and Walter Scheel agreeing on a new programme. Brandt was re-elected as Federal Chancellor by 269 votes to 223 with one invalid ballot.

Brandt continued as Chancellor until the spring of 1974, when he resigned over the affair of one of his aides suspected of spying for the German Democratic Republic (GDR). Brandt accepted political responsibility over the question of his aide Gunter Guillaume, and admitted he had known for some months that Guillaume was under suspicion. Brandt announced his decision to resign out of 'respect for the unwritten rules of democracy' on 6 May 1974.

Helmut Schmidt, Finance Minister in the SPD–FDP coalition, was unanimously elected SPD leader on 7 May 1974 to succeed Brandt; he was elected Federal Chancellor on 16 May by 267 votes to 225, with four deputies absent and no abstentions. Helmut Schmidt formed a new cabinet of Social Democrats and Free Democrats.

The election of 1976 held on 3 October resulted in a reduced majority for the SPD–FDP coalition of Helmut Schmidt, but his government continued in office. In 1976 the SPD lost 16 seats and the FDP lost two, while the CDU gained 13 seats and the CSU five seats. Voting patterns in 1976 showed the SPD continued with strong support in the northern *Länder* although that support was diminished somewhat in North Rhine-Westphalia compared to 1972. The CDU again became the dominant party in Saarland but only 0.1% (46.2% compared to 46.1%) separated the two major parties.

After the 1976 election Helmut Kohl, the CDU–CSU candidate for the Federal Chancellorship, claimed that as leader of the largest single party (CDU and CSU together in the Bundestag), he should be allowed an attempt to form a government. However, the FDP leader Hans-Dietrich Genscher indicated that he and his party wanted to remain in coalition with the SPD and thus the coalition continued with Helmut Schmidt as Chancellor. For the majority of SPD deputies the coalition with the FDP has been important not only in terms of a majority in the Bundestag but also to keep the left wing of the party from demanding too radical reforms; the 'FDP is not only a necessary ally in government but a welcome justification for the party's centrist image so vital in winning support amongst moderate, unaligned voters of the middle and skilled working classes'[2].

An SPD–FDP coalition has ruled the Federal Republic of Germany for over a decade. Whether this coalition could hold off the challenge of the CDU–CSU opposition in the federal elections of the autumn of 1980 was answered on 5 October. Franz-Josef Strauss, premier of Bavaria and leader of the CSU, had been nominated in July 1979 as the opposition candidate for the federal chancellorship in the 1980 elections and posed a threat to the continuance of socialist rule. Regional elections in March 1980 showed support for Die Grünen, the Green pro-Ecology party. Die Grünen managed to win more than 5% of the vote, enabling them to have representation in the provincial parliament Baden-Württemburg. It seemed in the spring of 1980 that electoral support for these smaller parties might further reduce the chance of the SPD–FDP coalition continuing, but the two parties went on to win another four years in power.

The SPD–FDP coalition increased its majority in the Bundestag and obtained 272 of the 397 seats. An extra seat was created after the 1980 election to deal with an anomaly in seat distribution in the *Land* of Schleswig-Holstein.

The FDP increased their share of the vote by 2.7% and gained 53 seats, compared to 39 in 1976. The two-vote system of the Federal Republic seems to have benefitted the FDP, who encouraged vote splitting; the party obtained 7.2% of first votes but

10.6% of the second ballots and consequently 'achieved their second-best result ever, essentially because they are seen as the guardians of centrism and as a counter-weight to the left wing of the Social Democratic Party'[3].

Helmut Schmidt was reconfirmed as Chancellor of the Federal Republic and is now one of Europe's more experienced statesmen.

Ecology parties

Ecology parties, which since 1979 have become known as green parties, were established in the late 1960s and early 1970s on the basis of environmentalist groups in Western Europe, or more notably in the case of the Federal Republic in opposition to the development of nuclear power. The nuclear power debate appeared to have been stronger and more intense in the Federal Republic than elsewhere in Western Europe and the desire to galvanize this response into some form of political action was a contributory factor in the establishment of ecology-oriented political groupings.

The first occasion when such a party contested an election was the *Land* (province) government elections held on 4 June 1978 for the *Länder* (provinces) of Lower Saxony and Hamburg. The Green List Ecology (GLU) presented candidates in both provincial elections, but gained only 3.9% in Lower Saxony and 1.0% in Hamburg.

In neither case was this vote sufficient for the grouping to achieve representation in the *Land* governments. The main theme of the Green List Ecology was their opposition to the development of nuclear power. In the rest of Western Europe, ecology parties and their supporters have tended to devote their attention to campaigns for specific environmental issues such as their efforts to promote the recycling of paper and glass: in these they have been more effective.

Elections to the *Land* parliament of Hesse were held on 8 October 1978 and Bavaria on 15 October. In the *Land* of Bavaria, the green parties reached agreement on a joint approach, but only secured 1.8% of the votes cast: in Hesse their total was 2.0% of the vote although there they had failed to reach any understanding on their policies.

The first real success in the Federal Republic came in the October 1979 elections to the Bremen Bürgerschaft (parliament), when the Bremen Grüne Liste (BGL) took more than 5% of the votes – the minimum required by federal law for representation

in any provincial assembly or in the Bundestag. The BGL had campaigned as opposing industrial growth and nuclear power and won four seats with a total of 20 911 votes or 5.1% of votes cast. In January 1980 the various ecology-oriented political groupings in Germany held a conference in Karlsruhe and formally constituted themselves into a national political party to be known as Die Grünen, the Green Party. In March 1980 the party fought the Baden-Württemberg *Land* election and achieved 5.3% of votes cast, with a total of 241 176. As this was above the required threshold the party gained six seats in the Baden-Württemberg parliament. This remains as the Green party's best electoral achievement to date; at the general election for the Bundestag in October 1980 the party received only 1.5% of the national vote.

Ecology parties have succeeded in provoking a greater general awareness of the environment in the last ten years in Europe and this remains their most significant achievement; however, they have found it difficult to translate this awareness into political support. In a period of continuing economic recession, the electorate is more concerned with employment issues rather than the problems of environmental protection. Ecology parties appear to have decided to move closer to the governmental system that they are attacking in order to become politically effective. This creates a problem for them as the political establishment may absorb them and their ability to persuade government and industry to take environmentally desirable decisions will be severely limited in the 1980s. Most commentators forecast a continuing high level of unemployment throughout the 1980s in Western Europe and therefore sympathy for environmental decisions which limit the creation of employment opportunities is likely to be at best, limited, and at worst, to generate positive hostility and reduced support for any ecology party. The Green Party in the Federal Republic appears as the best hope for electoral success for an ecology party in the 1980s.

References

1. Norpoth, H. (1980). Choosing a Coalition Partner: Mass Preferences and Elite Decisions in West Germany. *Comparative Political Studies* **12** (No. 4), 425 and 424–440
2. Allum, P. A. (1979). In *Political Parties in the European Community*, p. 101 (ed. by S. Henig). Allen & Unwin/Policy Studies Institute; London
3. *The Economist*, 11 October 1980, p. 51

Table 2.5 *The German electoral system 1969–1980*

Assembly	Bundestag
Members	518 (519 in 1980), of which 22 are nominated by West Berlin House of Representatives on the basis of parliamentary strength there. These 22 deputies do not possess voting rights
	Effective membership of the Bundestag: 1969, 1972, 1976 – 496; 1980 – 497
	The 1980 election produced an extra seat to give a total of 497 deputies, in accordance with the Basic Law (Constitution). This consisted of a so-called 'overhang' seat in Schleswig–Holstein
Dates of elections	28 September 1969 19 November 1972 3 October 1976 5 October 1980
Method	Combination of proportional representation (PR), d'Hondt system and plurality system. Each voter has two ballots: one in the constituency for a candidate, the other for a party list
Voting age	21, reduced to 18 in 1970, and effective at 1972 general election
Voter participation (turnout)	1969 86.7% 1972 91.1% 1976 90.7% 1980 87.8%

Sources: Keesings Contemporary Archives; Statistisches Jahrbuch 1979 für die Bundesrepublik Deutschland, pp. 83–86; Statistisches Jahrbuch 1980 für die Bundesrepublik Deutschland, pp. 84–86

Table 2.6 *Number of seats won in German elections 1969–1980*

Party	Number of seats (excluding West Berlin representatives who do not vote)			
	1969	1972	1976	1980
SPD	224	230	214	218
CDU	193	177	190	174
FDP	30	41	39	53
CSU	49	48	53	52
Die Grünen	–	–	–	0
NPD	0	0	0	0
DKP	–	0	0	0
KPD	–	–	0	–
AUD	–	–	0	–
KBW	–	–	0	0
EAP	–	–	0	0
CBV	–	–	0	0
BP	–	–	–	0
Volksfront	–	–	–	0
Total	496	496	496	497

Table 2.7 *Percentage of votes cast in German elections 1969–1980*

Party	Percentage of votes			
	1969	1972	1976	1980
SPD	42.7	45.8	42.6	42.9
CDU	36.6	35.2	38.0	34.2
FDP	5.8	8.4	7.9	10.6
CSU	9.5	9.7	10.6	10.3
Die Grünen	–	–	–	1.5[a]
NPD	4.3	0.6	0.3	0.2
DKP	–	0.3	0.3	0.2
KPD	–	–	0.1	–
AUD	–	–	0.1	–
KBW	–	–	0.1	
EAP	–	–	–	
CBV	–	–	–	0.1
BP	–	–	–	
Volksfront	–	–	–	
Other	1.1	0.0	0.0	0.0
Total	100.0	100.0	100.0	100.0

[a] *Die Grünen (Green Party) won 6 seats in the 16 March 1980 Land election of Baden-Württemberg*

Table 2.8 *Number of votes cast in German elections 1969–1980*

Party	Number of votes			
	1969	1972	1976	1980
SPD	14065716	17175169	16099019	16262096
CDU	12079535	13190837	14367302	12992334
FDP	1904422	3129982	2995085	4030608
CSU	3115652	3615183	4027499	3908036
Die Grünen	–	–	–	568265
NPD	1422010	207465	122661	67798
DKP	–	113891	118581	72230
KPD	–	–	22801	–
AUD	–	–	22272	–
KBW	–	–	20018	8285
EAP	–	–	6811	7814
CBV	–	–	6686	4019
BP	–	–	–	11623
Volksfront	–	–	–	9344
Other	379689	27223	58414	–
Total	32966024	37459750	37867149	37942452

Switzerland

Switzerland has long been a rare example of stability within Central Europe in terms of its politics and political geography.

Coalition government is the norm in Switzerland; the four largest parties constitute the Swiss Federal government throughout the period 1968 to 1979. *Figures 2.9* to *2.11* for the three elections of 1971, 1975 and 1979 show the large number of parties represented as do the relevant electoral statistics. The most outstanding feature of Swiss national elections is the low level of voter participation or what is usually referred to as voter turnout. By 1979 this figure had fallen to below half the eligible electorate, with only 48% of the electorate casting their votes, and in certain cantons this figure can be as low as 25%. These low voting figures and the fact that they have been declining during the 1970s can be explained by Switzerland's high degree of devolved government, which has been shared out to Swiss cantonal parliaments who take the decisions affecting the daily lives of their inhabitants; it can also be attributed to the lack of any substantial issue for the parties to contest. The election statistics show similar percentage votes for the parties, although here the lack of election issues, compared to neighbouring Austria, is not necessarily a contributing factor. Austria maintained a similar electoral pattern at its federal elections throughout the 1970s, but several issues were hotly contested at each election. The unique nature of devolved politics in Switzerland is the main reason for the low voter turnout; political commentators

Political parties	
CVP	Christian Democratic People's Party
EVP	Evangelical People's Party
FDP	Radical Democratic Party
LdU	Independents Party
LIDUS	Liberal Democratic Union of Switzerland
LPS	Liberal Party
NA	National Action against the Foreign Infiltration of People and Homeland
PdA	Party of Labour (Communist Party)
POCH	Progressive Organizations of Switzerland
PSA	Autonomous Socialist Party
Rep	Republican Movement
SPS	Social Democratic Party
SVP	Swiss People's Party

blame the tradition of consensus politics in Berne which has taken the interest out of federal affairs. The country has no Prime Minister, but the government ministers take turns at serving as Swiss president for a year. Policies associated with a particular leader cannot be identified as in other countries.

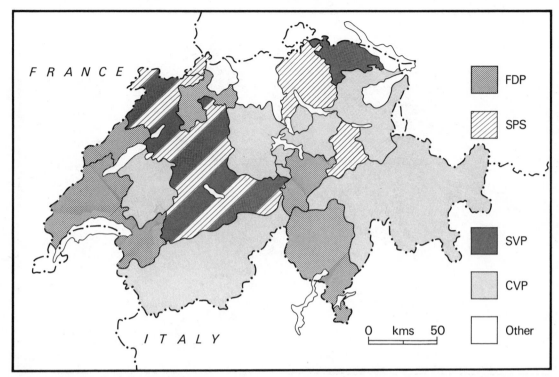

Figure 2.9 *Switzerland: the general election of 1971*

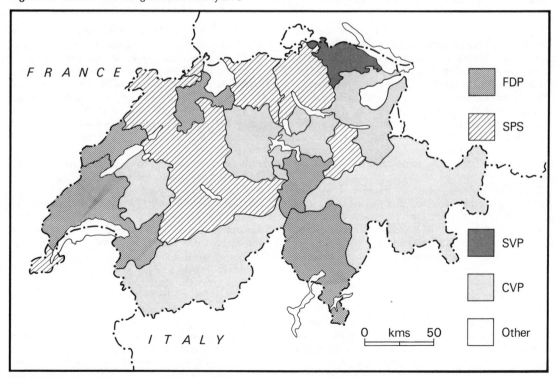

Figure 2.10 *Switzerland: the general election of 1975*

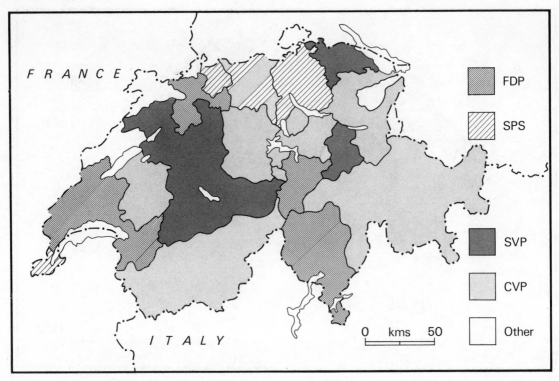

Figure 2.11   *Switzerland: the general election of 1979*

Since 1891 any Swiss citizen has been able to demand a national referendum on any issue provided a number of citizens sign the proposal. Formerly this figure was 50 000, but in September 1977 the Swiss voted to double the number of signatures required to 100 000. At the same time they voted in favour of requiring 50 000 signatures, instead of 30 000 to challenge existing laws. The country relies on the methods of direct democracy, namely the personal initiative and the referendum and this helps to explain the low level of voter participation in national elections[1].

The other striking point in Swiss politics and electoral geography is that, despite the country's reputation for stable democracy, it is only during the period under study that the franchise was extended to include its adult female population. This change to the constitution was approved following a national referendum to enfranchise women for federal affairs on 7 February 1971. In the first universal suffrage election in October 1971, the main outcome was the continued decline of support for the four parties in the coalition government with the loss of six seats. Women were also allowed to stand as candidates and eleven were elected. The Social Democrats (SPS) lost five seats, while the Christian Democrats (CVP) lost one. Other parties in the coalition governments have been the Radical Democratic Party (FDP) and the Swiss People's Party (SVP). The latter was actually formed just before the 1971 election in September and October of that year; it was previously an amalgamation of two parties known as the Farmers, Traders and Citizens party and the Democrats. The SPS, CVP, FDP and SVP comprise the Swiss coalition governments from 1971 to 1979, so that there has not been any opposition in the assembly and no grouping capable of forming an alternative administration. However, it has been suggested that there should be an opposition to the federal government[2].

In 1971 there was a net gain of six seats by the Republican Movement and four seats by the National Campaign against Foreign Domination of People and Homeland (Nationale Aktion gegen die Uber-freudung von Folk and Heimat); both parties had campaigned for a reduction in the number of for-eigners employed in Switzerland.

The trend of declining voter participation, which has been apparent since the introduction of prop-ortional representation in 1919 and was 80% of the electorate at that time, has been accentuated during the 1970s. In that decade the three elections show a voter participation of 56.9% in 1971, 52.4% in 1975 and, as mentioned above, the figure fell to 48% in 1979. In the 1975 elections there was a sharp increase in the Social Democrats (SPS) representation as the party increased its total from 46 to 55 and therefore regained the position it had lost in 1971 as the largest in the Nationalrat. The 1975 election did not change the composition of the Swiss government (the Bundesrat) with the SPS, CVP and FDP each having two of the seven seats and the SVP one.

In 1975 the FDP and SVP lost two seats each and the CVP gained two seats; the overall result was the four-party coalition of SPS, CVP, FDP and SVP had a net gain of seven seats. The four-party coalition remained in power for the period 1975 to 1979.

In the 1979 election the results for four-government coalition parties again changed little. The Republican movement, which had argued in 1975 for a reduction in the number of foreign workers, saw its support decrease in 1979 following the rejection of its proposals in a national referendum held in 1977.

Switzerland's government for the past twelve years has been a centrist coalition. The 200 seats in the Nationalrat are contested by some 30 political parties, and the electoral system is the Hagenbach –Bischoff method of proportional representation. In 1979 the Social Democrats (SPS) dropped four seats to have a total of 51, the same number as the liberal-inclined Radical Democrats (FDP). The centrist Swiss People's party (SVP) gained two for a total of 23, while the Christian Democrats (CVP) lost two to give them a total of 44. However, together these four governing parties had the same number of seats as in the previous legislature. Local rather than national issues dominated the 1979 election, reflecting the traditional Swiss reluctance to give more power to central government. A slight shift to the right was discernible, but the Alpine Confederation of cantons simply does not believe in giving too much power to the federal government.

Since 1959 the SPS (Social Democrats), FDP (Radical Democrats), and CVP (Christian Democrats) have each placed two members in the seven-seat federal cabinet on the basis of their representation in both houses of the Swiss parliament, these being the Nationalrat, National Council or Lower House and Ständerat, Cantonal Council or Upper House.

The Swiss People's Party (SVP) has the seventh cabinet post, and this line-up continued after the 1979 elections.

In 1979 Swiss women took part in the federal poll for the third time and eleven of their number were successful. The mass circulation Swiss newspaper *Blick* denied suggestions that Switzerland's election in 1979 was 'the world's most boring election', but admitted the truth of the predictions that everything would be just the same before and after the polls.

With less than 50% voter turnout and no change in the composition of the four-party government coalition, there appears to be little chance of change in the Swiss electoral pattern. The majority of Swiss electors appear already to have decided that there is indeed little point in their casting of votes in federal elections; the devolved nature of political power in the Alpine confederation allows its inhabitants a direct say in the decisions affecting their lives; it therefore seems to them unnecessary to cast a vote for a centrist coalition national government which is unlikely to change in the foreseeable future.

References

1. Mowlam, M. (1979). Popular Access to the Decision-making Process in Switzerland: The Role of Direct Democracy. *Government and Opposition*, **14** (No. 2), 180–197. However, this concept is not accepted by all students of Swiss politics: see discussion in Mowlam's article p. 183
2. *The Economist*, 3 February 1979. Switzerland: The Everlasting League, a Survey. Jean Ziegler of the Social Democratic Party is a notable supporter of the concept of an opposition

Table 2.9 *The Swiss electoral system 1971–1979*

Assembly	Nationalrat
Members	200 seats
Dates of elections	31 October 1971 26 October 1975 21 October 1979
Method	Proportional representation (PR); Hagenbach–Bischoff system. Every canton or half canton has one representative
Voting age	Men over 20; women enfranchised in 1971 for general elections for the first time by referendum
Voter participation *(turnout)*	1971 56.9% 1975 52.4% 1979 48.0%

Sources: Keesings Contemporary Archives; Annuaire Statistique de la Suisse 1979, pp. 543–545; Annuaire Statistique de la Suisse 1980, pp. 541–547

Table 2.10 *Number of seats won in Swiss elections 1971–1979*

Party	Number of seats		
	1971	1975	1979
SPS	46	55	51
FDP	49	47	51
CVP	44	46	44
SVP	21	21	23
LdU	13	11	8
LIDUS	6	6 LPS	8
Republican Movement	7	4	1
PdA	5	4	3
EVP	3	3	3
NA	4	2	2
POCH/PSA	0	1	4
Democrats	2	–	–
Progressives	–	–	2
Total	200	200	200

Table 2.11 *Percentage of votes cast in Swiss elections 1971–1979*

Party	Percentage of votes		
	1971	1975	1979
SPS	22.8	24.9	24.4
FDP	21.5	22.2	24.1
CVP	21.0	21.1	21.5
SVP	10.0	9.9	11.6
LdU	7.6	6.1	4.1
LIDUS	2.1	2.4 LPS	2.8
Republican Movement	4.0	3.0	0.6
PdA	2.5	2.4	2.1
EVP	2.2	2.0	2.2
NA	3.2	2.5	1.4
POCH/PSA	–	1.3	2.1
Democrats	0.8	–	–
Other	2.3	2.2	3.1
Total	100.0	100.0	100.0

Note: There are no vote totals available for Switzerland

Maritime Europe

Belgium

No study of modern Belgian politics is possible without first examining the historical background that has led to the linguistic strife threatening to tear this artificially created country in two. Belgium was formed in 1830, following the Walloon revolution against the short-lived United Kingdom of the Netherlands. It was created as a unitary French-speaking state when Flanders, to the north, was largely rural and politically dormant, while Wallonia was one of Europe's more industrialized areas with French the natural language for cultural and political life.

The weight of the Flemish majority was felt from the turn of the twentieth century when universal suffrage was introduced. The volatile language struggle has been exacerbated, some would argue superseded, since the 1960s by the diverging economic fortunes of Flanders and Wallonia. While Wallonia's traditional coal and steel industries have declined, Flanders has enjoyed a build-up of modern manufacturing industries and foreign investment so that Flanders output per head is 18% above that of Wallonia[1].

Instead of encouraging assimilation of different groups into a common culture, the more centralized control over economic and political decisions necessary in modern industrialized countries is far more likely to increase the rivalry between ethnic and linguistic groups competing for resources such as political power and investment. The Belgian problem is further divisive because of the sheer size of the ethnic minority; as Francophones or French speakers comprise 41% of the population and are thus able to compete for resources on a scale inconceivable for other European minorities such as the Basques, Bretons and even the Scots[2].

Political parties	
BSP–PSB	Belgian Socialist Party
CVP–PSC	Christian People's Party
FDF	Democratic Front Francophone
LIB	Independent Liberal
PCB–KPB	Belgian Communist Party
PL	Liberal Party
PLP	Party for Liberty and Progress (Walloon Liberals)
PRLW	Party for Reform and Liberty in Wallonia
PVV	Party for Liberty and Progress (Flemish Liberals)
RW	Walloon Assembly
Volksunie	Volksunie (Flemish Nationalist)

The increasing conflict of interests between the Flemish and their southern compatriots, the Walloons, was reflected in the 1960s by the growing strength of regionalist parties at the expense of big national parties. In the period under study from 1968 to 1979, all the large parties have split along linguistic lines, and have not always cooperated with their counterparts. Thus the tension between the Flemish and Walloons complicates every government decision, and the multiplicity of parties has made it increasingly difficult to form a government acceptable not just to a parliamentary majority, but to a majority on each linguistic side of the chamber.

The present seemingly intractable crisis was precipitated by demonstrations in 1966 at the bilingual University of Louvain by Flemish students against what they saw as the dominating presence of French-speaking students. Troubles increased until 1968, leading to the downfall of Paul Vanden Boeynants' Christian Social–Liberal coalition government, when the Christians split along linguistic lines into the CVP and PSC and the Flemish wing (CVP) supported their students. A general election was called for March 1968, a year ahead of time.

Belgium, along with its neighbour Luxembourg, is one of the few European countries where voting is compulsory; absence from casting one's vote at the ballot box is punishable by a fine of 400 Belgian francs.

The 1968 election strengthened support for the smaller federalist parties. The Volksunie (Flemish Nationalists) gained nearly 10% of the vote and increased its number of deputies from 12 to 20. Just before the election the Rassemblement Wallon was formed in the south to defend Walloon interests in the face of Flemish demands for autonomy. The Rassemblement Wallon (RW) aligned itself with the Brussels-based Front Democratique des Francophones (FDF) and between them took 15 seats.

The split Christian Socials, Socialists and Liberals all lost ground, and a further example of the increasing fragmentation of Belgian political life was that a ballot had to be held for the first time in the country's political history for the 24 co-opted senators in the second chamber. The elections, as was increasingly to become the case, solved nothing. After 132 days, a coalition was eventually formed between the Christian Socials and the Socialists in June 1968 under the premiership of the veteran politician Gaston Eyskens.

But the election did force a striking concession to the idea of federalism, then the dominant question in Belgian politics and still true at the present time. The government list comprised separate ministers of education and culture, as before, but now there were also two ministers for relations between the linguistic communities and two minister-secretaries of state for regional development in Flanders and Wallonia. The rest of the government list was a careful balance between 14 Flemings and 14 Walloons. The coalition partners also agreed on similar parity in the top ranks of the civil service and the army[3].

The conflicting interests of the two sides, Flanders seeking greater political autonomy and Wallonia seeking greater help for its economic problems,

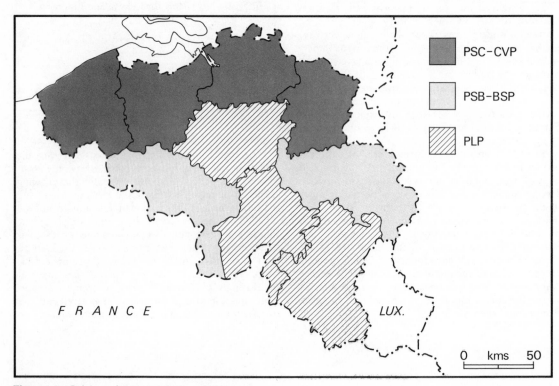

Figure 3.1 *Belgium: the general election of 1968*

increased with a related problem: the capital Brussels, a largely French-speaking enclave in Flanders. The Francophones sought to increase the size, and therefore influence, of Brussels in the face of strong opposition from the Flemish speakers in the surrounding countryside. The government firmly resolved to limit the growth of the capital. In the month before the general election of 7 November 1971, local elections allowed the militant FDF to make startling gains of between 20 and 25% in Brussels, making it the dominant grouping in many constituencies. However, the coalition could take comfort from socialist gains of up to 4% in the provinces. The other extremist regionalist parties also made gains, particularly in large cities. The 1971 election was the first national election since the electoral reforms of June 1969, which had reduced the voting age from 21 to 18 years.

Mr Eyskens went into the election having failed three times to get a vote on the limitation of Brussels. In the November 1971 election the moderate regionalists made substantial gains, the largest being the FDF–RW which increased its representation from 13 to 24, while the Christian Socials (CVP–PSC) lost and the Socialists BSP–PSB) gained slightly.

The Christian Socialists–Socialist coalition lasted until 1974 with Edmond Leburton as Prime Minister. A premature general election was caused by a cabinet crisis in connection with a Belgian–Iranian project to establish an oil refinery. Leo Tindemans, chairman of the Flemish wing of the Christian Socials (CVP), was deputy Prime Minister in the 1971–1974 coalition and attempted to form a minority coalition government of the CVP and the Liberals (PVV, Flemish Liberals and PLP, Walloon Liberals). A general election was held on 10 March 1974 after Mr Tindemans failed to form an administration; the Christian Socials gained five seats while the socialists lost two. The FDF and RW which made substantial gains in 1971 at the expense of the Liberals, lost two seats in 1974, but the FDF remained the strongest party in Brussels. Foreign press reports of the election indicated a degree of geographical polarization of supporters of the two largest traditional parties. Leo Tindemans became Prime Minister at the head of a Christian Socials (CVP–PSC) and Liberal (PVV–PLP) coalition which was announced on 24 April 1974, thus constituting a change in the pattern of coalition government in Belgium. The Socialists (BSP–PSB) went into opposition. On 11 June 1974 the minority coalition under Leo Tindemans was broadened to include the Rassemblement Wallon,

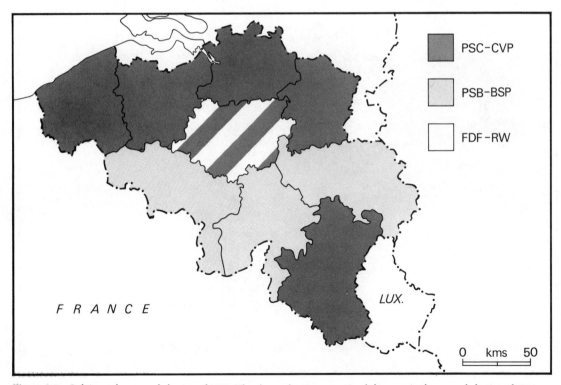

Figure 3.2 *Belgium: the general election of 1971. The electoral pattern remained the same in the general election of 1974*

thus making it a majority administration. This was the first occasion in Belgian politics that a federalist party had become part of the government coalition.

The municipal elections of October 1976 precipitated a change in the Tindemans government. The RW split after the party had suffered serious losses in the October elections. The founder members of the Rassemblement Wallon joined the Walloon wing of the Liberal Party (PLP) to form a new party the PRLW, Parti des Reformes et de la Liberté en Wallonie. This new party put itself forward as a pluralist group working for federalism in Belgium. The Tindemans coalition government was reorganized on 8 December 1976 and became the grouping of the Christian Socials, PRLW, the Flemish Liberals PVV and the RW.

By 1977 only the Socialist Party remained nationally united, although even it had two presidents representing the linguistic division and issued separate lists of Flemish and French-speaking candidates. The linguistically split but cooperating parties gained from their new identities, pushing the regionalist parties down slightly in the election of 17 April 1977; the Christian Socials made the largest gains from 72 seats in 1974 to 80 in 1977.

Leo Tindemans, Prime Minister since 1974, called after the election for a government of national unity in a grand coalition of Christian Socials, Liberals and Socialists to solve the devolution issue and the country's economic problems. Belgium's experience of the oil price quintupling and subsequent recession in 1974 was worse than other West European countries, with unemployment running then at 8%, one of the highest rates in the European Economic Community.

The results in 1977 could also be seen along linguistic lines: the Liberals fell back in Flanders but gained in Wallonia, while the socialists advanced in their traditional stronghold of Wallonia, but lost ground in Brussels.

Mr Tindemans formed a coalition with all the main parties except the Liberals and promised to produce a once-and-for-all settlement to the Flemish–Walloon conflict. Intense negotiation between the parties on devolution got under way immediately, culminating in the ill-fated Egmont Pact several weeks later. This was agreed by the six parties of the coalition: the CVP, PSC, BSP, PSB, FDF and Volksunie (Flemish Nationalist).

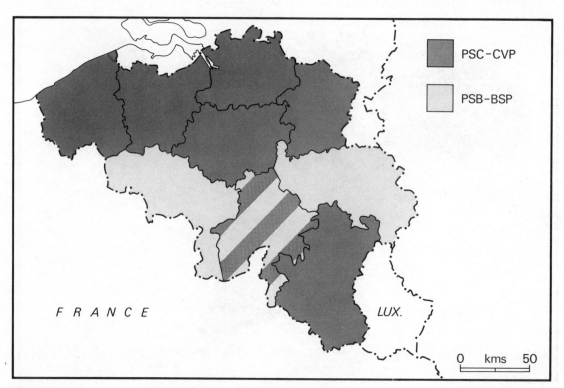

Figure 3.3 *Belgium: the general election of 1977. The electoral pattern remained the same in the general election of 1978*

The Pact envisaged five tiers of government with the following powers:

(1) The National Parliament retaining full control over foreign affairs, defence, justice, taxation and economic policy with the power of the Senate reduced to leave the Chamber the main legislative body;
(2) Regional Councils to be set up to take care of all regional questions with the old Cultural Councils reorganizing into Community Councils, but with the provinces and communes left untouched;
(3) An Arbitration Court to be set up to settle all conflicts arising between the tiers.

But the Pact floundered on Brussels. While the capital would not expand beyond its 19 communes, it would be given regional status on the same level as Flanders and Wallonia. The Flemings opposed this, arguing that the minority Francophones would have two regions, with all the economic advantages that entailed, to their one. Mr Tindemans, a Fleming, did not like the Pact either but agreed to it because he believed he could cut back on provisions that were over-generous to the Francophones when it came to working out the details[4]. A Constitutional Court ruled the following August that full implementation of the Pact was impossible without changing the constitution. This ruling caused an outcry in the chamber of deputies; Mr Tindemans, faced with his own CVP against the Pact, but miscalculating the mood of the country, resigned in October 1978 and provoked another early general election. Throughout the 1970s, the devolution question forced Belgium into early elections. A transitional government, led by Paul Vanden Boeynants, former Prime Minister from 1966 to 1968, operated until the general election could take place between three weeks and two months from the Tindemans' resignation.

The election of 17 December 1978, fought along the lines of 'The battle for Brussels' again solved nothing. It produced the same electoral pattern as the previous one, although the two wings of the Socialist Party BSP and PSB had become separate in October 1978 (*Figure 3.3*). Both Christian Social Parties gained ground slightly, each with one seat more to total 57 and 25, while the socialists lost four seats. The regionalist parties held their ground, except the Volksunie which dropped from 20 to 14 deputies. One lesson to be learned from this Belgian election was that if the politicians were obsessed by the devolution problem, the electorate was more concerned with unemployment, the economic situation and taxation. The communists doubled their representation from two to four seats, the anti-tax RAD –UDRT (Respect voor Arbeid en Democratie/Union

Democratique pour Respect du Travail) and the extreme right Vlaams Blok for the first time each won a seat.

Following the general election of 1978, three and a half months of protracted negotiations were necessary for the formation of a government. A coalition emerged on 3 April 1979 comprised of the two Christian Social parties, two Socialist Parties and the FDF under the premiership of Wilfred Martens, a Flemish Christian Social lawyer with no ministerial experience. The Volksunie had taken part in the Vanden Boeynants transition government but decided to go into opposition following its poor showing in the election.

On 23 January 1980 Martens announced that FDF had withdrawn from the coalition: this meant that the remaining parties still had a majority in the 212 seat assembly, but the loss of the 11 FDF members had reduced the effective voting total below the two-thirds majority required for the passage of constitutional amendments. In April, Martens resigned as Prime Minister after the Upper Chamber, the Senate, did not approve proposals for devolution of some powers to a regional assembly. However, he formed a new coalition of six parties on 18 May. This consisted of the two Christian Social Parties, two Socialist Parties and two Liberal Parties PRL and PVV. The six-party coalition under Martens has made progress towards financial autonomy for Flanders and Wallonia and directly elected regional councils are planned for October 1982. Brussels has retained its status until a decision on a regional assembly is taken, which is also planned for 1982. The result could be a third autonomous region for the Belgian capital, recognizing it as a separate entity within Flemish-speaking Flanders.

Little headway has been made since on devolution and there are no prospects for sudden change, given that the same politicians are continuing with the same arguments. However, with the extremist parties, for the moment, confined to small minorities and the main parties all walking so close to the middle of the road, there is no strong likelihood of one side or the other losing patience and unilaterally declaring an independent state.

References

1. *The Economist*, 19 January 1980, Survey of Belgium, p. 4
2. Rayside, D. M. (March 1979). The Impact of Linguistic Cleavage on the Governing Parties of Belgium and Canada. *Canadian Journal of Political Science*, p. 61
3. Huggell, F. E. (March 1969). More troubles in Belgium – Note of the Month. *The World Today*, p. 93
4. *The Economist*, op. cit., p. 8

Table 3.1 *The Belgian electoral system 1968–1978*

Assembly	Kamer der Volksvertegenwoordigers Chambre des Representants Chamber of Representatives
Members	212
Dates of elections	31 March 1968 7 November 1971 10 March 1974 17 April 1977 17 December 1978 Parliamentary term is 4 years
Method	Proportional representation (PR); d'Hondt system. Number of seats awarded to each party decided by dividing its total vote by electoral divisor. Each voter selects an integral list for preferred candidate or for candidate and an alternative
Voting age	21, reduced to 18 in June 1969. Voting is compulsory under penalty of a fine for all citizens over age 21 and domiciled in same municipality for at least six months; absence from ballot is punishable by a fine of 400 francs. Voters may cast a blank or spoiled ballot if they do not wish to support any candidate
Voter participation *(turnout)*	1968 90.1% 1971 91.7% 1974 91.6% 1977 95.1% 1978 94.9%

Source: Annuaire Statistique de la Belgique, 1970, 1971, 1976, 1978 pp. 110–115, 1979 pp. 110–111; Keesings Contemporary Archives

Table 3.2 *Number of seats won in Belgian elections 1968–1978*

Party	Number of seats				
	1968	1971	1974	1977	1978
CVP	45 ⎫		50	56	57
PSC	15 ⎬	67	22	24	25
BSP–PSB	59	60	59	62	58 BSP 26[c] PSB 32
PVV			⎧	17	22
PLP[a]	47	31	⎨ 33		
PRLW			⎪	14	14
PL			⎩ 2	1	
Volksunie	20	21	22	20	14
FDF ⎫	12	24	9	10	11
RW ⎬			13	5	4
PCB–KPB	5	5	4	2	4
Cartel VDB[b]	9	–	–	–	–
Other	0	4	0	0	2

[a] PLP contested 1968 and 1971 elections
[b] Cartel VDB contested 1968 election only
[c] PSB and BSP became separate parties in October 1978

Table 3.3 *Percentage of votes cast in Belgian elections 1968–1978*

Party	Percentage of votes				
	1968	1971	1974	1977	1978
CVP	20.0 ⎫	30.0	32.3	36.0	36.3
PSC	7.1 ⎭				
BSP–PSB	28.0	27.2	26.7	27.0	25.4 BSP 12.4 / PSB 13.0
PVV				8.5	10.3
PLP	20.9	16.4	⎧ 33		
PRLW			⎨ 15.2	5.9	5.2
PL			⎩	1.1	1.3
Volksunie	9.8	11.1	10.2	10.0	7.0
FDF ⎫	5.9	11.2	5.1	4.3	4.2
RW ⎭			5.9	2.8	2.8
PCB–KPB	3.3	3.1	3.2	2.1	3.3
Cartel VDB	4.6	–	–	–	–
Other	0.4	0.9	1.5	2.2	4.1

Table 3.4 *Number of votes cast in Belgian elections 1968–1978*

Party	Number of votes				
	1968	1971	1974	1977	1978
CVP	1 037 309 ⎫	1 587 195	1 700 855	2 005 812	1 447 131
PSC	370 193 ⎭				560 540
BSP–PSB	1 449 172	1 438 626	1 401 725	1 507 014	1 404 991
PVV					572 558
			798 818	866 306	
PLP	1 080 894	865 657			
PRLW					287 947
Volksunie	506 697	586 917	536 287	599 567	387 988
FDF ⎫	305 444	593 245	575 487	395 277	231 197
RW ⎭					158 602
PCB–KPB	170 625	161 517	166 008	118 085	180 233
Cartel VDB	236 283	–	–	–	–
Other	21 335	48 476	79 351	122 997	304 977
Total	5 177 952	5 281 633	5 258 531	5 575 058	5 536 164

Ireland

The Republic of Ireland is unique among the countries of Western and Southern Europe in the electoral system it employs to elect the members of the Dail Eireann, the Irish Parliament. The system is one of proportional representation known as the single transferable vote or STV: it means the country is divided into multi-member constituencies and voters effectively rank the candidates in their constituency in order of preference. The STV system therefore differs from the d'Hondt or Hagenbach–Bischoff system of lists as the voters have the opportunity to show their preferences for individual candidates rather than giving support to a party list of candidates.

In order to qualify for election to Dail Eireann, each candidate must obtain a quota of votes, usually referred to as the Droop quota, which consists of the votes cast for each candidate divided by the seats to be elected plus one, the result of this division being added to the figure of one[1]. A candidate who fulfils the quota in his or her first preference votes is declared elected; a second count is then taken with votes given for the already successful candidate being transferred to the remaining candidates in accordance with second preferences expressed by the voters. This procedure continues until all available seats have been filled. In Ireland, three-seat constituencies are the minimum, with larger constituencies having four or five seats.

Three general elections have been called during the period under examination, in June 1969, February 1973 and June 1977, and have seen the Fianna Fail party in government at the beginning and end of the period, but out of office for the period 1973 to 1977.

Figures 3.4, 3.5 and *3.6* indicate the extent of electoral support for the two major parties, Fianna Fail and Fine Gael, although in the case of the 1973 election it is relevant to show the constituencies where Fine Gael and Labour had a majority over Fianna Fail, as the two parties campaigned together and subsequently formed the government. The north and west of the Republic are the strongholds of Fianna Fail and its dominant position in the politics of the Republic is illustrated by the pattern of its support in 1973 in the north and west when it went into opposition. At the elections of 1969 and 1977, Fianna Fail has an overwhelming lead in the constituencies where its members are in a majority; on both these occasions it had a majority in the Dail Eireann and formed the government.

In 1968 Fianna Fail was in power, led by Jack Lynch who was Prime Minister or Taoiseach which is the Irish title for the leader of the assembly. Fianna Fail had won more seats than any other party in the Dail in the 1965 election, but had a majority of only one over all other parties: the party had been in

Political parties	
FF	Fianna Fail (Warriors of Destiny)
FG	Fine Gael (Tribe of Gaels)
Lab	Labour Party
	Democratic Labour Party
	Independent Party
	Independent Fianna Fail
	Independent Labour Party

power since 1957. In the election of June 1969 Fianna Fail campaigned on its record and was successful, as it won 75 of the 144 seats in the Dail to give it a majority of five over all other parties combined. Jack Lynch remained as Prime Minister and Taoiseach, an office which he continued to hold until the next election in 1973.

By that time Fianna Fail had been the governing party for 16 years: it has been noted in a study of Irish elections that 'it may even be suggested that the regime was excessively stable and it does not seem to support the suggestion that the single transferable vote method or proportional representation in some way leads inevitably to instability in government'. The study continues, 'it may be unlikely that the voting system itself has very much to do with governmental stability or instability'[2].

Both major parties Fianna Fail and Fine Gael supported the proposed accession of the Irish Republic to the EEC: on 10 May 1972 a national referendum was held on an amendment to the constitution for accession to the EEC and 71.0% of the electorate voted in favour of membership. The Irish Labour Party opposed entry but, following the referendum, accepted the decision of the electorate. The Common Market issue was never as divisive in Ireland as it was in neighbouring Britain nor was the 'anti' campaign successful as it was in Norway. Early discussions between Fine Gael and Labour appear to have been held in November 1970[3] but it was not until after the amendment to the constitution allowing for EEC membership that serious discussions took place.

In the 1973 election Fianna Fail increased their percentage of first preference votes from 45.7% to 46.2%, but their share of the seats obtained dropped from 51.7% to 47.5%. The combined share of seats in the Dail for the National Coalition, as Fine Gael and the Labour party had termed their alliance, increased from 47.6% in 1969 to 51.1% although it must be noted that the 1969 figure is purely notional as the parties campaigned separately for that election.

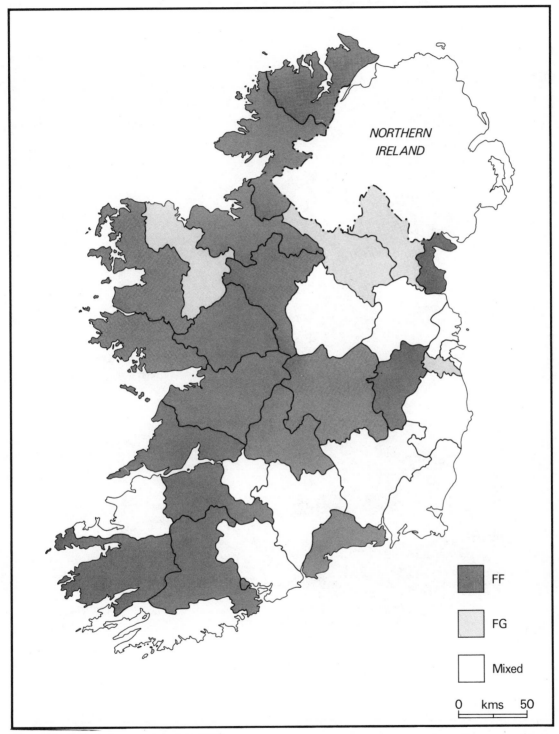

Figure 3.4 *Ireland: the general election of 1969*

40

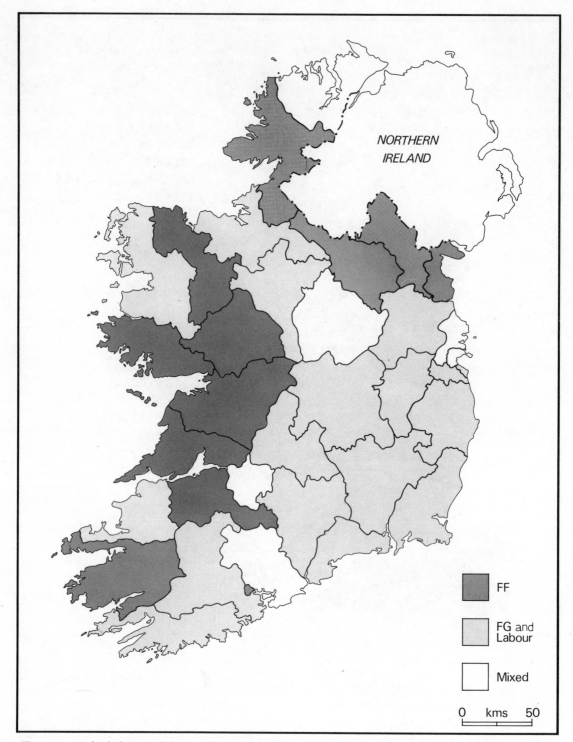

Figure 3.5 *Ireland: the general election of 1973*

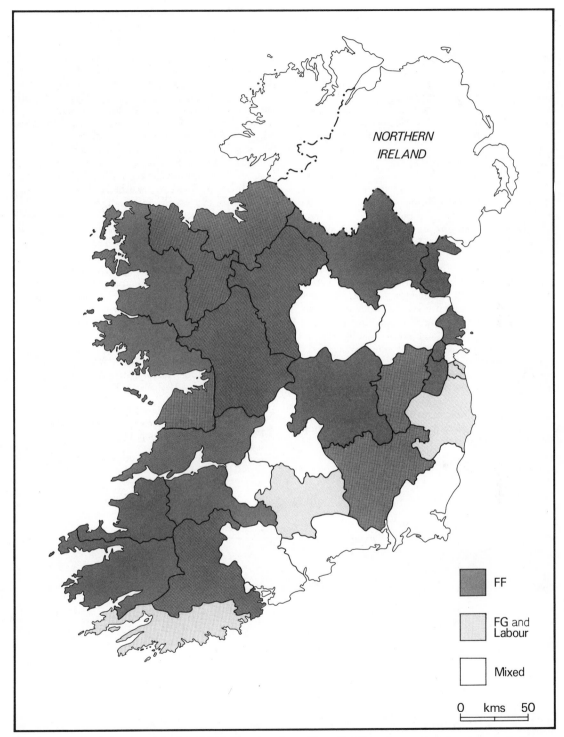

NORTHERN
IRELAND

FF

FG and
Labour

Mixed

0   kms   50

Figure 3.6 *Ireland: the general election of 1977. Note that electoral boundaries have been revised since the 1973 election*

The National Coalition gained 73 of the 144 seats in the Dail, sufficient for it to form an administration and force Fianna Fail for the first time in 16 years into opposition.

The leader of the Fine Gael, Liam Cosgrave became Prime Minister at the head of the coalition and Taoiseach; the administration was the twentieth Dail and continued in office until May 1977 making it the longest sitting Dail in the Republic's history. During its period in office the National Coalition had to contend with the impact of the quintupling of crude oil prices and the world commodity price boom; the problem of relations with the British Government over Northern Ireland and various attempts to solve the situation. It is doubtful, however, whether attempts at power sharing in Northern Ireland have had any impact on the electoral patterns of the Republic.

In 1977, the National Coalition led by Liam Cosgrave campaigned on its record as a government which had steered Ireland through four years of crisis and had succeeded for the first time in over a century in halting emigration. It promised a national development corporation and economic planning as well as support for agriculture and fisheries if it was re-elected. However, the voters turned away from the centre-left coalition and gave a decisive victory to Jack Lynch and Fianna Fail. Fianna Fail took 84 seats in the new 148-seat Dail, where boundary revision appears to have favoured the party (*see Figure 3.6*). It increased its first preference to more than 50%. Fine Gael and Labour could only total 60 seats in the new Dail and both parties saw their percentage vote decrease.

Jack Lynch became Taoiseach again and remained at the head of the Fianna Fail until December 1979. He resigned as leader of Fianna Fail and as Prime Minister and his place was taken on 7 December 1979 by Charles Haughey, who had suffered disgrace and dismissal from government in April 1970 over an unproved arms scandal. While Mr Lynch appeared to be moving his party towards closer cooperation with the British government over the Northern Ireland question, initially Charles Haughey was expected to adopt a tougher line towards any discussions, as he was well known for his commitment to the ideal of a united Ireland. 'His reputation was that of a hard-liner, an uncompromising republican. The reality has been different, however, and he is obviously a man the British can work with'[4]. This aspect of Mr Haughey's character was exemplified by the summit meeting at Dublin Castle in December 1980 with British Prime Minister Margaret Thatcher.

The next election is due in Ireland in 1981 and Fianna Fail would appear to be in a strong position; Ireland has benefitted considerably from EEC membership and Mr Haughey should be able to campaign on a successful economic record.

References

1. Mackie, T. T. and Rose, R. (1974). *The International Almanac of Electoral History*, Macmillan, London. *See* the Appendix: The Mechanics of Electoral Systems, p. 434
2. Knight, J. and Baxter-Moore, N. (1973). Republic of Ireland – The General Elections of 1969 and 1973, Arthur McDougal Fund, London, p. 11
3. Ibid., p. 15
4. *The Times*, 25 February 1981, Republic of Ireland: A Special Report

Table 3.5 *The Irish electoral system 1969–1977*

Assembly	Dail or Dail Eireann
Members	144 seats increased to 148 for 1977 election with revision of constituency boundaries
Dates of elections	18 June 1969 28 February 1973 16 June 1977
Method	Single transferable vote; multi-member constituencies with 3, 4 or 5 members elected by transferable vote
Voting age	In 1968 21 years, reduced to 18 in December 1972
Voter participation (turnout)	1969 76.9% 1973 76.6% 1977 76.3%

Source: Election Results and Transfer of Votes, Dublin, Stationery Office 1969, 1973, 1977; Keesings Contemporary Archives

Table 3.6 *Number of seats won and number and percentage of first preference votes in Irish elections 1969–1977*

Party	Number of seats		
	1969	1973	1977
FF	75	69	84
FG	50	54	43
Lab	18	19	17
Other	1	2	4
Total	144	144	148

Party	Number of first preference votes		
	1969	1973	1977
FF	602 200	624 500	811 615
FG	449 700	473 800	488 767
Lab	224 500	185 100	186 410
Other	42 500	67 100	116 235
Total	1 318 900	1 350 500	1 603 027

Party	Percentage of first preference votes		
	1969	1973	1977
FF	45.7	46.2	50.6
FG	34.1	35.1	30.5
Lab	17.0	13.7	11.6
Other	3.2	5.0	7.3

Table 3.7 *Percentage of seats obtained in Irish elections 1969–1977*

Party	Percentage of seats		
	1969	1973	1977
FF	51.7	47.5	56.8
FG	35.0	37.8	29.0
Lab	12.6	13.3	11.5
Other	0.7	1.4	2.7

Additional Data	1969	1973	1977
Persons entitled to vote	1 735 388	1 783 604	2 118 606
Total votes	1 334 963	1 366 474	1 616 770
Votes recorded as % of number entitled to vote	76.9	76.6	76.3
Valid votes as % of votes recorded	98.8	98.8	99.2

Luxembourg

Political parties

CSV   Christian Social Party/Christian Socialists

LCR   Revolutionary Communist League

LSAP   Socialist Workers Party

PD   Democratic Party (Liberals)

        Communists

        Enrôlés de Force

        Independent Socialists

        Social Democrats

Luxembourg presents an example of stable coalition government; its politics and government from 1945 to 1974 have been dominated by the Christian Social Party (CSV). The country is divided into four electoral constituencies; three elections have taken place during the period 1968–1979 and following each election a coalition government has been formed. *Figure 3.8* shows the electoral pattern if a Socialist –Liberal Coalition had been formed in 1968. This pattern suggests a joining of political forces might have been able to remove the Christian Social Party from their dominant position at that time, although this did not happen until 1974.

In 1968 the Luxembourg government was a coalition of the Christian Social Party (CSV) and the Socialists (LSAP). It resigned in October 1968 over the issue of finance for the social-welfare programme; the elections held on 15 November for a new chamber of deputies resulted in the CSV losing one seat, the LSAP lost three seats while the Liberals gained five to increase to 11. The CSV had ruled continuously in the Grand Duchy from 1945.

Following the election there was a three months crisis in the formation of an administration, which ended on 27 January 1979 when the CSV and the Liberals agreed on the formation of a coalition. A revival of the previous coalition between the CSV and the LSAP was not possible due to issues concerning State schools and the problem of workers' participation in the management of enterprises.

The new government was headed by Pierre Werner, leader of the CSV and outgoing Prime Minister. The coalition comprised 32 of the 56 deputies in the chamber and took office on 31 January 1969. This coalition remained in power for more than five years. In 1971 the Social Democratic Party was formed by a number of right-wing deputies from the Luxembourg

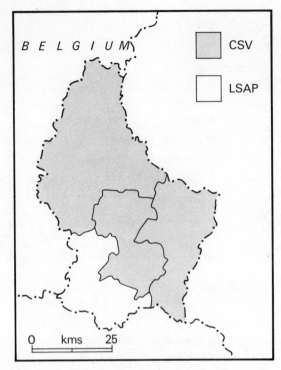

Figure 3.7 *Luxembourg: the general election of 1968*

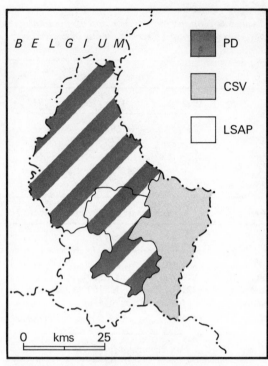

Figure 3.8 *Luxembourg: a theoretical electoral pattern based on an idealized coalition following the 1968 general election. Figure 3.9 shows the actual result*

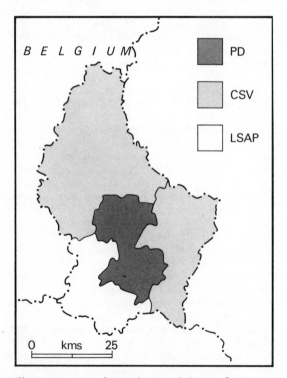

Figure 3.9 *Luxembourg: the general election of 1974*

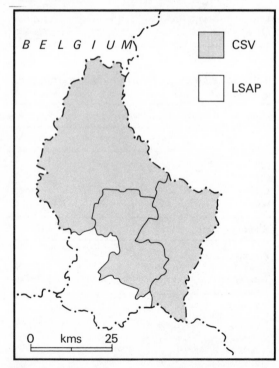

Figure 3.10 *Luxembourg: the general election of 1979*

Socialist Workers Party (LSAP). Six of the 18 LSAP deputies, elected in 1968, broke away from the party and were led by Henry Cravatte, previously chairman of the LSAP and deputy Prime Minister from 1964 to 1968. The LSAP were reduced to 12 deputies in the chamber. The deputies who moved away to form the Social Democratic Party were opposed to what they regarded as the leftist tendency in LSAP policies they felt had appeared in the party following the 1968 elections. In 1971 the more immediate issue, which precipitated the actual break, was the question of cooperation with the communists at local government level.

The election of 26 May 1974 produced a major change in Luxembourg's coalition government as, for the first time since 1945, the CSV were not part of the coalition. The CSV Liberal coalition was replaced by a Liberal–Socialist (LSAP) coalition headed by the Liberal leader Gaston Thorn. In the previous administration he had been foreign affairs minister. The major issues in the 1974 election were inflation, the liberalization of abortion laws, women's rights and agricultural problems.

The question of worker representation on boards of management again featured as an issue, following a one-day general strike in October 1973.

The chamber of deputies had been enlarged from 56 to 59 and the franchise extended to the 18 to 21 year olds. This added 13 000 voters to a total electorate of 206 000.

The new coalition government headed by Gaston Thorn had an equal number of Liberal and Socialist ministers in the eight-member cabinet, and support of 31 of the 59 deputies in the chamber. The Social Democrats won 5 seats in the 1974 election, the first they had contested as a separate party, and obtained 9.1% of the vote.

The Liberal–Socialist coalition lasted five years and the most recent election took place on 10 June 1979. With only a quarter of the votes counted, Gaston Thorn announced he would resign as the results were going against the coalition parties. He subsequently became President of the European Communities Commission. The 59 seats were contested by 11 party lists in 1979; voting is compulsory in Luxembourg and took place on the same day for elections for the European Assembly. Even though there is a legal obligation to vote, only 188 900 of the 211 000 electors went to the polls, giving an 84% turnout.

Opposition leader Pierre Werner's challenge had focused on liberal-sponsored reforms of the abortion, divorce and death penalty laws. Of the coalition partners, the Socialists (LSAP), lost three seats, although the Liberals, Democratic Party, gained one. The LSAP and Liberals had undertaken to form another coalition if they received a majority in the chamber, but their majority was removed.

Four weeks of negotiations followed the elections and resulted in a coalition of the CSV, in opposition from 1974 to 1979, and the Liberals. Agreement for a joint programme was announced on 9 July 1979. Pierre Werner again became Prime Minister, with outgoing premier Gaston Thorn taking the office of deputy Prime Minister, with foreign and economic affairs. This example of coalition in the cabinet formation is a situation unthinkable in the adversary politics of other West European countries, notably Great Britain.

The Christian Social Party resumed its role as part of the government, which had been uninterrupted in the Grand Duchy from the end of World War II until 1974.

Two new parties each gained one seat in the new chamber. The Independent Socialists gathered votes in Luxembourg city and the Enrôlés de Force (enforced enrolment) Party polled well in the south of the country. The latter party demands compensation from the Federal Republic of Germany for the 12 000 Luxembourgers who were forced to join the Nazi army when the country was annexed during World War II.

The new government was headed by Pierre Werner, and the coalition parties controlled 39 of the 59 seats in the chamber.

This model of coalition government would appear likely to continue in Luxembourg in the future.

Table 3.8 *The Luxembourg electoral system 1968–1979*

Assembly	Chambre des Deputes Chamber of Deputies
Members	In 1968 56 seats in the Chamber, increased in 1974 to 59 seats
Dates of elections	15 December 1968 26 May 1974 10 June 1979
Method	Proportional representation (PR); Hagenbach–Bischoff system. Four constituencies in Luxembourg; voting is compulsory
Voting age	In 1968 21 years, reduced in 1972 to 18
Voter participation (*turnout*)	1968 88.6% 1974 85.0% 1979 84.1%

Source: *Annuaire Statistique 1975, pp. 277–280; Statec, Luxembourg; Keesings Contemporary Archives; Annuaire Statistique 1979, pp. 313–316*

Table 3.9 *Number of seats won in Luxembourg elections 1968–1979*

Party	Number of seats		
	1968	1974	1979
CSV	21	18	24
PD	11	14	15
LSAP	18	17	14
Social Democrats	–	5	2
Communists	6	5	2
LCR	–	0	0
Liberals	–	0	0
Euroles	–	–	1
Independent Socialists	–	–	1
Other	0	0	0
Total	56	59	59

Table 3.10 *Percentage of votes cast in Luxembourg elections 1968–1979*

Party	Percentage of votes		
	1968	1974	1979
CSV	35.3	28.0	34.5
PD	16.6	22.1	21.3
LSAP	32.3	29.0	24.3
Social Democrats	–	9.1	6.0
Communists	15.5	10.4	5.8
Euroles	–	–	4.4
Independent Socialists	–	–	2.2
Other	0.4	1.4	1.4

Table 3.11 *Number of votes cast in Luxembourg elections 1968–1979*

Party	Number of votes		
	1968	1974	1979
CSV	915 944	836 990	1 049 390
PD	430 262	668 043	648 404
LSAP	837 555	875 881	737 863
Social Democrats	–	276 495	181 805
Communists	402 610	314 635	177 286
Euroles	–	–	135 360
Independent Socialists	–	–	66 909
Other	10 355	33 194	44 236
Total	2 596 726	3 005 238	2 041 253

Netherlands

Political parties	
AR	Anti-Revolutionary Party
BP	Farmers Party
CDA	Christian Democratic Appeal (comprising the AR, CHU, KVP)
CHU	Christian Historical Union
CPN	Communist Party of the Netherlands
D'66	Democrats '66
DS'70	Democratic Socialists 70
GPV	Reformed Political Union
KVP	Catholic People's Party
PPR	Radical Political Party
PSP	Pacifist Socialist Party
PvdA	Labour Party
SGP	State Reformed Party
VVD	Party of Freedom and Democracy (Liberal)

The Netherlands is unique in the European political scene in that, although it has 18 constituencies spread across the country, the members of the Lower Chamber (the Tweede Kamer of the States General) are elected in multi-member constituences on the basis of a country-wide vote.

Between 1968 and 1980 three general elections were held in 1971, 1972 and 1977. Although the country votes together, it is possible to make regional comparison of electoral support for the major parties.

Figure 3.11 shows the pattern for 1971. This did not change in the election of 1972. *Figure 3.12* shows the changed position after the 1977 election.

Political parties in the Netherlands are divided on a religious and secular basis, known as the confessional parties and the non-confessional parties. A recent study notes that 'In other European countries . . . it is religious voting that dominates. This is particularly true of countries straddling Europe's Protestant/Catholic divide, such as the Netherlands and Switzerland'. It continues 'this suggests that instead of the most recent cleavage (labour market) superseding the earlier religious factor, in these countries religion remains the most important social basis of voting'[1].

From 1917 to 1970 voting was compulsory in the Netherlands. The first elections with voluntary voting were held in March 1970 for local councils.

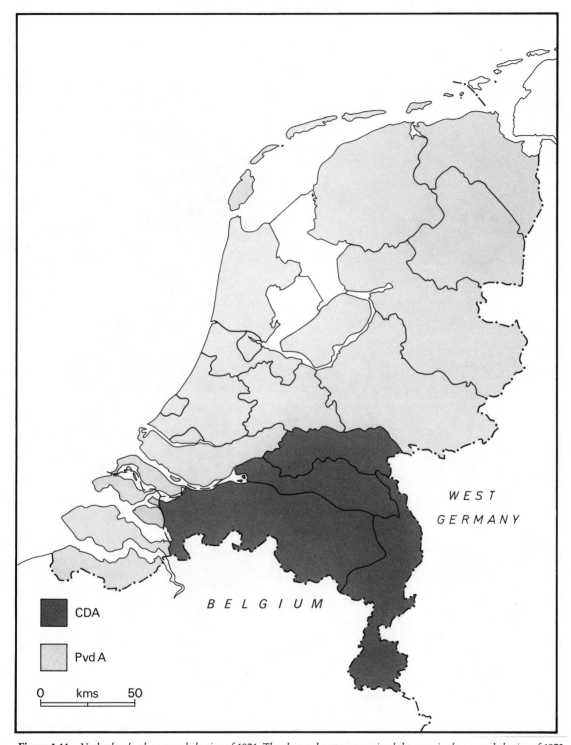

CDA

PvdA

0   kms   50

Figure 3.11   *Netherlands: the general election of 1971. The electoral pattern remained the same in the general election of 1972*

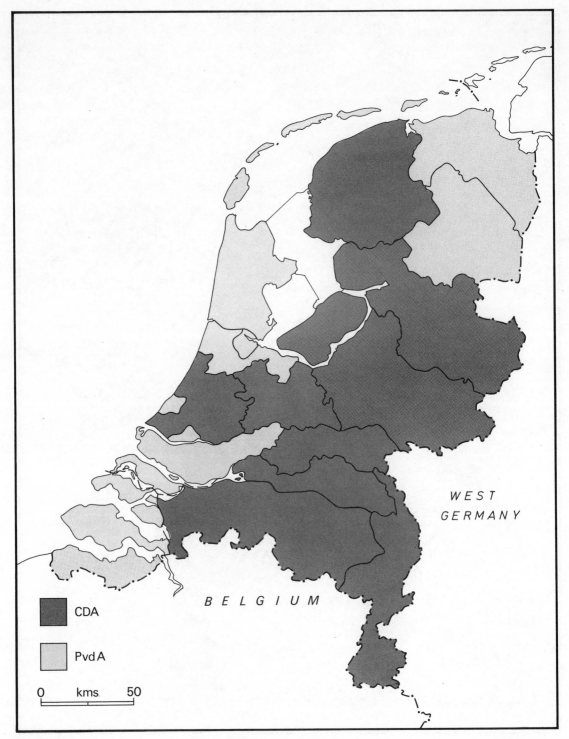

Figure 3.12 *Netherlands: the general election of 1977*

Although the Netherlands would appear to be a model social democracy in Europe, with high living standards and a tolerant open society, in the political field each election has been followed by substantial political infighting and argument before a coalition government has emerged. The Dutch themselves recognize this in their saying: 'Put two Dutchmen in a room and you will get at least three political parties.' After the March 1971 election Queen Juliana asked Piet Steenkamp, professor of social law at Eindhoven University to investigate the possibilities of forming a cabinet. He was a member of the Catholic People's Party (KVP), which gained 35 of the 150 seats in the Lower Chamber. The 1971 election produced political deadlock since neither the ruling coalition of KVP, Protestants (AR and CHU) and Liberals (VVD) nor the opposition bloc headed by Labour (PvdA) won sufficient seats for a working majority in the Lower House. In 1967 KVP, AR, CHU and VVD had gained 86 of the 150 seats, but in 1971 won 74 seats. The prospects appeared likely for an extension of the old coalition with the new Democratic Socialist Party (DS'70) which had gained eight seats. This five-party coalition emerged from the negotiations: Anti-Revolutionary Party (AR). Christian Historical Union (CHU), Catholic People's Party (KVP), Liberals (VVD) and DS'70 with Barend Biesheuvel as Prime Minister. A total of 28 parties had contested the elections, and with 14 parties represented in the Lower Chamber there were several combinations of parties possible.

A cabinet crisis in July 1972, when two ministers from DS'70 resigned from the five-party coalition, began the process towards a premature election. Rows over the 1973 budget caused the resignations. Biesheuvel tried to form a four-party minority coalition but failed, and his centre-right coalition was defeated in the November 1972 election. The Dutch Left picked up support from the 18 to 21 year olds who were voting for the first time.

However, no party group had more than 43 of the 150 seats, so numerous combinations remained possible. At the time, commentators feared that protracted haggling by the parties would hurt the nation, plagued as it was by spiralling inflation and high unemployment – the same problems that brought down the Biesheuvel coalition after only 16 months in office.

In numerical terms the biggest winners in 1972 were the Liberals (VVD) who picked up six seats to make a total of 22. The biggest losers were the KVP who lost eight of their 27 seats. The Liberals could have entered a possible coalition with DS'70 which would have kept the confessional parties in office with a one-seat majority.

The biggest winners in percentage gain were the breakaway Catholic Radicals (PPR) increased from two seats to seven. This advance was attributed to the youth vote and to progressive Catholics disenchanted with the traditional blocs. The Labour Party (PvdA) emerged with the most seats, 43, a gain of four over 1971. Dutch political commentators at the time said there was complete deadlock[2] and went on to argue that since nothing had been solved, the main lesson was that it was time to revise the whole Dutch election system.

The leader of the victorious Labour Party, Joop den Uyl, argued for a progressive minority cabinet which would be able to count on the support of a majority in the Lower House. After six months of negotiations, den Uyl became Prime Minister at the head of a five-party coalition of the PvdA, KVP, AR, PPR and Democrats 66 (D'66). The 164 day delay, which at that time was the longest in Dutch political history, was caused by the three progressive parties' reluctance to negotiate with parties with which no agreement had been reached prior to the election. However, this proved necessary in order to form a government.

The provincial elections of March 1974 showed that Dutch electors endorsed the den Uyl's government policies in the wake of the Yom Kippur war of October 1973 and the subsequent Arab oil embargo on the Netherlands. In 1974 the Labour Party showed gains of 2% over the 1972 general election, rising from 27.3% to 29.3%. The VVD which became the main opposition party after 1972, also made striking gains of 4.5%, but most of the smaller opposition and splinter parties lost ground. The provincial elections of 1974 were seen as a barometer of public feeling over the socialist-dominated government's handling of the oil embargo crises to which the Netherlands had been subjected.

In the 1972–1977 parliament, 14 separate parties were represented. The Dutch system of proportional representation only requires small parties to reach two-thirds of 1% of a nationwide vote to secure one parliamentary seat.

By 1977 the three confessional parties, the AR, the CHU and the KVP had united to form the Christian Democratic Appeal (CDA) with a total of 47 seats. It was led by Andreas Van Agt, a controversial Catholic Justice Minister in the outgoing cabinet. The CDA had a moderate position on most issues but was strongly anti-abortion. The VVD or People's Party for Freedom and Democracy had been the opposition since 1973. It was a business-oriented party, urging a cutback in the growth of government spending, higher profits and a less egalitarian incomes policy. The junior partner in the den Uyl coalition, the Radical party (PPR), was committed to stay out of any new centre-left coalition.

The Communist Party (CPN) had won seven seats in 1972; it is an isolationist party opposed to Euro-communism and in 1977 moved back closer to a pro-Soviet position after years without links to the

USSR. It has been opposed to Dutch membership of the EEC.

As the results came in for the 1977 election, Premier den Uyl and his CDA rival, Andreas Van Agt, remained in the Justice Ministry dealing with a double hostage seizure in northern Holland by South Moluccan gunmen. 87.5% of the electorate voted, an increase of 4.5% on 1972; spokesman for the three major parties (CDA, PvdA, VVD) welcomed a move away from the chronic trend towards splinter groups and divisions. The left liberal D'66 party, junior partner in the outgoing government, was the only small party to improve its position, increasing from six to eight seats. The CPN dropped nearly two-thirds of its previous vote and declined from seven seats to two.

After the 1977 election, Joop den Uyl indicated he would seek to form another centre-left alliance with the CDA, and described the results as the biggest single shift in Dutch political life in 30 years. PvdA won 53 seats, an increase of 10, and at the time it appeared certain that the Labour Party would hold a dominating role in the next coalition government. 'All observers in the Netherlands agree that a new government led by Mr den Uyl in partnership with the CDA will eventually emerge'[3]: this seemed to summarize political opinion.

The CDA totalled 49 seats, having obtained an additional seat and the VVD increased from 22 to 28.

However, despite this personal endorsement for Premier den Uyl, five months of negotiations were necessary before a government emerged. This suggests that the election was inconclusive, but really points to the protracted negotiations necessary to form an administration in the Dutch fragmented political arena.

Den Uyl undertook a marathon attempt to reach a new pact with the CDA but this collapsed, and the Labour Party found itself relegated to the opposition in December 1977. CDA and the Liberals (VVD) quickly hammered together a partnership, amid Labour party cries of 'we were robbed'. Andreas Van Agt became Prime Minister, but his coalition commanded the support of only 77 of the 150 members. His worst problems were related to a massive package of public-spending cuts which involved large-scale reductions in welfare expenditure. However, his government's survival so far is based on the fact that none of the Dutch parties wants another general election. Opinion polls showed many voters to be disillusioned by the protracted bargaining session from May to December 1977 on the formation of the government. The May 1978 municipal elections proved to be a vote of confidence for premier Van Agt and his party. The CDA polled 32% against 28.8% in the 1974 municipal elections. In March 1978 CDA took 35.1% in the provincial council elections, overtaking the Labour opposition as the country's biggest single party. The Labour Party polled 30.7% against 33.9% in the March provincial council elections.

The increased vote for the major parties could indicate a change in Dutch politics: 'Holland may be taking the first steps towards a more normal European pattern of division amongst Social Democrats, Christian Democrats and Liberals'[4].

References

1. Taylor, P. J. and Johnston, R. J. (1979). *Geography of Elections*, p. 166, Penguin Books
2. *Algemeen Dagblad, Rotterdam,* 30 November 1972 (a daily newspaper)
3. Wheaton, M. (July 1977). Holland: Polarization of Political Forces. *The World Today,* pp. 247–250
4. Ibid., p. 249

Table 3.12 *The Dutch electoral system 1971–1977*

Assembly	Tweede Kamer (Second Chamber) of States General
Members	150
Dates of elections	28 March 1971 20 November 1972 25 May 1977
Method	Proportional representation (PR); d'Hondt system; highest average 18 constituencies but taken on a country-wide basis
Voting age	23 in 1967, lowered to 21, lowered again in 1972 to 18. Voting was compulsory in the Netherlands from 1917 until 4 March 1970
Voter participation (turnout)	1971 79.1% 1972 82.9% 1977 87.5%

Source: Statistical Yearbook of the Netherlands 1979, (1980) p. 95, The Hague; Keesings Contemporary Archives

Table 3.13 *Number of seats won in Dutch elections 1971–1977*

Party	Number of seats		
	1971	1972	1977
PvdA	39	43	53
CDA	(58)[a]	(48)[b]	49
AR	13	14	
CHU	10	7	
KVP	35	27	
VVD	16	22	28
D'66	11	6	8
SGP	3	3	3
PPR	2	7	3
CPN	6	7	2
GPV	2	2	1
PSP	2	2	1
BP	1	3	1
DS'70	8	6	1
RKPN	–	1	0
Other	2	0	0

[a, b] *Notional number of seats, since AR, CHU and KVP united in 1977 to form CDA*

Table 3.14 *Percentage of votes cast in Dutch elections 1971–1977*

Party	Percentage of votes		
	1971	1972	1977
PvdA	24.7	27.3	33.8
CDA	(36.8)[a]	(31.3)[b]	31.9
AR	8.6	8.8	
CHU	6.3	4.8	
KVP	21.9	17.7	
VVD	10.4	14.4	17.9
D'66	6.8	4.2	5.4
SGP	2.3	2.2	2.1
PPR	1.8	4.8	1.7
CPN	3.9	4.5	1.7
GPV	1.6	1.8	1.0
PSP	1.4	1.5	0.9
BP	1.1	1.9	0.8
DS'70	5.3	4.1	0.7
RKPN	–	0.9	0.4
Other	2.4	0.6	1.5
Additional parties	14	5	12
Middle party	1.5	0.4	0.0

[a, b] *Notional totals of voters, since AR, CHU and KVP united in 1977 to form CDA*

Table 3.15 *Number of votes cast in Dutch elections 1971–1977*

Party	Number of Votes		
	1971	1972	1977
PvdA	1 554 280	2 021 454	2 813 793
CDA	(2 321 520)[a]	(2 313 473)[b]	2 655 391
AR	542 742	653 609	
CHU	399 106	354 463	
KVP	1 379 672	1 305 401	
VVD	653 370	1 068 375	1 492 689
D'66	428 067	307 048	452 423
SGP	148 192	163 114	177 010
PPR	116 049	354 829	140 910
CPN	246 569	330 398	143 481
GPV	101 790	131 236	79 421
PSP	90 738	111 262	77 972
BP	69 656	143 239	69 914
DS'70	336 714	304 714	59 487
RKPN	23 047	67 658	33 227
Other	228 155	77 245	123 987
Total	6 318 147	7 394 045	8 319 705

[a, b] *Notional number of votes cast, since AR, CHU and KVP united in 1977 to form CDA*

United Kingdom

Political parties	
C	Conservative Party
CPGB	Communist Party of Great Britain
L	Liberal Party
Lab	Labour Party
NF	National Front
PC	Plaid Cymru (Welsh Nationalist Party)
SDLP	Social Democratic and Labour Party
SDP	Social Democratic Party
SLP	Scottish Labour Party
SNP	Scottish National Party
UU	Ulster Unionists (comprising the DUP, OUP, UUUP)
DUP	Democratic Unionist Party
OUP	Official Unionist Party
UUUP	United Ulster Unionist Party

Britain stands apart from the rest of Europe not only physically but in its electoral procedure. Alone among the countries of Western and Southern Europe, the British government, through the two major political parties that control the electoral procedure, clings doggedly to the simple plurality system of elections which most of Britain's European neighbours abandoned in favour of some form of proportional representation in the first quarter of the twentieth century.

France and the Federal Republic of Germany continue to use plurality for part of their electoral process. In France a two-round contest allows voters to express some preference for candidates of smaller parties. In Britain the major political parties, the two largest parties in terms of support, the Conservative or Tory party and the Labour (socialist) party resolutely refuse to consider any electoral reform in favour of a system of proportional representation. They hide behind the facade of a personal relationship between the British member of the lower chamber of parliament (The House of Commons) and his constituents, while most voters in Britain cannot even name their elected representative. It is clear that the parties are conservative in their attitude to electoral reform because of the diminution of parliamentary power which would accompany it. Both parties are strongly élitist in character and appear to be prepared to go to great lengths to deny

the third major party, the Liberals, any representation in the House of Commons which would resemble the 5 300 000 (October 1974 election) or 4 300 000 (May 1979 election) votes which the electorate gave the party. British politicians of the two largest parties refuse to believe there could be any benefit in a form of coalition government, claiming they need a majority in the 635 seat House of Commons to govern effectively. In this they express their peculiar brand of élitism and are remote from the population: a major British party in power with a majority, such as the Conservative party under Margaret Thatcher at the time of writing, constitutes what the senior Tory politician Lord Hailsham has termed 'an elective dictatorship'. This grouping of one of the two major parties, providing it has a comfortable majority, cannot be dislodged for a period of up to five years, and while the major party out of power can draw attention to policy changes of the government, it is impotent to prevent the passage of government bills, as the ruling party's whips simply ensure enough of their members are in the chamber at the right time. Only a controversial piece of legislation, where there is dissent among members of the ruling party, can be prevented; members of parliament may then vote against their own party, though they may face disciplinary action.

Under these circumstances the British political and electoral system can be seen to be politically archaic and in some ways moribund; as British society reverts to its more vigorous and aggressive nature, such as existed prior to Victorian Britain of 1840 or thereabouts, more confrontations can be expected in industrial relations in all sectors of manufacturing, processing and service industries. The inadequate method of electoral representation, with a chamber which likes to style itself the mother of parliaments, is long due for overhaul; failure to reform has created a sense of alienation between governments and the electorate, and may have contributed to Britain's lack of success in the modern world. (The emergence of a Social Democratic Party in March 1981 can be attributed, in part, to the lack of electoral reform.)

During the period under study, four British general elections (*Figures 3.13* to *3.16*) have taken place and the country has seen two attempts at coalition government. In the first example Edward Heath, the Prime Minister and leader of the Conservative Party, invited Jeremy Thorpe, then leader of the Liberal Party, to consider joining a coalition government following the inconclusive February 1974 election, in which the Conservative Party had failed to obtain a majority. Thorpe declined, although his party had won 6 000 000 votes in the February 1974 election, and this caused some loss of electoral support as the liberal vote fell to 5 300 000 in October 1974.

The other coalition in all but name was during the premiership of Labour leader James Callaghan, when

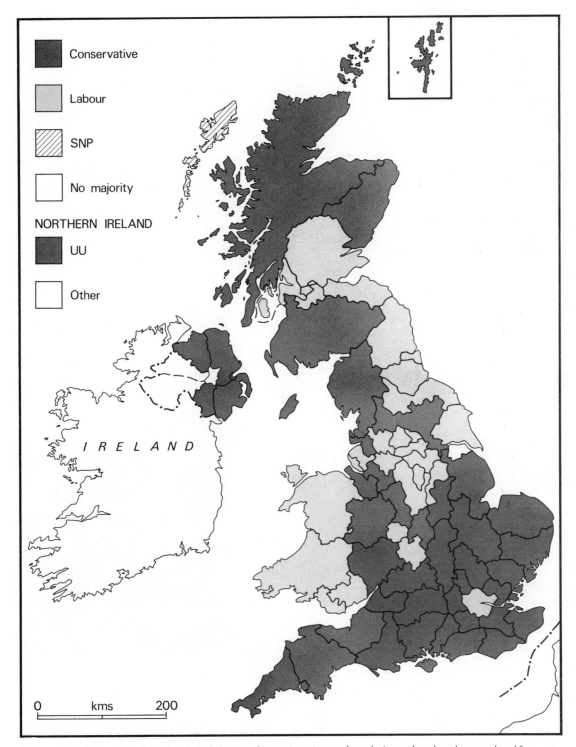

Figure 3.13 *United Kingdom: the general election of 1970. Constituency boundaries are based on those employed for elections to the European Parliament, except for Northern Ireland. Inset is Shetland*

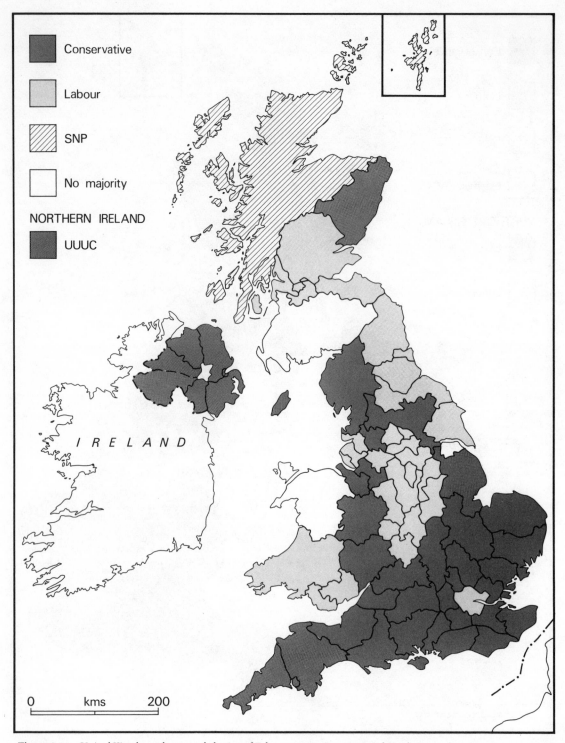

Figure 3.14 *United Kingdom: the general election of February 1974. Constituency boundaries are based on those employed for elections to the European Parliament, except for Northern Ireland. Inset is Shetland*

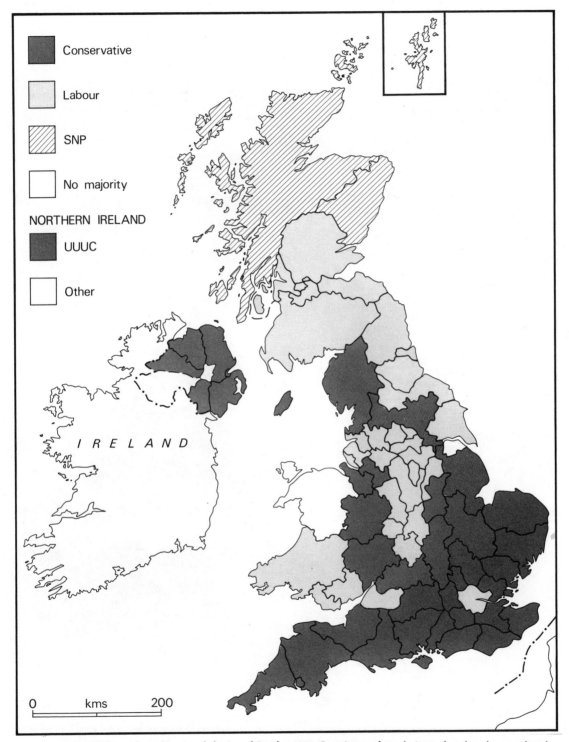

Figure 3.15 *United Kingdom: the general election of October 1974. Constituency boundaries are based on those employed for elections to the European Parliament, except for Northern Ireland. Inset is Shetland*

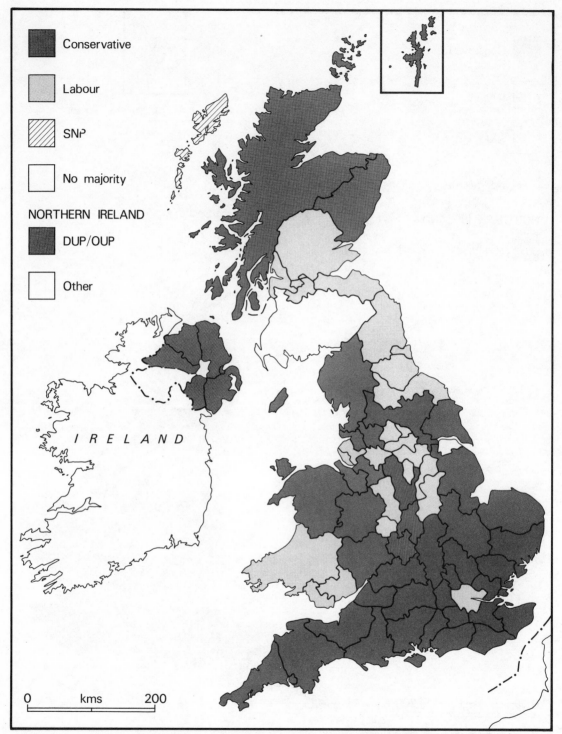

Figure 3.16 *United Kingdom: the general election of 1979. Constituency boundaries are based on those employed for elections to the European Parliament, except for Northern Ireland. Inset is Shetland*

a pact or understanding was formed between the minority Labour administration and the Liberal Party led by David Steel, who had taken over from Jeremy Thorpe in 1976. This 'Lib–Lab' pact, as it was called, lasted from March 1977 to August 1978 and enabled Callaghan to continue in office.

In 1968 the Labour Party was in office with a massive majority of 98 over all other parties, holding 364 seats in the chamber, which at that time had a total of 630 members. Under the leadership of Harold Wilson, the party had improved its performance at the March 1966 election over the narrowly won October 1964 election which had brought Wilson and the Labour Party to power after 13 years of Conservative government. Wilson was in a confident mood as Prime Minister and felt that his policies of allowing substantial wage increases over the winter of 1969/70 would more than compensate for the inflationary pressures which existed in the British economy, and were causing prices to rise at 8–9% a year. Wilson thought he would win a summer election and thus become the first British Prime Minister in the twentieth century to win three consecutive general elections. At the time, opinion polls indicated Wilson and the Labour Party would win virtually up to the day before polling.

As the results came in, it became clear that the British electorate had showed their traditional support for the underdog, in this case the first Conservative leader elected by other Tory members of parliament, Edward Heath. He swept to power with a majority administration of 330 seats, to Labour's 288. Harold Wilson, after the profound shock of not winning and remaining premier, fell back to writing his record of the two Labour administrations he had headed from October 1964 to June 1970.

Heath had employed the slogan of 'cutting prices at a stroke', but his policies and the impact of world commodity prices proved this was not to be the case. The Conservative Party wanted to introduce an industrial relations bill in an attempt to solve the thorny problem of workers' disputes, but it provoked bitter opposition from British trade unions. Throughout the 1970s, the power and influence of trade unions in the British political scene has developed, but unfortunately this power often takes the form of a negative or opposing mood. Trade unions appear reluctant to initiate changes in industrial relations, although considering the influence they wield, they could be considered a 'fourth estate' of the British realm.

In an attempt to prevent inflation reaching what at the time seemed unacceptable levels, the Heath government imposed a wage and prices freeze for six months in November 1972. Heath's economic policies, put into practice by his finance minister Anthony Barber, were in large measure responsible for the subsequent inflation. Barber expanded the money supply dramatically in an attempt to stimulate growth in the British economy, but unfortunately all the major Western world economies were growing sharply during 1973. The Heath government might have succeeded, but the Yom Kippur war of October 1973 and the subsequent quintupling of crude oil prices prevented their success. When the government introduced an austerity package in December 1973 after several weeks of media discussion of the so-called oil and energy crisis, it completely misjudged the mood of the nation. This was supposed to be the worst economic crisis since 1945 and the remedy was to be cuts in government spending and the imposition of a three-day week. Government spending cuts in 1973 were not the familiar terminology that they had become by the end of the decade; in fact they meant little to the electorate, who had been told this was a great crisis, and reacted by asking 'what crisis?'. Petroleum prices were increased and the British economy went into recession, which lasted until the end of 1977. The next eighteen months saw British inflation rise to unprecedented levels, peaking at 27.8% on an annual basis in the summer of 1975, although if measured on a six-month basis the true rise was around 36% per annum. Otherwise things continued as normal, and possibly the last occasion when the British nation could have been roused to arrest its declining industrial performance was lost.

In January 1974 the British miners came out on strike for the second time since 1926 and Heath refused to agree to their pay demands. The first miners' strike had also been under Heath's government administration; this was settled mainly by preparing a blank cheque and allowing a government commission to determine that the miners were 'a special case'.

The February 1974 election was unusual in British political experience: 'Government uncertainty and public speculation as to the possibility of a "who governs" election removed any element of surprise, whilst the introduction of the three-day working week to meet the coal shortage and appeals to the "Dunkirk spirit" had little appeal in the Britain of the 1970s'[1].

The Heath government had made progress towards a power-sharing executive in Northern Ireland. However, the Ulster Unionists did not want to see the Catholic minority have any political influence, and so proceeded to wreck the Sunningdale agreement of December 1973 concluded between Mr Heath, Liam Cosgrave the Irish Prime Minister and members of the Northern Ireland executive-designate, led by Brian Faulkner.

Before 1974 three loyalist parties, the Official Unionists, Vanguard Unionists and Protestant Unionists existed. They all opposed the Sunningdale agreement and the new executive-designate; in February 1974 they contested the election under the

UUUC title (United Ulster Unionist Council) and won all the province's seats, except one which went to the Social Democratic and Labour Party (SDLP). The outcome of the election was that the Conservative Party lost support with their number of seats dropping to 297, while Labour gained to have a total of 301, but neither party had an overall majority. The Liberals improved their vote total dramatically to 6 060 000, but had only 14 seats because of the plurality system used in Britain.

After Heath's attempt to form a coalition with the Liberals, Wilson became premier again at the head of a minority administration. Another election had to be held in October 1974 and this time Labour improved its showing to take 319 seats to the Conservatives' 277, which gave Labour a small majority in the 635 seat House of Commons. The total number of seats had been increased with electoral boundaries redrawn in some cases since the 1970 election. Wilson became Prime Minister for the fourth time and presided over a period of rapid inflation and substantial wage increases under the terms of Labour's 'social contract' with the trade unions. After the rapid inflation, the level of price increases was reduced not by direct government action, but by agreement between government and trade unions on a £6 a week pay increase for all workers in the autumn of 1975 to last for the period of a year.

In March 1976 Wilson resigned from the leadership of the Labour Party and James Callaghan, then foreign minister, became leader of the Labour Party and Prime Minister. By March 1977 the Labour Party had lost its parliamentary majority in a series of by-election defeats, but the pact with the Liberals kept the Callaghan government in power.

Callaghan surprised most commentators and members of his party by announcing in September 1978 that his government would continue in office for a fifth term. The subsequent industrial unrest, combined with a bad winter in terms of weather contributed to Callaghan's failure to remain in power in May 1979. *Figures 3.13* to *3.16* show the extent of Labour support in the conurbations of Britain and the Conservative traditional support in the rural areas: in 1979 the Conservative Party made inroads into the major cities and, led for the first time by a woman, took power with 339 seats to a Labour total of 268, the largest majority of any party for twenty years. Margaret Thatcher had been education minister in the Heath administration from 1970 to 1974 but had never held a senior cabinet post: she had ousted Heath from the leadership of the Conservative Party in February 1975 and in May 1979 the Conservative Party, under her leadership, won an outright majority of 44 over all other parties allowing them complete control of the House of Commons. With the Thatcher administration in office, dedicated to cuts in public spending, the revitalization of private industry and an attempt at limitation of the corporate nature of the British economy, Britain took a sharp turn to the right in the political arena. It remains to be seen if these policies will succeed: by December 1980 Britain was in its severest recession since the slump of the 1930s with private industry in considerable difficulty. If Britain did somehow manage to reverse the seemingly inevitable trend towards a corporate state where the government controls more than 60% of the gross national product, it would then be a model for other countries in Western Europe. In order to succeed, the Conservative Party must hope for at least a second term in office, but on the basis of the Heath government in the early 1970s this would appear to be unlikely.

Following the Dublin Castle summit in December 1980 between Thatcher and Irish Prime Minister Haughey, a new approach to the problem of Northern Ireland may emerge, but it would have to be a joint initiative. Electorally the Protestant loyalist parties still dominate the province.

By February 1981 it had become clear that a major realignment was occurring in British politics with the establishment of the Council for Social Democracy, which led to the founding of a Social Democratic Party in March, the first new political party for 80 years which could be expected to have mass support. The Labour Party lost a number of its members to the new party; it remains to be seen how the Social Democratic Party will fare at the next general election. The party might expect to benefit from its new image at that election, so that the real test of its support will be the election after the next one.

References

1. Henig, S. (ed.), (1979). *Political Parties in the European Community*, p. 215, Allen & Unwin/Policy Studies Institute

Studies of each British general election since 1951 have been produced by David Butler and his co-authors. The relevant publications for elections included in this atlas are detailed below:

Butler, D. E. and Pinto-Duschinsky, M. (1971). *The British General Election of 1970*, Macmillan, London
Butler, D. E. and Kavanagh, D. (1975). *The British General Election of February 1974*, Macmillan, London
Butler, D. E. and Kavanagh, D. (1975). *The British General Election of October 1974*, Macmillan, London
Butler, D. E. and Kavanagh, D. (1980). *The British General Election of 1979*, Macmillan, London

The most recent edition of a useful compendium relating to elections and political matters, updated after each British general election, is:

Butler D. and Sloman, A. (1980). *British Political Facts 1900–1979*, Macmillan, London

Table 3.16 *The UK electoral system 1970–1979*

Assembly	House of Commons Lower chamber of Parliament
Members	630 in 1970, increased to 635 in 1974; single-member constituencies
Dates of elections	18 June 1970 28 February 1974 10 October 1974 3 May 1979
Method	Simple plurality: the candidate with the highest total in the constituency, even when this is less than 50% of the votes cast
Voting age	In 1968 21 years, reduced in 1969 to 18; voters may cast their ballot at the first election after their 18th birthday
Voter participation (turnout)	1970 72.0% 1974 February 78.7% 1974 October 72.8% 1979 76.0%

Source: Craig, F. W. S. (1976). British Electoral Facts 1885–1975, pp. 28–30, Macmillan, London; Butler, D. and Sloman, A. (1980), British Political Facts 1900–1979, pp. 209–210, Macmillan, London; Keesings Contemporary Archives

Table 3.17 *Number of seats won in UK elections 1970–1979*

Party	Number of seats			
	1970	Feb. 1974	Oct. 1974	1979
C	330	297	276	339
Lab	287	301	319	268
L	6	14	13	11
SNP	1	7	11	2
PC	0	2	3	2
UU[a]	–	11	10	10
NF	–	0	0	0
SDLP	1	1	1	1
Other (includ. Speaker)	5	2	2	2
Total	630	635	635	635

[a] *Ulster Unionists, plus Vanguard Unionist Progressive Party and Democratic Unionist Party. 1979 comprised: Official Unionist 5, Democratic Unionist 3, United Ulster Unionist 1, Ulster Unionist 1*

Table 3.18 *Percentage of votes cast in UK elections 1970–1979*

Party	Percentage of votes			
	1970	Feb. 1974	Oct. 1974	1979
C	46.4	37.9	35.8	43.9
Lab	43.0	37.1	39.2	36.9
L	7.5	19.3	18.3	13.8
SNP	1.1	2.0	2.9	1.6
PC	0.6	0.6	0.6	0.4
NF	–	0.3	0.4	0.6
CPGB	0.1	0.1	0.1	0.1
Other	1.3	2.7	2.7	2.7
Total	100.0	100.0	100.0	100.0

Table 3.19 *Number of votes cast in UK elections 1970–1979*

Party	Number of votes			
	1970	Feb. 1974	Oct. 1974	1979
C	13 145 123	11 872 180	10 462 565	13 697 753
Lab	12 208 758	11 645 616	11 457 079	11 509 524
L	2 117 035	6 059 519	5 346 704	4 313 931
SNP	306 802	633 180	839 617	504 259
NF	–	76 865	113 843	191 267
PC	175 016	171 374	166 321	132 544
CPGB	37 970	32 743	17 426	15 521
Other	354 094	848 685	785 549	855 991
Total	28 344 798	31 340 162	29 189 104	31 220 790
Electorate	39 342 013	39 798 899	40 072 971	41 093 264

Mediterranean Europe

France

France has both national and presidential elections, although the latter tend more to show voters preferences for an individual. Theoretically, the French power structure lies somewhere between the British parliamentary system and the American presidential system. In practice, given an assembly obligated to follow the President, the Elysée Palace can outdo the White House for power and patronage. The President of France is a republican monarch: he makes policy in every sphere, internal and foreign, and makes sure it is carried out by a government he names. He can send his Prime Minister instructions

Political parties			
CD	Democratic Centre Party	RAD	Radical Party
CDP	Centre for Democracy and Progress	REF	Reformist Movement
CDS	Central Social Democratic Party	RI	Independent Republicans (Republicains Independents)
CERES	Centre for Study of Research and Education of Socialists (Left wing of PS)	RPR	Assembly for the Republic (Rassemblement pour la République)
CIR	Convention of Republican Institutions	UC	Centrist Union
FGDS	Federation of the Democratic and Socialist Left	UDF	Union for French Democracy (Union pour la Démocratie Française)
MRG	Movement of Left Radicals	UDR	Union for Defence of the Republic (1968) (Union pour la Defence de la République)
MRP	Popular Republican Movement		
MSDF	French Democratic Socialist Movement	UDR	Union of Democrats for the Republic (Union des Démocrates pour la République)
PCF	French Communist Party (Parti Communiste Français)		
PDM	Progress and Modern Democracy	UGSD	Socialist and Democratic Union of the Left
PR	Republican Party	URP	Union of Republicans for Progress (1973) (Union des Républicains pour le Progrès)
PRRS	Radical Socialist Party		
PS	Socialist Party (Parti Socialiste)		
PSU	United Socialist Party	Union of the Left	Comprising the PCF, PS, PRRS

and indeed dismiss him at will: the President runs cabinet meetings, can call referendums, can dissolve parliament and rule by emergency decree. The French seem to have an entrenched need for a monarchical system that the Revolution did not destroy. The President is elected every seven years, while the term of office for the national assembly is five years.

France uses a two-ballot, single-member system of voting whereby a candidate for the Chamber of Deputies in the National Assembly must win both more than 50% of the vote and have the support of 25% of the registered electorate in that constituency. If no outright winner emerges on the first ballot, a second vote is taken a week later. Candidates with less than 12.5% of the vote on the first round are eliminated, and the second vote is on the plurality system. In practice, candidates usually drop out in favour of political allies and recommend their voters to choose their ally. Presidential elections are also on the two-ballot system, except that if no outright winner is chosen on the first round, only the two front-running candidates go forward to the second ballot.

One of the problems of any study of French politics is the regularity with which new parties are formed and old ones disappear, or re-emerge under different labels[1]. The list of current parties represented in the National Assembly at the present time is outlined here.

(1) RPR: Rassemblement pour la République

The Gaullist party, led by the mayor of Paris, Jacques Chirac, was between 1968 and 1976 the UDR, the Union of Democrats for the Republic. The RPR grouped Gaullists and three smaller centrist parties together who signed an electoral pact and joint manifesto in 1977, but ended on the eve of the 1978 elections, when the non-Gaullist (majorité) parties formed their own group.

(2) UDF: Union pour la Démocratie Française

This party is Giscardian and centrist and was formed in 1977 as an electoral umbrella for non-Gaullist 'majorité' candidates. It comprised the Radical Party and the Independent Republicans, the latter being Giscard d'Estaing's party. It took its name from Giscard d'Estaing's book *Démocratie Française*.

(3) PS: Parti Socialiste

Since the general election of 1978, when the PS won the highest single percentage of votes, the PS has claimed to be the largest party in France.

Created in 1905 and currently led by François Mitterrand, the PS has traditionally espoused social-democratic politics and policies. Its partners in the 1978 elections, the MRG, are left-wing radicals, fragments of the old Radical Party.

(4) PCF: Parti Communiste Français

The PCF is led by Georges Marchais and was formed in 1920 after disenchanted socialists broke with the PS. It is the only Latin communist party that has enjoyed legal status almost continuously since its formation. Along with the communist parties of Italy and Spain, it embraced the pluralistic ideals of Eurocommunists in the mid-1970s, but has since begun returning to its traditional strictly disciplined communist policies and can no longer be considered a Eurocommunist party. Firmly implanted in the working class, it can claim a steady 20% of the French vote.

France in 1968 was at the forefront of what promised to be radical change throughout Europe. The disenchantment which swept Western Europe in the year of student revolt began in Paris with uncoordinated street revolts by university and school students climaxed in May 1968 in workers' strikes which looked like forcing the downfall of the Gaullist government.

But the elections called for June 1968, far from spurring the 'revolution', gave the Gaullists a larger majority than ever. General Charles de Gaulle's party had won in a country which believed it had a choice between only Gaullism and chaos. But his own authority was badly shaken; he tried to weaken the upper chamber of the National Assembly, the Senate, but the reforms put to the electorate in a referendum in April 1969 were soundly rejected, and de Gaulle immediately announced his retirement, plunging the country into its fifth national election contest in less than four years.

The election of Georges Pompidou as the second President of the Fifth Republic, chosen by universal suffrage in 1969, followed a campaign in which intricate manoeuvering between the parties resulted in six sponsored candidates and one independent.

Gaullist Pompidou and centrist Alain Poher were the frontrunners, while leftists Jacques Duclos, socialist Gaston Defferre and PSU candidate Michel Rocard were more concerned with demonstrating their individual electoral strength to each other and so better influence future arrangements on the Left, rather than having any confidence of their victory. Communist Alain Krivine and independent Louis Ducatel simply wanted to show they were capable of attracting some votes at least[2]. In the second round run-off between Pompidou and Poher, Pompidou

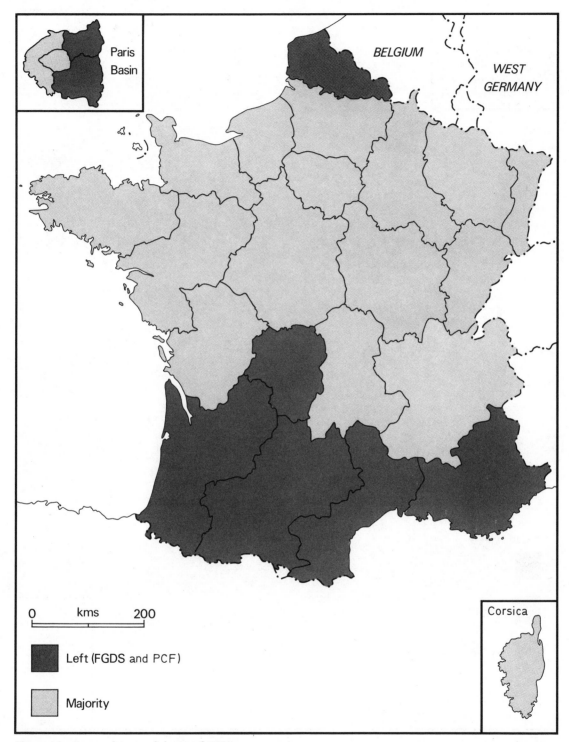

Figure 4.1 *France: the general election of 1968*

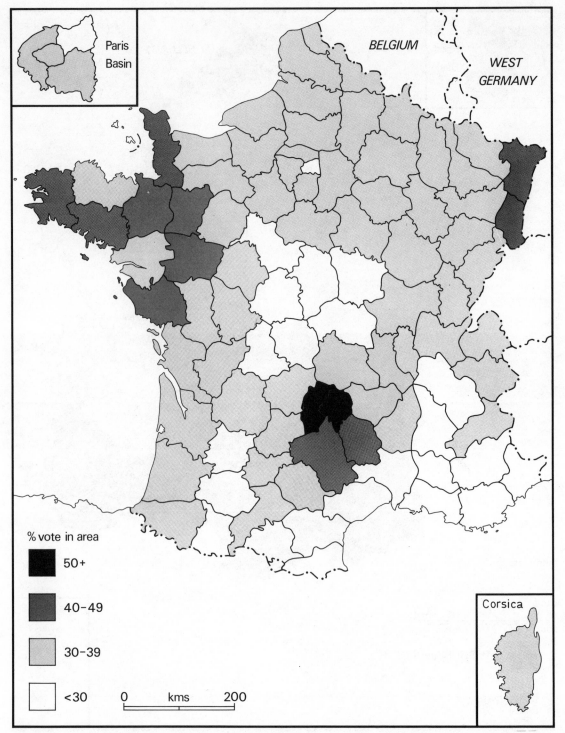

Figure 4.2 *France: the presidential election of 1969. The first ballot, held on 1 June 1969, showing support for Georges Pompidou. The second ballot produced a vote of overwhelming support for Pompidou in all regions*

won through advocating his policy of maintaining the institutions and stability of the Fifth Republic against Poher who, he argued, would not have a parliamentary majority, which in turn would lead to political instability.

In the national election of March 1973 the ruling coalition parties led by the Gaullists had an overall majority in the National Assembly, although the left-wing, which had joined in an electoral alliance, made substantial gains. The PS increased from 57 to 102 seats, the PCF gained 73 compared to 33 in 1968 and the Gaullist UDF lost its overall majority. Pierre Messmer, Prime Minister of the Gaullist coalition before the elections, formed a new government of the UDF and the centre-right parties.

President Pompidou did not survive his seven-year term of office and by early 1974 it became apparent that he was gravely ill. He died in April 1974 and a presidential election was called for May. This contest centred on the two candidates of the centre-right and the left, François Mitterrand of the PS and Valery Giscard d'Estaing of the Independent Republicans, who had won 55 seats in the 1973 general election. On the first round, Mitterrand was ahead of Giscard, but in the second round with just the two candidates, Giscard d'Estaing emerged as victor with 50.7% of the votes to 49.3% for Mitterrand, possibly because of traditional West European fears of allowing the left any real power.

In the preparations for the 1978 election all political groupings in France were being torn by dissension: to the right and centre, personal rivalries between Jacques Chirac, who still felt himself to be the rightful successor as a Gaullist to the late general and Pompidou, and the charismatic newcomer Giscard, who had so easily taken on his predecessors' mantle. The campaign on the right was marked by attempts by Prime Minister Raymond Barre to assume leadership of the ruling coalition, a move supported by Giscard but strongly resisted by Chirac and his RPR. Within the RPR itself, dissension was rife. This culminated in the party's withdrawal from an agreement with the three smaller parties, the grouping by which the 'majorité' had planned to present single candidates in each constituency. This resulted in 90% of France's 491 seats being contested in the first round by more than one 'majorité' candidate. On 1 February 1978, the 'majorité' rift became official with the creation of the Union pour la Démocratie Française.

With the Union of the Left comprising the PCF, PS and close socialist supporters, the Left Radicals, dissension over their 1972 common platform which had been simmering since 1974, deepened until it was abandoned in September 1977, with each side accusing the other of sabotaging the left-wing union for party advantage in the forthcoming election. The breakup of the left's common platform centred on the question of the number of French companies to be nationalized by a left government when it came to power, a question that had been settled by compromise in 1972. In 1977 the PS wanted a total of 200 firms to be nationalized, but the communists wanted the number to reach over 700. More than that, the socialist star was on the ascendancy, while the communists, for all their embracing Eurocommunism and appearing flexible to the extent of supporting Mitterrand in the 1974 presidential election, still found themselves firmly entrenched in the working class, and therefore unable to increase their share of the poll.

Despite such well-publicized rifts within the left, France seemed on the brink of ending a 40-year tradition of centre-right government and voting for the left. Up till Giscard banned them just before the election, public opinion polls consistently put the left ahead of the 'majorité'. Another reason for hope on the part of the left was that this was the first election in which 18 to 21 year olds were allowed to vote and the left traditionally captured the majority of young voters' support. The results were a success for the centre-right who gained 291 seats to the left's 200: the PS increased to 113 and the PCF to 86 but this did not give the expected victory of the left.

If the French decided to abandon their ten-year appointment with revolution, as in 1958 de Gaulle destroyed the Fourth Republic, and in 1968 students and workers eventually forced de Gaulle out, the left can certainly blame themselves. Their internal squabbles did nothing to instil confidence that they were ready to govern the country. The socialists had taken over as the largest left party, but the communists, although officially in the Eurocommunist camp, had failed to persuade many that their move to democracy was sincere. The hurried reconciliation between the parties in the week between the first and second ballots fooled no one. The left can also thank president Giscard's appeal to the deep-rooted conservatism of Catholic France, and the emphasis placed on his difficulty in governing the country without a working majority in the National Assembly and the consequent political instability which all French fear.

Giscard, strengthened by the 1978 election to an extent that he was more or less free to do as he wanted, developed into one of the most articulate, clear minded and effective Western leaders. His initial support of Spain and Portugal's entry into the EEC in the face of ensuing economic and political problems it would bring to France, his economic leadership within the EEC, did much to build up his prestige and a belief that no other man could rule France.

However, the French electorate were not completely satisfied with President Giscard d'Estaing's record and the victory the left had hoped for in 1978 was delayed for three years.

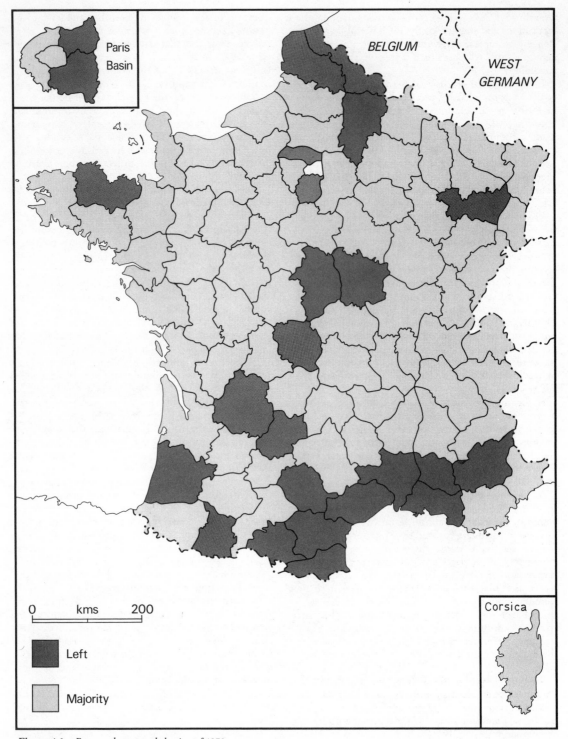

Figure 4.3 *France: the general election of 1973*

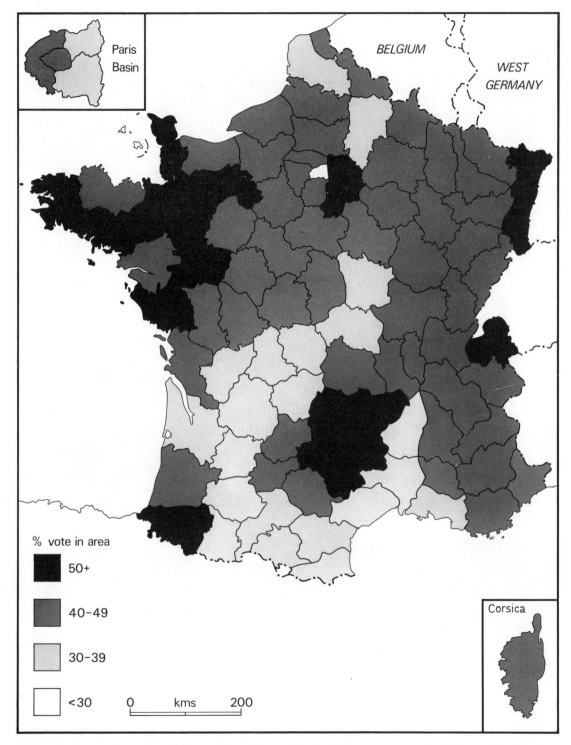

Figure 4.4 *France: the presidential election of 1974. The second ballot, held on 19 May 1974, showed support for Valery Giscard D'Estaing*

68

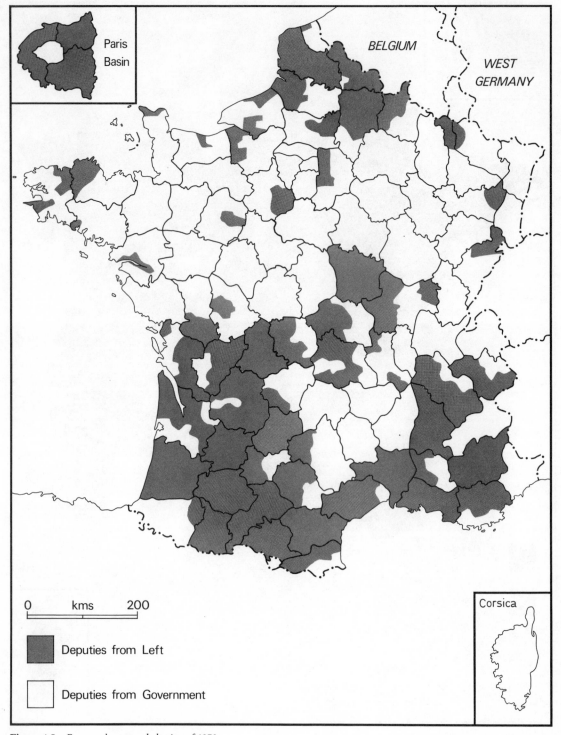

Figure 4.5 *France: the general election of 1978*

The first six months of 1981 have confirmed that France and the French people still retain the ability to cause political surprise and upheaval with important implications, probably more so than any other European electorate. The double election victory of socialist François Mitterrand in May and June 1981 represents a dramatic political rebirth: the Socialist Party (Parti Socialiste, PS) is a phoenix-like creation of a decade which grew out of the old FGDS (Fédération de la Gauche Démocratique et Socialiste). Mitterrand was the FGDS presidential candidate at his first attempt in 1965. The PS was reborn electorally in alliance with the PCF (French Communist Party) at the March 1971 municipal elections. It held a congress at Epinay-sur-Seine in June 1971 at which Mitterrand was elected the new first secretary. Exactly ten years later he became the first socialist President of France since 1954 and had gained an overwhelming majority for his party in the national assembly at the June 1981 general election to give France its first socialist administration for 45 years.

Opinion polls of October 1979 had suggested that the second and decisive round of the 1981 presidential election would be a repeat of the 1974 contest between François Mitterrand and Valery Giscard d'Estaing. The polls suggested that Giscard would beat Mitterrand by a 52:48 split of the vote, and thus Mitterrand would be a 'three times' loser of the presidential contest. The reality was the opposite, with Mitterrand achieving 51.8% of the vote to Giscard's 48.2%, after trailing in the first round with 25.8% to Giscard's 28.3%. At the third attempt Mitterrand became President of the French Republic and was inaugurated on 21 May 1981.

One of his first actions was to dissolve the National Assembly and announce a general election with voting on 14 June and 21 June 1981. The French constitution, formulated in 1958, is based on the assumption that the President and the majority in the National Assembly have the same political persuasion, so that the period between Mitterrand's election as President and the June general election caused much speculation as to what would happen, if, as expected, the socialists failed to gain an outright majority in the National Assembly. In particular, the possible role of the French Communist Party was focused upon and memories of the Union of the Left were revived. However, in the election, the French people made their preferences clear: the socialists increased their representation from 107 seats obtained in 1978 to an absolute majority of 285 of the 491 deputies. Their partners in the 1978 general election, the communists, decreased from their total of 86 to 44 seats. But President Mitterrand thought it expedient to include the PCF in Pierre Mauroy's administration and accordingly the PCF was given four ministries in the new government. This was the first time that communist ministers had held office in France since May 1947. So, following his success at the Presidential contest, Mitterrand had demonstrated the political power and influence of the French Presidency, that to all intents and purposes the holder is a republican monarch. The *Economist* of 20 June 1981 wrote: 'The result of the election illustrates the pulling power of the French Presidency'.

The socialist change in France has acted as a significant pointer on the political map of Western Europe: socialist parties everywhere have drawn considerable comfort from Mitterrand's success, particularly at the June general election. After a move to the right of the political spectrum in 1978 and 1979, the French electorate have spearheaded a move to the left which is likely to continue throughout the electorates of Western Europe at least until the mid-1980s.

References

1. Sallnow J. and John, A. (1978). France Divided Right and Left. *Geographical Magazine*, **L** (No. XII), 792
2. Jackson, R. J. (April/June 1970). The Succession of Georges Pompidou: the French Presidential Election of 1969. *The Political Quarterly*, pp. 156–168
3. Howorth, J. (April 1980). The French Communist Party – Return to the Ghetto. *The World Today*, pp. 139–146

Table 4.1 *The French electoral system 1968–1981*

Assembly	Chambre des Députés Chamber of Deputies
Members	In 1968, 470 seats; 1973, 490 seats and 1978 and 1981, 491 seats
Dates of elections	23 and 30 June 1968 1 and 15 June 1969 (presidential) 4 and 11 March 1973 5 and 19 May 1974 (presidential) 12 and 19 March 1978 26 April and 10 May 1981 (presidential) 14 and 21 June 1981
Method	Two ballots; single member constituency with combination of percentage vote and plurality. On first ballot an absolute majority of votes and support of 25% of electorate is required. No new candidates are allowed at the second ballot. Candidates winning less than a minimum percentage of votes in the first round are eliminated. In 1968 this minimum was 10%; in 1973 it increased to 12.5%
Voting age	18

Voter participation *(turnout) in* *general elections*	1968	80.0%
	1973(1)	79.1%
	(2)	79.9%
	1978(1)	82.8%
	(2)	84.6%
	1981(1)	70.4%
	(2)	74.5%
Voter participation *(turnout) in* *presidential elections*	1974(1)	84.2%
	(2)	87.3%
	1981(1)	81.0%
	(2)	85.9%

Source: Keesings Contemporary Archives

Table 4.2 *Number of seats won in French elections 1968–1981*

Party	Number of seats			
	1968	1973	1978	1981
UDR/RPR	349	183	154	88
UDF			124	63
RI		55		
UC		30		
REF		34		
Conservatives	31			
PS	57	102	113	285
PCF	33	73	86	44
Other	0	13	14	11
Total	470	490	491	491

Table 4.3 *Percentage of votes cast in French elections 1968–1978*

Party	Percentage of votes				
	1968	1973(1)	1973(2)	1978(1)	1978(2)
UDR/RPR	43.6	23.9	31.3	22.6	26.1
UDF	–	(23.2)	(17.7)	21.5	23.2
RI	4.1	6.9	7.7		
CDP	–	3.8	3.9		
REF	10.3	12.5	6.1		
Various majority	–	3.5	3.2	2.4	1.2
PS	16.5	19.0	21.9	22.6	28.3
PCF	20.0	21.4	20.6	20.6	18.6
Left Radicals	–	2.7	3.8	2.1	2.4
Various Left	0.7	–	–	–	–
Extreme Left	3.9	3.3	0.3	3.3	–
Ecologists	–	–	–	2.1	–
Other	0.9	3.0	1.2	2.8	0.2

Table 4.4 *Number of votes cast in French elections 1968–1978*

Party	Number of votes				
	1968	1973(1)	1973(2)	1978(1)	1978(2)
UDR/RPR	9 667 532	5 759 580	6 730 147	6 462 462	6 651 756
UDF				6 128 849	5 907 603
RI	917 758	1 674 016	1 658 060		
CDP	–	901 136	841 576		
REF	2 289 849	2 995 383	1 325 058		
Various majority	–	843 429	706 942		
PS	3 660 250	4 579 888	4 438 834	6 451 151	7 212 916
PCF	4 434 832	5 148 579	4 722 886	5 870 402	4 744 868
Left Radicals	–	663 172	823 084	603 902	595 478
Various Left	163 482				
Extreme Left	873 581	794 056	85 678	953 088	
Ecologists	–	–	–	612 100	
Other	139 931				
Total	22 539 743	23 359 239	21 332 265	27 081 984	25 112 621

Table 4.5 *Results of French presidential elections 1969*

First ballot

Candidate	Votes	Percentage
Pompidou	10051816	44.5
Poher	5268651	23.3
Duclos	4808285	21.3
Defferre	1133222	5.0
Rocard	816471	3.6
Ducatel	286447	1.3
Krivine	239106	1.0
Total	22603998	100.0

Second ballot

Pompidou	11064371	58.2
Poher	7943118	41.8
Total	19007489	100.0

Table 4.6 *Results of French presidential elections 1974*

First ballot

Candidate	Votes	Percentage
Mitterrand	11044373	43.25
Giscard d'Estaing	8326774	32.60
Chaban-Delmas	3857728	15.11
Royer	810540	3.17
Laguiller	595247	2.33
Dumont	337800	1.32
Le Pen	190921	0.75
Muller	176279	0.69
Krivine	93990	0.37
Renouvin	43722	0.17
Sebag	42007	0.16
Héraud	19255	0.08
Total	25538636	100.00

Second ballot

Giscard d'Estaing	13396203	50.8
Mitterrand	12971604	49.2
Total	26367807	100.0

Source: Penniman, H. R. (ed.), (1975). France at the Polls, Foreign Affairs Study 22, American Enterprise Institute for Public Policy Research, pp. 255–315

Table 4.7 *Results of French presidential elections 1981*

First ballot

Candidate	Votes	Percentage
Giscard d'Estaing	8223432	28.32
Mitterrand	7505960	25.85
Chirac	5225846	18.00
Marchais	4456922	15.35
Lalonde	1126254	3.88
Laguiller	668057	2.30
Crepeau	642777	2.21
Debre	481821	1.66
Garaud	386623	1.33
Bouchardeau	321344	1.10
Total	29038036	100.00

Second ballot

Mitterrand	15708262	51.76
Giscard d'Estaing	14642306	48.24
Total	29350568	100.00

Greece

In the period under study Greece has returned to Democracy, elections and referendum[1]. The Colonels, having taken over in 1967 to prevent communist leader George Papandreou from coming to power, saw their regime fall in disarray in 1974 following student resistance and an abortive counter-coup in the previous year. They asked former Prime Minister Constantinos Karamanlis, exiled in Paris since 1963, to return and lead the country back to parliamentary democracy. He arrived in the summer of 1974 to a hero's welcome.

But the years of Greece's 'economic miracle' from 1963 to 1973, when its GNP grew at an average annual rate of 7.6%, were over and Karamanlis faced instead the oil crisis and the consequences of Turkey invading and occupying northern Cyprus with United States arms. In August 1974 Greece withdrew from NATO's integrated military structure in protest at the Cyprus invasion; attempts to return were blocked by fellow-NATO member Turkey until October 1980 when Greece rejoined the military alliance.

Constantinos Karamanlis immediately demonstrated his commitment to democracy by legalizing the communist parties in Greece. He formed a government with his New Democracy Party, and although political groups complained there was not enough time to get organized, quickly formed parties and alliances to fight the elections he called for 17 November 1974. The result was an overwhelming victory for Karamanlis, with New Democracy (ND) winning 220 seats with 54.4% of the vote; its nearest rival the Centre Union–New Forces (EK–ND), then led by George Mavros gained 60 seats and 20.5% of the vote. The Pan Hellenic Socialist Movement (PASOK) had 12 seats with 13.6% of the vote and the United Left (EA) eight seats with 9.5%.

The voting pattern was more or less consistent throughout the regions with the marked exception of Crete, where the EK–ND took the highest percentage of votes, 36.9%, followed by the ND with 25.4%, just pipping PASOK with 23.9%. The EA won 6.3%. The traditional support in Crete for the old Centre Union Party had evidently reasserted itself strongly.

PASOK suffered its lowest share of the vote in the Thessaloniki sub-area, where the EA won its highest vote. As expected, EA had a significantly higher share of the vote in the urban electoral areas and in Greece's Aegean islands, traditional left-wing strongholds.

Even taking these variations into account, the remarkable consistency of each party's share of the vote suggests that a similar view of the basic issues prevailed throughout the country. The election was quickly followed, on 8 December, by a referendum on the Greek monarchy. Asked whether they wanted a republic or a 'crowned democracy', the Greeks voted overwhelmingly for a republic, by 69.5% to

---

Political parties

EA	United Left
EDE	National Democratic Union
EDHK	Union of the Democratic Centre
EKKE	Revolutionary Communist Party
EK–ND	Centre Union – New Forces
KKE–Interior	Communist Party – Interior (Eurocommunist)
KKE–Exterior	Communist Party – Exterior (pro-Moscow)
LDE	Popular Democratic Unity
ND	New Democracy
PASOK	Pan Hellenic Socialist Movement
	Alliance of Progressive and Left-Wing Forces
	Liberal Democratic Union
	National Camp
	Neo-Liberal Party

30.5%, decisively ending a question that had divided Greece throughout the twentieth century. Again there was little regional variation except in Crete, noted for its republicanism. where the royalists could muster only 9.3% of the poll.

Karamanlis lost no time either in drafting a new constitution. Based on the 1952 constitution, it included many new articles to increase the power of the executive, safeguard human rights (despite a clause prohibiting strikes for political reasons) and allow for the election of a presidential head of state. The new Greek government approved the constitution on 23 November 1974. Greece, with its new democratic system installed in 1974, was readmitted to the Council of Europe in November of that year, ending seven years of political and cultural isolation.

Prime Minister Karamanlis, secure in his massive majority in parliament, now had the clear confidence of the people to tackle Greece's considerable problems: not least, the task of depoliticizing the army without weakening the country's fighting potential in the face of confrontation with Turkey over Cyprus and territorial rights in the Aegean Sea. Careful not to provoke hard-core rightist backlash, Karamanlis confined himself to eliminating the ringleaders of the 1967 coup. He exiled the original troika of the Colonels' regime, Papadopoulos, Parrakos and Makarezos, to the island of Kea. By January 1975, less than 100 army officers had been compulsorily retired, compared with the forced retirement of some 1500 officers of the three armed forces in 1967 and 1968[2].

Greece's economy was also in grave difficulty. It had the highest rate of inflation in Europe and a crippling balance of payments deficit. Karamanlis saw his way round these problems by keeping Greece firmly in the Western camp through remaining in NATO and joining the EEC. Although the left generally wanted to withdraw from NATO and was against joining the EEC, Karamanlis' strong parliamentary majority allowed him to follow his pro-Western centrist reformist policies through.

However, between the elections of 1974 and 1977, the left-wing opposition parties continued to criticize the government as unrepresentative for the following reasons: the shortness of the electoral campaign in 1974 had not given them enough time to get organized, the system of reinforced proportional representation was unduly discriminatory against small parties and coalitions, voting was based on an outdated electoral register and the voting age had not been lowered from 21 to 18, thereby excluding a large potential of left-wing votes expressed in elections to student bodies one week before the November 1974 general election.

The left also accused premier Karamanlis of picking up 'scare votes' by projecting himself as the one man who stood between democracy and the return of

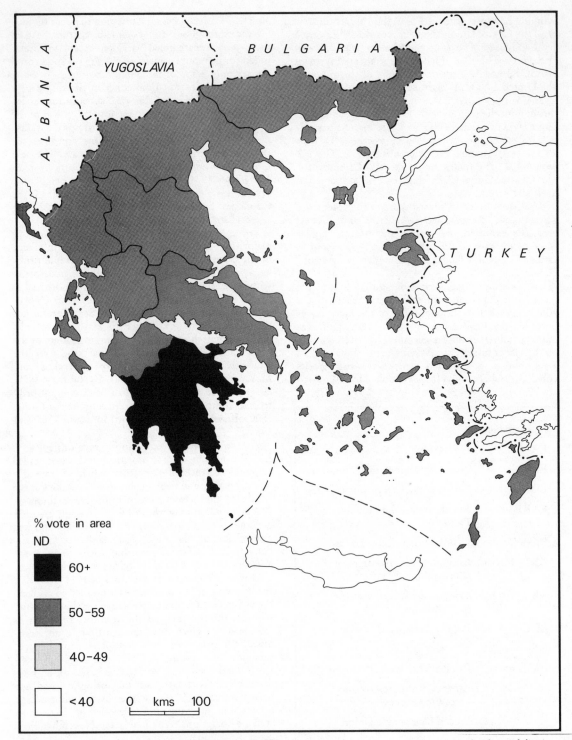

Figure 4.6 *Greece: the general election of 1974 showing the ND (New Democracy) percentage vote in the electoral districts*

the tanks. The left maintained that this, the huge vote against the monarchy in the referendum when the ND refused to commit itself either way, and the significant leftward swing in the municipal elections in the spring of 1975 more accurately reflected the country's political leanings. The charges were borne out, if only partly, in November 1977, in Greece's second general election since the fall of the Colonels. PASOK, led by Andreas Papandreou, made dramatic advances, apparently indicating an increased radicalization of the Greek electorate as memories of the dictatorship, and threats of its reimposition, faded.

Why Karamanlis decided to call the election a year ahead of time is not clear. With his majority in parliament, he was under no domestic pressure to call it although he himself argued that crucial decisions in foreign affairs during 1978 could only be taken by a government armed with a fresh mandate from the electorate. These issues were the Turkish occupation of northern Cyprus, territorial disputes with Turkey in the Aegean Sea, and Greece's application for accelerated membership of the EEC to take effect from 1981 rather than 1984.

Party coalitions and alliances had changed somewhat in the intervening three years: the far right National Rally had emerged in the summer of 1977, founded by veteran politician Stephanos Stephanopoulos, and directing its appeal at royalists and supporters of the fallen dictatorship.

A new party had also appeared on the centre-right: Constatinos Mitsotakis' New Liberals, claiming to represent orthodox liberalism as espoused particularly by the people of Crete as against the by then socialist course of George Mavros' Centre Union. The Centre Union and the New Forces group, which had fought the 1974 election in coalition, had fused to fight this election as the Union of the Democratic Centre (EDHK).

The United Left coalition (EA) of 1974, comprising the two wings of the Greek Communist Party (KKE–Exterior and KKE–Interior) and the pre-coup United Democratic Left (EDA), which essentially had been a cover for the then-illegal communists, soon broke into its constituent parts. The KKE–Interior had formed a coalition with the EDA and three other small groups to make up the Alliance of Progressive and Left-Wing Forces.

There was never any question that Karamanlis would be returned to power with a comfortable majority in the 1977 election. This he did with a reduced share of the vote, down from 54.4% to 41.9%, but this meant he still had control of 173 of parliament's 300 seats. It was PASOK's dramatic advance that provided the sirprise: it almost doubled its share from 13.6% to 25.3%, capturing 93 seats in the process, compared with a previous 13, and moved from being the third party to the majority opposition (*Figure 4.9*). The voting pattern was again fairly even throughout the country, except in individualist Crete where the ND won 24.1% of the vote, little more than half its national average. The strongly liberal island was the only region to give the EDHK its 1974 level of voting, 23.6%. The New Liberals also made their best showing in Crete, 13.4%, compared with a nationwide average of 1.1%.

PASOK made its best gains in the predominantly rural areas of North West Peloponnese and South West Rumeli, Crete and Epirus. It is also significant that the combined left-wing vote, namely that of PASOK, the communist party and the Alliance of Progressive and Left-Wing Forces, at 37%, was the highest in Greek electoral history. But this was balanced by the fact that the combined right-wing vote, of National Rally, the ND and the New Liberals, at 50% had registered only a small decline since 1974.

PASOK's success had largely been achieved at the expense of the EDHK. Leader George Mavros acknowledged responsibility for his party's serious decline and immediately resigned the leadership.

However, any drop in support must weaken the political leader and Karamanlis' strategy of calling for an increased mandate from the people for his foreign policies had seriously misfired. He could no longer use the argument based on the 1974 election results that three-quarters of the Greek electorate supported entry to the EEC. The pro-EEC vote had been reduced to just over 60%, and he could expect more vigorous opposition to his full range of policies: Cyprus, relations with Turkey, NATO and the United States. However, a more telling reason for calling early elections could be that the ultra-right National Rally may well have cut further into his electoral support if they had had another year to get organized. National Rally's 6.8% showing was a remarkable achievement considering it had been formed as recently as the summer before the November 1977 election.

The results certainly led to a more fluid political situation, meaning less power for Karamanlis while none of his problems had diminished: the Greek–Turkish dispute continued with little sign of either side being prepared to compromise under an air of mutual distrust. Relations improved in the autumn of 1980 and Greece returned to full membership of NATO.

While Karamanlis saw EEC membership, which took place in January 1981, as the best insurance against the kind of political instability that brought the Colonels to power, he had to contend with a large body of anti-EEC opposition which could be mobilized if the ND government ran into difficulties. With Karamanlis' move to the presidency in May 1980 and his successor for the premiership being George Rallis, it remains a problem. An election may be called before the cracks appear in the ND and push the

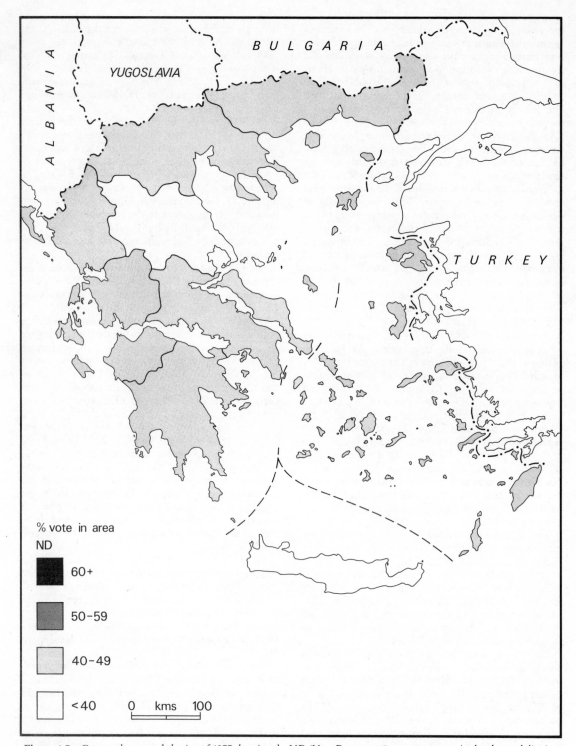

Figure 4.7 *Greece: the general election of 1977 showing the ND (New Democracy) percentage vote in the electoral districts*

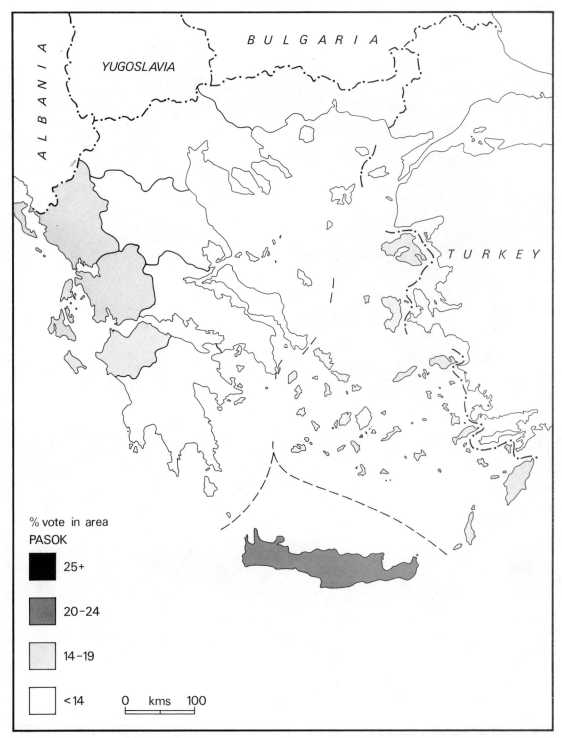

Figure 4.8 *Greece: the general election of 1974 showing the PASOK (Pan Hellenic Socialist Movement) percentage vote in the electoral districts*

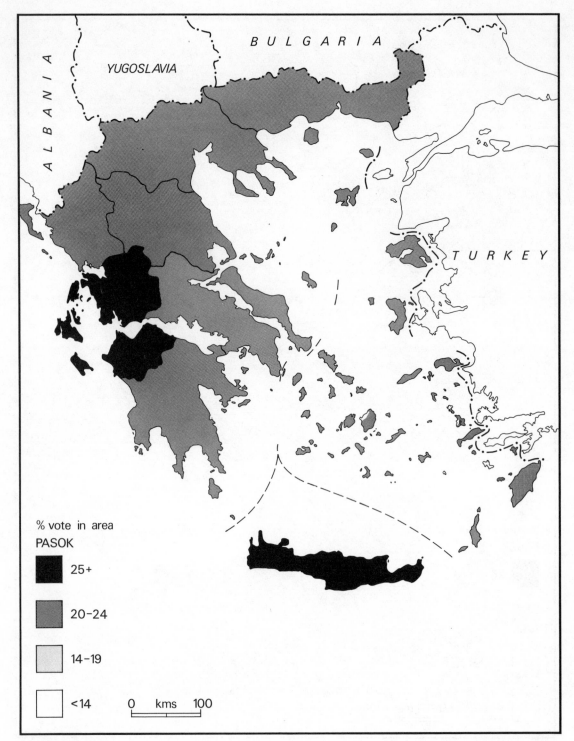

Figure 4.9 *Greece: the general election of 1977 showing the PASOK (Pan Hellenic Socialist Movement) percentage vote in the electoral districts*

electorate towards PASOK or the extreme left. The next election is scheduled for November 1981, but most commentators believe it will be held earlier.

Greece employs the system of reinforced Proportional Representation, that is, for a candidate to win an electoral district outright, he or she must obtain a higher number of votes than the district's margin, or the total number of votes in the district divided by the number of its parliamentary seats, plus one. Any remaining seats are allotted to parties polling more than 17% of the national vote or coalitions of two parties winning 25%. Coalitions of three or more parties must win at least 30%. This system has been used in both elections since the fall of the Colonels' regime in 1974, although there were modifications between the general elections of 17 November 1974 and 20 November 1977.

The electorate of 6 703 834 is divided into nine electoral districts which elect 300 deputies, who, according to the constitution, cannot change allegiance once elected, and in such an event may only resign.

References

1. Sallnow, J. and John, A. (1979). Grecian Lifestyle in a 'New Democracy', *Geographical Magazine*, **LI** (No. 4), 257–262
2. Clogg, R. (January 1975). Greek Perspectives after the Elections. *World Today*, pp. 7–14 and footnote p. 8
3. *General Secretariat of Press and Information*, October 1978, Athens

Table 4.8 *The Greek electoral system 1974–1977*

Assembly	Parliament (Vouli)
Members	300 seats
Dates of elections	17 November 1974 20 November 1977
Method	Proportional representation (PR); reinforced system of PR with party lists; d'Hondt system. In 1974 Divisor – total number of votes by number of seats; in 1977 Divisor – total number of votes by number of seats plus one
Voting age	21 in 1974, lowered to 20 on 6 June 1977. Voting is compulsory for all persons aged between 21 and 70 and living within 200 kilometres of their constituency
Voter participation (turnout)	1974 77.6% 1977 74.3%

Source: Greek Press and Information Office, Nos. 5, 6, 7, December 1974 and December 1977

Table 4.9 *Percentage of votes cast in Greek elections 1974–1977*

Party	Percentage of votes	
	1974	1977
ND	54.37	41.85
PASOK	13.58	25.33
EDHK/EK–ND	20.52	11.95
KKE–Exterior	–	9.36
EA	9.45	–
National Camp	–	6.82
Alliance of progressive and Left-Wing Forces	–	2.72
Neo-Liberal Party	–	1.08
EKKE	0.02	0.23
EDE	1.10	–
LDE	–	0.17
Other	0.96	0.49

Table 4.10 *Number of seats won in Greek elections 1974–1977*

Party	Number of seats	
	1974	1977
ND	220	173
PASOK	12	92
EDHK/EK–ND	60	15
KKE–Exterior	–	11
EA	8	–
National Camp	–	5
Alliance of progressive and Left-Wing Forces	–	2
Neo-Liberal Party	–	2
EKKE	0	0
EDE	0	–
LDE	–	0
Other	0	0
Total	300	300

Table 4.11 *Number of votes cast in Greek elections 1974–1977*

Party	Number of votes	
	1974	1977
ND	2670804	2146687
PASOK	666806	1299196
EDHK/EK–ND	1002908	613113
KKE–Exterior	–	480188
EA	464331	–
National Camp	–	349851
Alliance of Progressive and Left-Wing Forces	–	139762
Neo-Liberal Party	–	55560
EKKE	1053	11962
EDE	54162	–
LDE	–	8826
Other	52292	24739
Total	4912356	5129884

Political parties

DC	Christian Democratic Party
DP	Proletarian Democracy
MSI	Italian Social Movement
MSI–DN	Italian Social Movement – National Right (comprising the MSI and PDIUM)
PCI	Italian Communist Party
PDIUM	Democratic Party of Monarchist Unity (1968 only)
PDUP	Party of Proletarian Unity for Communism
PLI	Liberal Party
PR	Radical Party
PRI	Republican Party
PSDI	Social Democratic Party
PSI	Italian Socialist Party
PSIUP	Socialist Party of Proletarian Unity
PSU	United Socialist Party (comprising the PSI, PSDI, 1968 only)
SVP	South Tyrol Peoples Party

Italy

The international background of the late 1960s and early 1970s is probably more relevant to understanding Italy's political moves than any other European country. The late 1960s saw the Soviet Union build up a massive fleet in the Mediterranean and achieve nuclear parity with the United States, which had become weakened by growing disillusionment with its involvement in South East Asia, by its return to an isolationist policy in the second half of the 1970s and wracked with guilt over Watergate.

There was considerable fear among Italy's western allies that the country, which for political and geographical reasons is the most exposed of western nations, would turn communist and become a lonely outpost, or be the Finland of the south.

Internally, Italy was facing up to the imbalances of its post-war development and the 1960s *Dolce Vita* years. This can be viewed in terms of four factors.

(1) *The rapid transfer of the country's economy from an agrarian to an industrial base*. In the mid-1950s more people were employed on the land than in industry, but by the late 1970s the agricultural sector had decreased to 15–20% of the labour force. Post-war Italy had to chose between spending to promote industrial advance or tackle the enormous social problems of building houses, hospitals, schools and prisons, establishing fair pension schemes and training the unemployed. The government decided the former was more pressing.

Therefore, as the peasants flocked north, Italian cities found their social services stretched beyond their limit, and as the factories became increasingly mechanized the unskilled jobs the peasants had come for no longer existed, while the south – Mezzogiorno – remained the underdeveloped land of old men, children and vendettas, despite a government fund set up to develop the area.

(2) *Italy's political experience.* It has been the widest and Roman culture is among the oldest in Europe. The *Economist*, in a survey in April 1978 put it this way: 'Renaissance Italy was the haven of the city states, whose forms of government – by family, by dictator, by merchant oligarchy, even by diplomacy – varies as widely from one another as their art. Garibaldi's Italy in the nineteenth century, if not the birthplace of nationalism, was at least its most romantic expression. Italy pioneered Fascism after the first world war; and it has pioneered its own increasingly democratic brand of communism after the second'[1].

(3) *The highly decentralized political system.* This has been especially so since the April 1970 decrees authorizing regional councils in 15 regions, the

other five regions being granted autonomy earlier. Regional elections have taken place in June 1970, June 1975 and June 1980 (*see Figures 4.11, 4.13, 4.17*). The constitution allows public pressure to force government to open up discussion on subjects it might otherwise choose to ignore: any individual or organization can demand a referendum on any issue providing they collect a petition of at least 500 000 signatures calling for it.

(4) *The mass involvement of the Italians in their electoral process.* Average turnout at general elections is 94–95%, regional elections of 1970 and 1975 was 92–95% and local elections over 80%. Voting in Italy is not compulsory, though failure to turn up at the polling station brings an official enquiry. The fact that Italy abandoned the plurality system, still used by Britain today, in 1919 in favour of proportional representation may indicate greater political maturity. The high turnout of voters combined with proportional representation means that the result of elections more closely reflect the choice of the electorate. This in turn has brought its own problems: no party in such a diverse society is likely ever to win an outright majority, thus Italy must always be run by a government of consensus if not actual coalition which forces collaboration between diametrically opposed ideologies and interests.

Italian electoral history is more a record of minor changes than of sudden increases and reversals. Since the end of World War II, the Christian Democrats (DC) have consistently polled the highest number of votes and headed every coalition government. Immediately prior to and following nearly all general elections, the DC has run a minority single-party government. Until 1972 every parliament ran its full five-year term, frequent changes of government notwithstanding; in 1972 and 1976 general elections were called one year early and in 1979 two years ahead of schedule.

The major feature of Italian political history since 1948 has been the underlying fear of allowing communists into government: 'Italy is a special type of democracy which cannot afford the luxury of alternating governments because the arrival of the opposition led by the Communist Party in power would, by definition, destroy it'[2]. This is despite the Communist Party's (PCI) impeccable record of democratic government in the cities and regions where it has been in power. For example, Bologna, communist-ruled since the end of the war, is frequently said to be the best-run city in Italy. In the period under study Italy has had four general elections, in 1968, 1972, 1976 and 1979, and three regional elections, affecting 15 of the country's 20 provinces in 1970 and 18 provinces in 1975. The student agitation which had begun in Italy and France in late 1967, and was the

forerunner of worker discontent in the 'hot autumn' of 1969, provided the background to the election in 1968.

The centre-left government of Christian Democrats and Socialists (PSI), Social Democrats (PSDI) and Republicans (PRI), faced the electorate in 1968 with a five-year record of non-achievement. This was summarized in the Italian word *immobilismo* – not getting anything done, due largely to the opposing interests of the socialists and the DC. Immobilismo in turn produced two more words to reflect the views of the day: *contestazione* or confrontation between social groups, between employer and employed, students and the already educated hierarchy; and *concilaire*, the need for opposing political factions to cooperate over Italy's economic problems.

In the 1968 mood of protest and confrontation, Italy was expected to polarize and return a government very much to the left; Italy's electorate thought otherwise and showed its political maturity by returning to power the only form of government all the factions of Italy could tolerate. The centre-left partners fought the election on separate lists: the DC, the PSU (United Socialist Party) and the Republicans slightly improved their position, winning 366 out of 630 seats in the chamber of deputies, compared with 359 in 1963.

The PCI won nearly 800 000 fresh votes and 11 more seats in the chamber to give them 177. With the left-wing Partito Socialista di Unita Proletaria (PSIUP) the two parties presented joint lists for the senate and won two more seats. Together they accounted for one-third of the electorate. The increase was mainly in the north, and largely from immigrants who had moved from the south and become politicized in the factories where they found jobs but low wages and poor accommodation. The PCI and PSIUP also attracted more young people who had reached the age of majority since 1963.

During the previous administration, from 1963 to 1968, Italy had four governments; from 1968 the crises deepened in the two years to 1970, especially following the uncontrolled immigration to northern cities which were at the root of the 'hot autumn' crisis of 1969. Italy endured four further governments: the fifth, a centre-left coalition, was formed in April 1970 and despite polling well in the June regional elections only lasted until July, when a sixth administration was formed. This again was a centre-left coalition.

It was against this background of class confrontation and unstable centre-left government that convergence began. The unions, divided by the cold war, began to unify through a common grudge against inefficient government. The PCI expelled its far left, very vociferous *Il Manifesto* group while the social democrats and socialists split again with the social democrats accusing the socialists of moving too close to the communists.

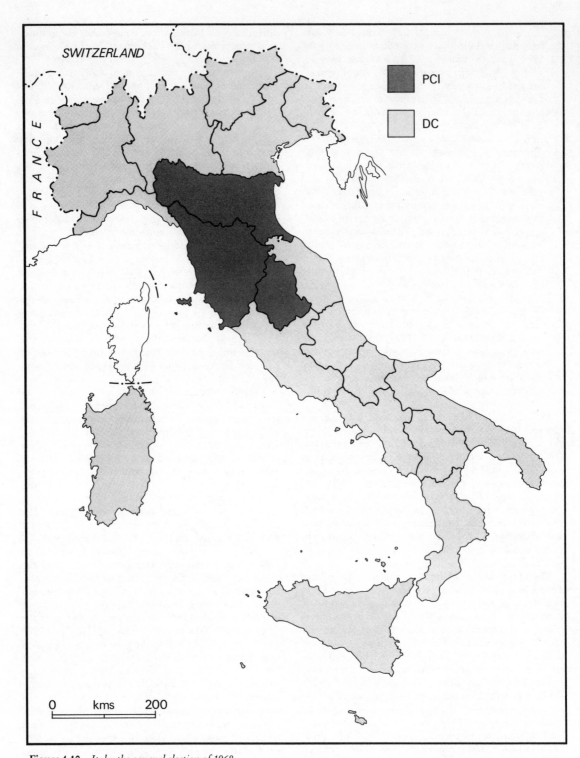

Figure 4.10 *Italy: the general election of 1968*

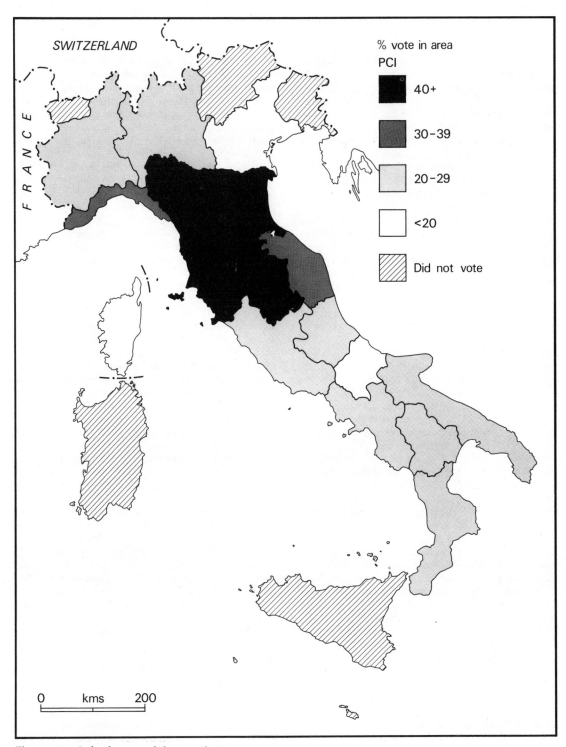

Figure 4.11 *Italy: the regional elections of 1970*

The first seeds of the historic compromise could be detected. Enrico Berlinguer, the architect of the historic compromise and disliked by the Soviet Communist Party, was not yet leader of the PCI, but an assistant to the ageing Luigi Longo. There was talk of a grand coalition between Catholics and Communists in a *Repubblica Conciliare*, a republic of conciliation, though many dismissed the idea out of fear that one side or the other would dominate.

The regional elections of June 1970 marked the beginning of nationwide regional administrations in Italy. Such regionalization had been provided for in the constitution of 1948 and can be read as a reaction to the over-centralized Fascist rule. Although four regions were given autonomy straight away, and a fifth in 1962, autonomy for the remaining 15 was delayed because of a fear that the PCI would win control in their strongholds of Emilia-Romagna, Umbria and Toscana, creating a 'red belt' across the centre of Italy. This proved to be the case in June 1970 and subsequent elections (*see Figures 4.11, 4.13, 4.14*).

The election of 1972 was the first election in the history of the republic to be held ahead of schedule, the last precedent being the ill-fated election of 1924 which consolidated Fascist power. That election haunted the political scene in 1972. The centre-left coalition which had ruled Italy for almost a decade was in disarray and the neo-Fascist Italian Social Movement (MSI) had made shock advances in the local elections of 1971. The Socialist Party (PSI) had declared it would not necessarily follow the same government coalition following the 1970 regional elections and declared it would be ready to collaborate with the PCI if it seemed inevitable. The DC government called the 1972 election in order to stave off a right-wing demand to hold a referendum on divorce, which had been legalized in Italy only in 1970. Under the constitution no referendum can be held within a year of a general election. Thus President Leone was left with no choice but to dissolve the chamber and announce elections for 7 May 1972. The results, as is the want of Italians, brought little change: the DC lost a little ground winning 38.8% of the vote, compared with 39.1% in 1968, but gained one seat in the chamber to give them 267, while the PCI gained slightly to follow their consistent pattern: 27.2% (26.9% in 1968) and gained two seats in the chamber to make a total of 179. The electoral pattern was the same in terms of regions (*Figure 4.12*).

The general trend, though slow moving, was now discernable. The PCI was the first communist party to condemn the Soviet-led invasion of Czechoslovakia in 1968; it began loosening its ties with Moscow and joined the national democratic process in its own country. Enrico Berlinguer became party secretary of the PCI in 1972 and demonstrated his independence from the Soviet bloc by skilfully representing his party as a bulwark of democracy against the threat from the extreme right and calling for a grand coalition between communists, socialists and left-wing Catholics. In his personal life, he also showed democratic Italian communism, driving his Catholic wife to mass on Sunday and waiting for her outside.

It was the overthrow in September 1973 of Salvador Allende's Marxist government in Chile with United States connivance that spurred Berlinguer to think out his strategy. The DC, with the assistance of the Catholic church and United States influence, had persuaded the majority of electors that the PCI was pledged to overthrow democracy. The role of the cold war had been crucial. It enabled the governing parties to identify the PCI with three bogies at the same time: the USSR, the anti-Christ and the destruction of Western civilization. Berlinguer became convinced after Allende's overthrow that even if the left won an outright majority it would not be allowed to run the country. The only solution he decided was an historic compromise – in Italian *compromesso storico* – between Catholics and communists, both cooperating in the national interest. The divorce referendum of 1974 set the scene for a DC decline and PCI gains of the local elections the following year. The government could not put the referendum off any longer: the Catholic-backed DC was forced to support the petition gatherers seeking to abrogate the divorce law and found itself uneasily in alliance with the MSI against all the other parties. With an 88% turnout, 59.1% voted to retain divorce. The vote cut across party lines, social class and was remarkably even throughout the country, with only areas in mainland southern Italy voting to end divorce.

The swing against the DC towards secular parties was further confirmed in Sardinia's June regional election where the DC vote declined by 6.23%. In June 1975 the regional elections, which marked the lowest point for the DC, cut back the DC vote from 38.7% to 35.3%, while the PCI went up from 27.2% (1970) to 33.4%. Socialist–communist governments took control in 24 of Italy's 47 cities with 100 000 plus inhabitants.

In 1975 the term Eurocommunism was coined by Yugoslav journalist Frane Barbieri in an article in *Giornale Nuovo*[3]. The word quickly caught on and was adopted by the parties themselves. The left was ready for a general election; the socialists withdrew from the government and demanded communist participation and for the second time Italy's parliament was dissolved a year ahead of schedule.

The PCI, pushing their historic compromise, went into the June 1976 election campaign confident of another spectacular advance though not the victory many Western commentators predicted. The results gave the PCI 34.4%, four percentage points behind the DC's 38.7%, although the DC had recovered

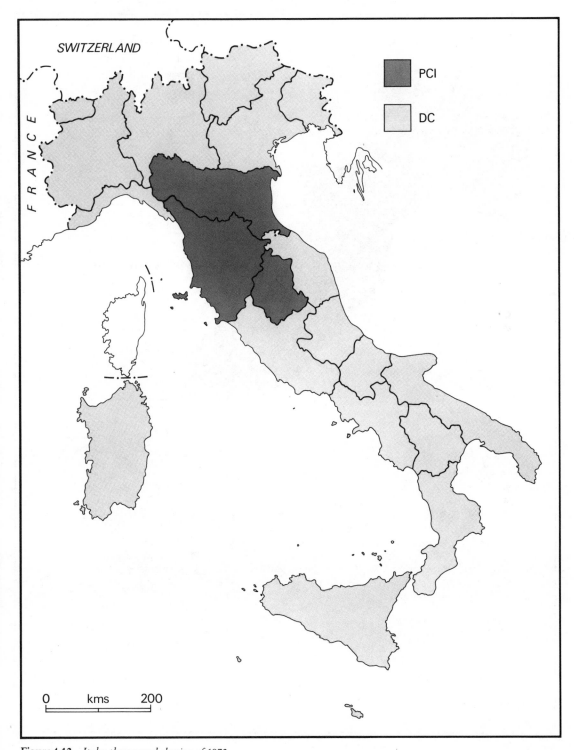

Figure 4.12 *Italy: the general election of 1972*

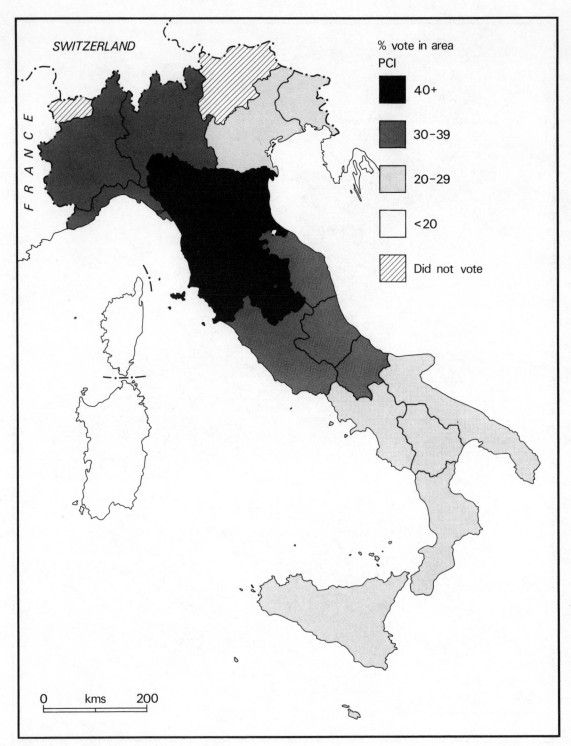

Figure 4.13 *Italy: the regional elections of 1975*

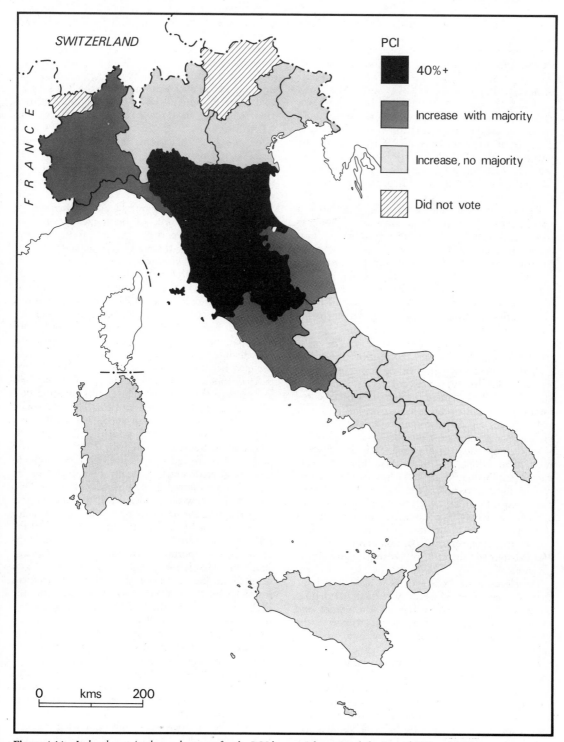

Figure 4.14 *Italy: change in electoral support for the PCI between the regional elections of 1970 and 1975*

votes lost in the 1975 regional elections to return exactly to their 1972 position. The results can be seen as a polarization of Italian society, the DC and PCI between them squeezing out the smaller parties: the PSI slipped back to its 1972 level of 9.6%, the Social Democrats (PSDI), Liberals (PLI) and MSI all suffered heavy losses. The small Radical Party, active on civil rights, feminism and conservation issues, gained its first representation in the chamber with four seats. It is important to compare the 1976 election not just with the results of 1972, but also the regional elections of 1975, because it was only in 1975 that the voting age for the chamber of deputies was lowered to 18.

A study by Gianfranco Pasquini[4] indicated a marked shift to the left by young voters, probably caused and sustained by a new type of political socialization taking place at work and in schools. Approximately 55% of under 25 year olds voted for the PCI, PSI, DP (Proletarian Democrats) and PR (Radical Party). In terms of percentage, the net gain for the left does not exceed 2% at best, but if the trend continued there would be a natural majority for the left in the making.

Because of the size of the PCI vote in 1976, with 228 deputies in the chamber, it could no longer be ignored. Consequently the widely respected Pietro Ingrao, a PCI deputy, was elected to the Presidency of the chamber of deputies, while eight other communist representatives became chairmen of powerful parliamentary legislative committees. These moves, while not satisfying communist demands to enact the historic compromise of allowing PCI into government, went a long way to appease them. No one wanted another election, and thus on 11 August 1976, a third government led by Guilio Andreotti was voted into office by a vast number of abstentions. It was Italy's 39th administration since the fall of fascism in 1943 and the first time since their eviction from the tripartite coalition in May 1947, the PCI abstained instead of voting against the government[5].

The elections of 1975 and 1976 had altered the political scene after 30 years of virtual status quo. While the PCI won its demand for consultation and an agreed programme of economic recovery, the electorate found parliament was without effective opposition.

The most obvious manifestation of this was the increased urban political violence, which culminated in the kidnap and murder of Aldo Moro in May 1978. He was one of Italy's most respected politicians, had been tipped as the next President after Giovanni Leone, and was responsible for bringing about agreement between the PCI and the DC on a government programme. Had Moro lived, Italy may well have witnessed the historic compromise, as Moro believed direct communist participation in the government to be inevitable.

The first phase of Andreotti's government had ended in January 1978 during which the PCI kept the minority DC administration alive by their abstention. When this clearly failed to meet PCI aspirations a new formula was devised under which the PCI was permitted into parliamentary majority supporting Andreotti. This consisted of five parties: DC, PCI, PSI, PSDI and PRI. The parties were consulted on government measures, but without direct participation in the cabinet.

By January 1979 the contradiction of this role for the PCI, in the words of Berlinguer 'a party of government and of struggle' became too great, and the disapproval of the party militants too big to ignore. The PCI withdrew from the parliamentary majority and Andreotti's government resigned on 31 January 1979. He then formed a coalition government of the DC, PSDI and PRI on 21 March but this lost a vote of confidence in the Senate ten days later. The result was the assembly was dissolved on 1 April in preparation for a general election two years ahead of schedule, an election in which the PCI vote declined for the first time since World War II: the party dropped 4% from 34.4% in 1976 to 30.4% and lost seats in the chamber. The results gave the PCI 201 seats compared to 228 in 1976. The DC polled 38.3%, marginally less than the 38.7% in 1976 and obtained the same number of deputies, 262. The PSI increased its representation from 57 to 62. Italy's politics of confusion showed itself in the attempts to create a government. Eventually Francesco Cossiga on 4 August formed an administration of the DC, PSDI and PLI, with the socialist (PSI giving support by abstention. Previous attempts following the ballot had been made by Andreotti, Craxi (secretary of the PSI) and Pandolfi (DC). When the socialists withdrew their support by abstention for the Cossiga coalition, negotiations between Cossiga and Craxi resulted in the return of the PSI to government formally, for the first time since 1974, along with the PRI. The PSDI and the PLI left the coalition when this occurred in April 1980. This government lasted from 4 April to 27 September when it was defeated in a vote on economic reforms. Arnaldo Forlani formed a four-party majority coalition of the DC, PSI, PSDI and PRI on 19 October 1980 with 360 of the 630 seats in the assembly. He had never been Prime Minister before but had been DC party secretary from 1969 to 1973 and foreign minister under Andreotti from 1976 to 1979. Forlani belongs to the right-wing majority faction of the DC. The Italian political kaleidoscope

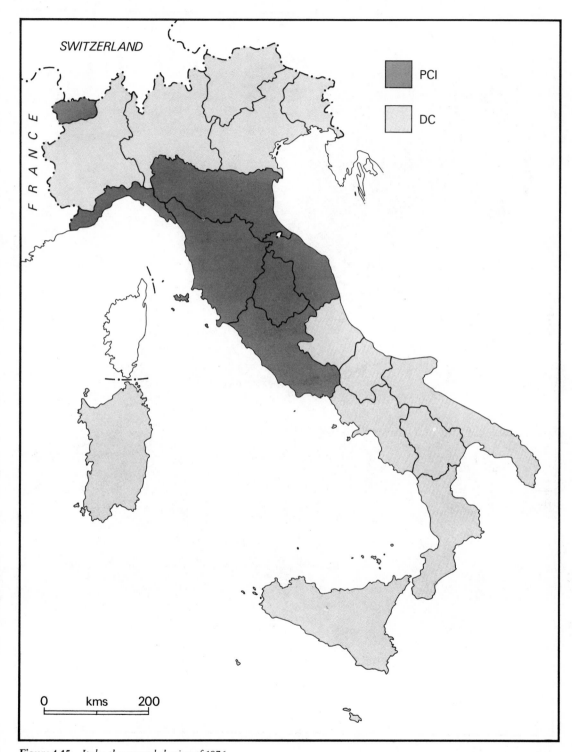

Figure 4.15 *Italy: the general election of 1976*

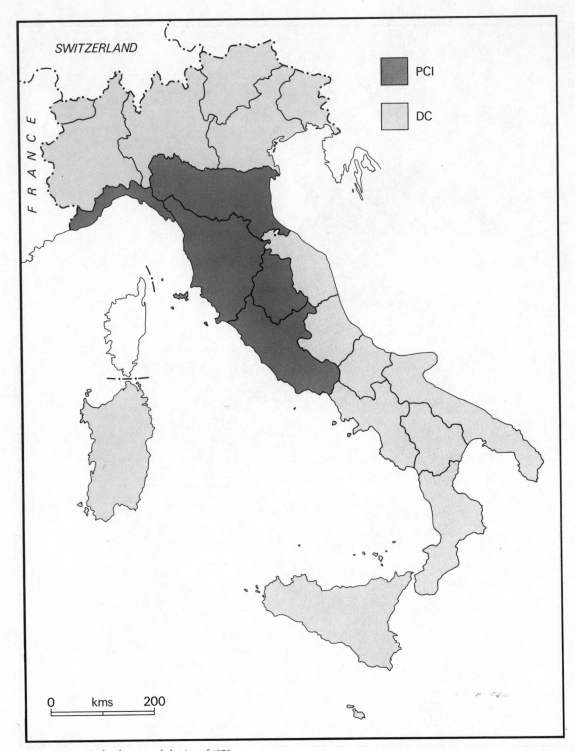

Figure 4.16 *Italy: the general election of 1979*

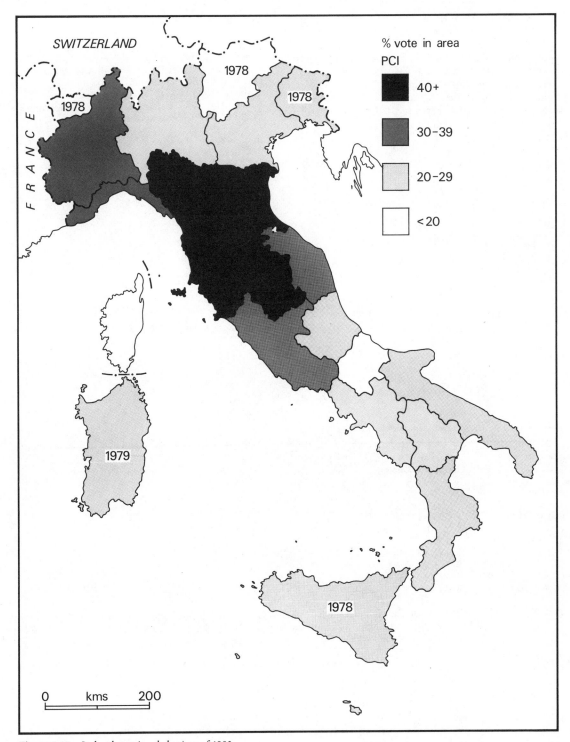

Figure 4.17 *Italy: the regional elections of 1980*

now is without Aldo Moro, the one politician who might have been able to prevent a rightward drift of the DC. The PCI feels it has no alternative to opposition, even though it lost ground at the last election. It has accused the DC of breaking the collaboration pact and of no longer following Moro's policies. The historic compromise of Berlinguer appears further away than ever, although he still professes faith in its eventual achievement.

References

1. *The Economist*, 1 April 1978, A Survey of Italy, p. 8
2. Allum, P. A. (1979). In *Political Parties in the European Community*, p. 135 (ed. by S. Henig). Allen & Unwin/Policy Studies Institute, London
3. Barbieri, F., 26 June 1975, *Giornale Nuovo*
4. Pasquini, G. (1977). Before and after the Italian National Elections of 1976. *Government and Opposition*, **12** (No. 1), 60–87
5. Ibid., p. 84

Table 4.12 *The Italian electoral system 1968–1980*

Assembly	Camera dei Deputati Chamber of Deputies
Members	630
Dates of elections	19–20 May 1968 7 June 1970 (regional) 7–8 May 1972 15–16 June 1975 (regional) 20–21 June 1976 3–4 June 1979 8–9 June 1980 (regional)
Method	Proportional representation (PR); d'Hondt system; 31 multimember PR constituencies (*collegi elettorali*). Single-member constituency for Aosta valley. Nation as a whole used for assignment of residual votes and seats
Voting age	21, reduced to 18 in 1975, although minimum age for eligibility for membership of Chamber retained at 21
Voter participation (turnout)	1968 92.8% 1972 93.2% 1976 93.2% 1979 89.9% 1980 88.5%

Source: Italy, Documents and Notes 1968–1976: Ministry of the Interior, Rome; Keesings Contemporary Archives

Table 4.13 *Number of seats won in Italian regional elections 1970–1980*

Party	Number of seats		
	1970	1975	1980
DC	287	277	290
PCI	200	247	233
PSI	67	82	86
MSI	34	40	37
PSDI	41	36	31
PRI	18	19	18
PLI	27	11	15
PDUP[a] }	–	4	8
DP }	–	4	2
PSIUP	16	–	–

[a] *In 1975, PDUP and DP members elected in alliance on PDUP ticket. In 1980, parties campaigned separately*

Table 4.14 *Percentage of votes cast in Italian regional elections 1970–1980*

Party	Percentage of votes		
	1970	1975	1980
DC	37.9	35.3	36.8
PCI	27.9	33.4	31.5
PSI	10.4	12.0	12.7
MSI	5.9	6.4	5.9
PSDI	7.0	5.6	5.0
PRI	2.9	3.2	3.0
PLI	4.7	2.5	2.7
PDUP[a] }	–	0.5	1.2
DP }	–	0.9	0.9
PSIUP	3.3	–	–.
Other	–	0.2	0.3

[a] *In 1975, PDUP and DP members elected in alliance on PDUP ticket. In 1980, parties campaigned separately*

Table 4.15 *Number of votes cast in Italian regional elections 1970–1980*

Party	Number of votes		
	1970	1975	1980
DC	10 303 236	10 707 682	11 153 439
PCI	7 586 983	10 149 135	9 555 767
PSI	2 837 451	3 636 647	3 851 722
PSDI	1 897 034	1 700 983	1 505 607
PRI	787 011	961 016	922 970
PLI	1 291 435	749 749	816 418
MSI	1 620 280	1 951 011	1 785 750
PDUP[a] }	–	417 725	372 102
DP }			374 100
PSIUP	878 697	–	–
Other	–	70 789	85 491
Total	27 202 127	30 344 737	30 423 366

[a] *In 1975, PDUP and DP members elected in alliance on PDUP ticket. In 1980, parties campaigned separately*

Source: *Keesings Contemporary Archives 1975, 27338–27339) Keesings Contemporary Archives 1980, 30520–30522. See the above source for a regional breakdown of votes for each party. See also other regions; 29910, 29686, 29222–23*

Table 4.16 *Number of seats won in Italian general elections 1968–1979*

Party	Number of seats			
	1968	1972	1976	1979
DC	266	266	262	262
PCI	177	179	228	201
PSI }[a]	91	61	57	62
PSDI }		29	15	20
PRI	9	15	14	16
PLI	31	20	5	9
MSI	24	56	35	30
SVP	3	3	3	4
PDUP	–	–	6[b]	6
PR	–	–	4	18
PSIUP	23	0	0	0
PDIUM	6	0	0	0
Valdostani	–	–	–	1
Per Trieste	–	–	–	1
Other	0	1	1	0

[a] *PSI and PSDI campaigned together as PSU in 1968*
[b] *6 seats in 1976 won by DP in alliance with PDUP*

Table 4.17 *Percentage of votes cast in Italian general elections 1968–1979*

Party	Percentage of votes			
	1968	1972	1976	1979
DC	39.1	38.7	38.7	38.3
PCI	26.9	27.1	34.4	30.4
PSI }[a]	14.5	9.6	9.6	9.8
PSDI }		5.1	3.4	3.8
PRI	2.0	2.9	3.1	3.0
PLI	5.8	3.9	1.3	1.9
MSI	4.4	8.7	6.1	5.3
SVP	0.5	0.5	0.5	0.6
PDUP	–	–	1.5	1.4
PR	–	–	1.1	3.4
PSIUP	4.5	1.9	–	–
PDIUM	1.3	–	–	–
Valdostani	–	–	–	0.1
Per Trieste	–	–	–	0.2
Other	1.0	1.6	0.3	1.8

[a]   *PSI and PSDI campaigned together as PSU in 1968*

Table 4.18 *Number of votes cast in Italian general elections 1968–1979*

Party	Number of votes			
	1968	1972	1976	1979
DC	12440156	12912466	14209519	14007594
PCI	8557077	9068961	12614650	11107883
PSI }[a]	4604603	3208497	3540309	3586256
PSDI }		1718142	1239492	1403873
PRI	626549	954357	1135546	1106766
PLI	1850796	1296977	480122	708022
MSI	1414194	2894862[b]	2238339	1924251
SVP	152991	153674	184375	206264
PDUP	–	–	557025	501431
RP	–	–	394439	1259362
PSIUP	1414982	648591	–	–
PDIUM	414517	–	–	–
Valdostani	–	–	–	33250
Per Trieste	–	–	–	62602
Other	324235	544886	113762	659031
Total	31800100	33401413	36707578	36566585

[a]   *PSI and PSDI campaigned together as PSU in 1968*
[b]   *MSI and PDIUM vote in 1972 under MSI–DN label*

Portugal

The Captain's coup of April 1974 was inevitable only with hindsight. The Salazar–Caetano dictatorship brought on its own destruction by sending its young men to defend an outmoded empire and fight a hopeless war. Worse still, it exposed its educated officers to the Marxist philosophy of Portuguese Africa's rebels.

However, as late as March 1974, following the abortive revolt at the army barracks at Caldas da Rainha, one British Diplomat filed a report saying the possibility of a coup could be ruled out for the foreseeable future[1]. What is of interest, however, is that following the takeover by the Armed Forces Movement (MFA) and during the 19 months of revolution up to the suppression of a far left insurrection in November 1975, a period when the country experienced six provisional governments, three Prime Ministers and two Presidents, there was no real threat of civil war. Neither was there any danger that the country, used to half a century of Fascist dictatorship, was in any way willing to swap one master for another, namely the well-organized, pro-Moscow Portuguese Communist Party (PCP), the only West European party openly to applaud the 1968 Soviet-led invasion of Czechoslovakia.

Two important elements helped prevent this:

(1) The intelligence and tactical ability of the MFA. Within 20 hours of the coup, on 25 April 1974, it

Political parties			
		PDA	Atlantic Democratic Party
		PDC	Christian Democratic Party
AD	Democratic Alliance	POUS	Workers' Party for Socialist Unity (Trotskyist)
AOC	Alliance of Workers and Farm Labourers	PPD	Popular Democratic Party (merged with PSD)
APU	United People's Alliance		
CDS	Social Democratic Centre	PPM	Popular Monarchist Party
FEC–ML	Electoral Front of Communists (Marxist–Leninist)	PRP–BR	Revolutionary Proletarian Party–Revolutionary Brigades
FRS	Republican and Socialist Front	PRT	Workers' Revolutionary Party
FSP	Popular Socialist Front	PSD	Social Democratic Party
LCI	International Communist League	PSP	Portuguese Socialist Party
		PSR	Revolutionary Socialist Party (Trotskyist)
MDP	Portuguese Democratic Movement	PT	Workers' Party
MDP–CDE	Democratic Electoral Committee	PUP	Popular United Party
MES	Movement of the Socialist Left	OCMLP	Marxist–Leninist Communist Organization of Portugal
MIRN	Independent Movement for National Reconstruction	UDP	Popular Democratic Union
MIRN–PDP	Independent Movement for National Reconstruction – Portuguese Party of the Right	UESD	Union of the Socialist and Democratic Left
		ASDI	Independent Social Democratic Association
MRPP	Movement for the Reorganization of the Proletarian Party	AD	Democratic Alliance (comprising the PSD, CDS, PPM)
PCTP–MRPP	Portuguese Workers' Communist Party	FRS	Republican and Socialist Front (comprising the PSP, UESD, ASDI)
PCP	Portuguese Communist Party		
PCP–ML	Portuguese Communist Party (Marxist–Leninist)	APU	United People's Alliance (comprising the PCP, MDP)

had taken control of the military, forced Prime Minister Marcello Caetano to resign and installed a Junta de Salvacao Nacional (National Salvation Committee) with the moderate general Antonio de Spinola as the country's new President. Spinola had only a few months before written a book in which he declared his opposition, albeit mild, to the Caetano regime.

On the morning of 26 April, the Junta presented itself to the nation on television and within 19 days a provisional government was formed with the participation of moderates, socialists and communists. With the communists sharing power, it was no longer in their interest to cause disruptions.

(2) Portugal's economic position. Under the Caetano regime, Portugal had encouraged massive loans and industrialization by foreign companies, especially the United States. This investment was hardly likely to remain in a country ruled by the extreme left, forcing those extreme leftists to face the very real possibility of finding Portugal a kind of Albania or Cuba of Western Europe. Even worse, in the new era of détente Portugal might have become more like Chile under Allende, isolated and receiving aid from no one.

Portugal had undergone four distinct phases of development since April 1974 when its soldiers emptied out the bullets and put carnations in their guns. The initial stage of the revolution was followed by a period of 14 months when it seemed the country might evolve into a communist state allied to the Soviet Union. This ended with the counter-revolution led by Colonel, later General Ramalho Eanes, one 25 November 1975. Eanes was subsequently elected Portugal's soldier President in June 1976 when he secured 61% of the vote in a four-cornered contest.

Portugal's second general election of April 1976 heralded the third stage, with Mario Soares becoming Prime Minister and heading the minority socialist administration with 107 of the then 263 seats in the National Assembly. Soares also signalled the start of the fourth phase the following December when he lost a motion of confidence for his economic reforms, resigned and was then forced into coalition with the conservative Centre Democrat (CDS) Party.

This phase of instability continued after Eanes dismissed Soares in July 1978, and through three subsequent Prime Ministers appointed by the President. During that time 'senior right-wing army officers were saying they would have to intervene in politics if the politicians did not put their house in order'[2]. Two non-party men, Alfredo Nobre da Costa and Carlos Mota Pinto, attempted to govern the country. The last of the three Prime Ministers, Maria de Lurdes Pintassilgo, was given the task of

forming a 100-day government, the eleventh since April 1974, in a run up to early general elections in December 1979.

A fifth phase has now commenced, with the majority administration of the right-wing Democratic Alliance (AD) elected on 2 December 1979. The AD consists of the centre-right Social Democrats (PSD), conservative Centre Democrats (CDS), the Monarchist Party (PPM) and a group of dissident socialists. The leader of the AD, Francisco Sa Carneiro, became Prime Minister. However, the present constitution made it compulsory for Portugal to stage fresh elections in October 1980. The leaders of the Democratic Alliance repeated their electoral success with an increased majority in October 1980, only to have it marred by the death of Sa Carneiro in an aeroplane crash in December 1980.

When the military took over in April 1974, it inherited a government system that existed more on paper than in reality. The Salazar dictatorship had been more a clerico-corporate regime than a Fascist dictatorship, and the military had been docile servants rather than power sharers. The revolution therefore created a vacuum, which the military was too little experienced to fill. The Communist Party (PCP), formed in 1921, was an underground organization before it was five years old, and the only political group sufficiently well organized, through their clandestine trade union work, to be capable of filling the vacuum. The Socialist Party, which was later to take power, had been formed only in 1973, and that in exile.

In many ways the PCP was only doing what no other organization was capable of doing at the time: to its credit, the communist trade union movement Intersindical did its best to bring order and discipline to the workers intent on celebrating their new freedom by striking, though it was later to take over as the vanguard of revolutionary seizures of land, factories and banks.

It should be remembered that the left wingers had also to work against any threatened right-wing backlash, and had Spinola been better organized, a right-wing government would certainly have been imposed against the general will of the people in September 1974. His plan for reactionary riots backfired and he was forced to resign on 30 September 1974. He was replaced by general Francisco da Costa Gomes. The following March, another attempted coup was quashed and the communists were firmly installed in power, but they were unable to find good enough reasons to prevent the scheduled April 1975 elections to the constituent assembly, the country's first free elections in half a century.

Here the military made a bid for power by calling the electorate to cast blank ballots in their favour, but the people of Portugal, having endured so long the rigged elections of Salazar, would not consider such a move and a mere 6% of the country's six million, voters returned blank or spoiled papers.

In an election turnout of 91.7%, Mario Soares' Socialist Party (PSP) took 38% of the vote, the centre-left Popular Democrats (PPD) 26% and the Communists (PCP) 12.5%. The conservative Centre Democrats (CDS) won 7.5% and the Portuguese Democratic Movement–Democratic Electoral Committee (MDP–CDE), 4%.

Portugal's first post-revolutionary election showed that nearly half a century of dictatorship had produced the most radical electorate in Western Europe, with over 80% of the total vote going to parties to the left of the political spectrum. The results also showed a strong antipathy to any form of authoritarian rule, giving the PCP and its running mate the MDP–CDE only 16% of the vote; its support was concentrated on the red industrial belt around Lisbon and the southern Alentejo region (*Figure 4.18*). In the north, the combined communist vote was under 10%. The MFA was not yet prepared to relinquish power and throughout 1975, Portugal seemed to be faced with the choice between pro-Soviet or anti-Soviet communism. A pact signed in the same month as the election between the political parties and the MFA acknowledged military control over Portugal's future for an indefinite period. During the summer of 1975, Portugal staggered through its government crises. In July Soares resigned from the government, followed quickly by the PPD. Amid July anti-MFA rallies, a military triumvirate was formed and August saw anti-communist riots in the north with local party officers sacked as the country's fifth post-revolutionary government was formed. Moderate officers called for a form of government mid-way between Soviet-style communism and West European social democracy. A sixth government was formed in September and in November a far left revolt was quickly quashed by the hitherto quiet figure of Antonio Ramalho Eanes.

Some say Eanes organized the left revolt so he could crush it and gain power himself. Certainly Eanes was ready for the uprising and therefore one could assume he had some kind of prior knowledge of it.

Politicians and the MFA immediately began talks on a new pact. Signed in February 1976, the Supreme Revolutionary Council now had power only to give its opinion on laws passed in the assembly, and to pass them back for further consideration. The military's safeguard now deepened on the politicians' tacit agreement to elect a soldier President with wide executive powers, including the right to appoint Prime Ministers (after consultations with the parties) and to veto legislation (although he could be overridden by a two-thirds majority in the assembly). The only other safeguard lay in the new constitution, passed in the same month by the assembly, which enshrined the MFA 'as a guarantor of the democratic conquests and the revolutionary process'.

The second election campaign began on 4 April 1976 with the communists calling on the socialists to join a popular front. But the confident socialists instead talked of consolidating the economic order, and neither conservative parties talked about rolling back the economic changes since 1974, although both argued that the private sector should be allowed to survive.

In a poll reduced in turnout by almost 9% to 83%, the socialists lost slightly with 35% of the vote compared to 38%, as did the Popular Democrats (PPD). The communists gained 2% while the Centre Democrats more than doubled their share of the poll from 7.5% to 16%.

The quiet and patriarchal Eanes was the obvious choice in the presidential elections two months later, taking 61% of the vote in a four-cornered contest.

Prime Minister Soares faced enormous economic problems: a trade deficit of 2000 million dollars, an annual budget deficit of 1000 million dollars, and an unemployment rate of 25%[3]. The economic chaos was exacerbated by the *retornados* – Portuguese refugees fleeing Africa and returning to Portugal penniless[4]. (Since then, one million have been forced to return.) Soares' government staggered on until December 1977, when he lost a vote of confidence over austerity measures and a spate of cabinet resignations. Eanes forced a coalition on Soares with the conservative CDS, which lasted until the following July, when the CDS withdrew and Eanes dismissed Soares.

Why Portugal should differ so much from Spain in its route to democracy from dictatorship and why their communist parties should differ so much must be seen in a geographic and historical context. The boom years of the 1960s hardly touched Portugal, a tiny country of 88 500 square kilometres lying on the edge of Europe, with a population of just over eight million and virtually no middle class. The Tagus (Tejo) river divides Portugal in two, both politically and geographically. To the north, conservative family-run smallholdings and what industry there is in the country, to the south the fertile Tagus delta and the Alentejo where landless labourers seized farms covering 1 000 000 hectares in the heady days following the revolution[5].

The influential communist party also had a greatly differing evolution. While the Spanish communist leaders fled abroad after the 1936–1939 civil war, leaving behind well-organized underground networks, the embryonic PCP in 1926 stayed. Its present secretary-general Alvaro Cunhal spent 13 years in prison, eight of them in solitary confinement. He went into exile only in 1962, and then to Czechoslovakia, while Carrillo of the Spanish party (PCE) lived in democratic Paris. By 1974, the members of the

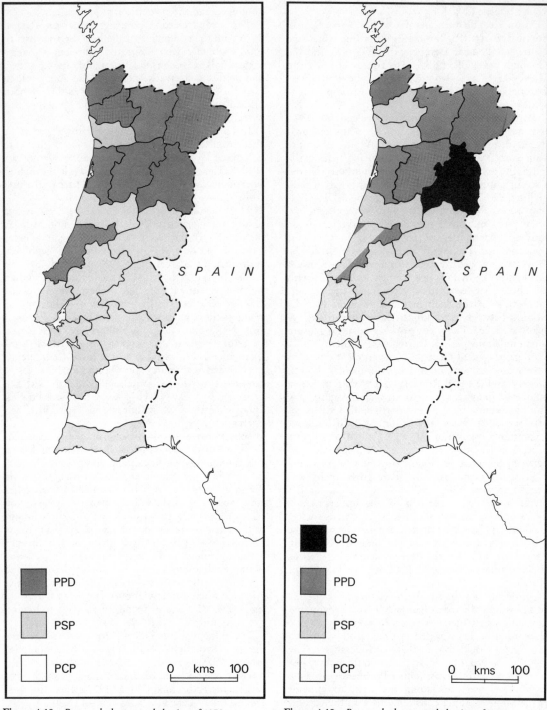

Figure 4.18 *Portugal: the general election of 1975*

Figure 4.19 *Portugal: the general election of 1976*

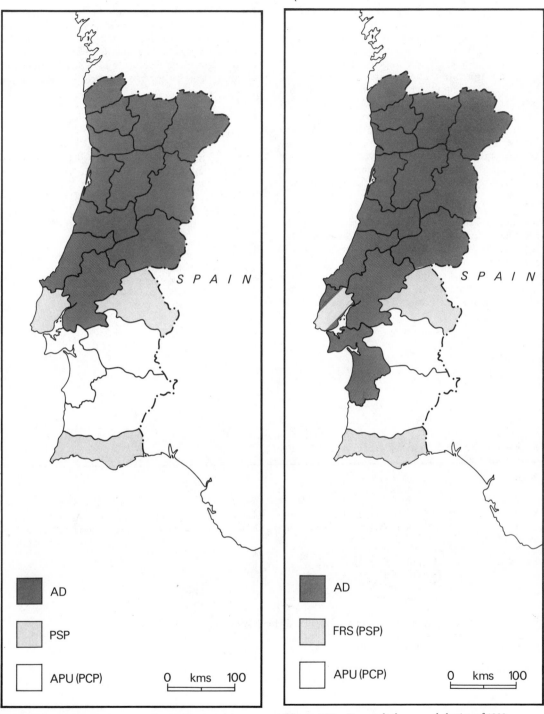

Figure 4.20 *Portugal: the general election of 1979*

Figure 4.21 *Portugal: the general election of 1980*

PCP central committee had spent between them 308 years in gaol[6]. Their years of repression and clandestine activity have turned them into tough, resourceful and well-organized tacticians.

The PCP is unlikely to change its Stalinist policies under the present, though ageing, leadership. But Portugal is moving closer to Europe. It has been a member of NATO since its inception, is a member of EFTA and expects to join the European Communities of the Coal and Steel Community, the Common Market and Euratom in 1983. Portugal has firmly rejected any move back to totalitarianism. A new leadership, reaching the top in a freer, more European atmosphere could change the shape of the party in time.

Figures 4.18 to *4.21* confirm the Tagus (Tejo) river division of Portugal's political geography with the Democratic Alliance (AD) taking the districts to the north of the river, while the communists and socialists continue to win areas in the south.

The country has swung from the far right to, in the early days of the revolution, the far left, and is now hovering around the centre. Two electoral successes for the AD in less than 12 months have helped to confirm it as a government party. As a country small enough to make participatory democracy work, Portugal could stay in the middle. The success of the centre-right at the December 1979 and October 1980 elections would appear to confirm this for the present.

References

1. Pimlott, B. (1977). Socialism in Portugal: Was it a Revolution? *Government and Opposition*, **12** (No. 3), 332–350 and 342 (footnote)
2. *The Economist, 14 June 1980*, Almost There. Portugal: A Survey, p. 8
3. Harvey R. (1978). *Portugal: Birth of a Democracy*, p. 119, Macmillan, London
4. *The Economist*, op. cit., p. 4
5. Sallnow, J. and John, A. (1978). Iberia Without Fascism, *Geographical Magazine*, **L** (No. 7), 428
6. Gallagher, T. (1978). Portuguese Communist Party and Eurocommunism, *The Political Quarterly*, **50** (no. 2), 205–218 and 206

Table 4.19 *The Portuguese electoral system 1975–1980*

Assembly	Assembleia da Republica Assembly of the Republic
Members	1975: Elections to the Constituent Assembly with 250 seats; 1976: Elections to the Assembly of the Republic (Assembleia da Republica) with 263 seats; 1979: Number of seats reduced to 250; 1980: As 1979
Dates of elections	25 April 1975[a] 25 April 1976 2 December 1979 5 October 1980
Method	Proportional representation (PR); d'Hondt system
Voting age	All citizens over the age of 18
Voter participation (turnout)	1975 91.7% 1976 83.3% 1979 87.5% 1980 84.4%

[a] *The 1975 general election was originally planned for 12 April, but was postponed for 'technical reasons'*

Source: Elections to the Assembly of the Republic, Ministry of the Interior, Lisbon, 1976; Keesings Contemporary Archives; Expresso, Lisbon, 11 October 1980

Table 4.20 *Number of seats won by major parties in Portuguese elections 1975–80*

Party	Number of seats			
	1975	1976	1979	1980
PSD (PPD in 1975, 1976)	81	73	75	82
CDS	16	42	42	46
PPM	0	0	5	6
PSP	116	107	74	66
PCP	30	40	44	39
MDP	0	0	3	2
UDP	1	1	1	1
UESD	–	–	0	4
ASDI	–	–	0	4
Reformists	–	–	5	–
Independent	–	–	1	–
FSP	0	0	0	0
MRPP (PCTP–MRPP)	–	0	0	0
Other	6	0	0	0
Total	250	263	250	250

Table 4.21 *Number of seats won and percentage of votes taken by electoral alliances in Portuguese elections 1979–1980*

Party	Number of seats		Percentage of votes	
	1979	1980	1979	1980
AD	182	134	45.0	47.3
PSD	75	82	24.3	
CDS	42	46	16.6	
PPM	5	6	1.3	
Other (PSD, CDS Islands)	6	0	2.8	
FRS	74	74	28.1	28.0
PSP	74	66	27.4	
UESD	0	4	0.7	
ASDI	–	4	–	
APU	47	41	19.0	16.9
PCP	44	39	16.5	
MDP	3	2	2.5	
UDP	1	1	2.2	1.4
Total	250	250	94.3	93.6

Table 4.22 *Percentage of votes cast in Portuguese elections 1975–1980*

Party	Percentage of votes			
	1975	1976	1979	1980
PSD (PPD in 1975, 1976)	26.4	24.0	26.7	27.7
CDS	7.6	15.9	17.0	18.0
PPM	0.6	0.5	1.3	1.6
PSP	37.9	35.0	27.4	24.0
PCP	12.5	14.6	16.5	14.9
MDP	4.1	2.0	2.5	2.0
UDP	0.8	1.7	2.2	1.4
UESD	–	–	0.7	2.0
ASDI	–	–	–	2.0
FSP	1.2	0.8	–	–
MRPP (PCTP–MRPP)	–	0.7	0.9	0.6
POUS	–	–	0.8	1.4
PSR	–	–	–	1.0
MES	1.0	0.6	–	–
PDC	–	0.5	1.1	0.3
LCI	0.2	0.3	–	–
PCP–ML	–	0.3	0.1	–
AOC	–	0.3	–	–
PRT	–	0.1	–	–
OCMLP	–	–	0.1	0.1
PT	–	–	–	0.7
Other	7.7	2.7	2.7	3.3
Total	100.0	100.0	100.0	100.0

Table 4.23 *Number of votes cast in Portuguese elections 1975–1980*

Party	Number of votes			
	1975	1976	1979	1980
PSD (PPD in 1975, 1976)	1495017	1296246		
CDS	433343	857179	2497019	2787089
PPM	31809	28161		
PSP	2145618	1886932	1621950	1658201 (FRS)
PCP	709659	785594	1121224	1000967
MDP	233380			
UDP	44546	91364	127825	81916
UESD	–	–	42200	
ASDI	–	–	–	
FSP	66163	41945	–	–
MRPP (PCTP–MRPP)	–	36231	51644	–
POUS	–	–	12573	–
MES	57695	31063	–	–
PDC	–	28178	65351	–
LCI	10732	16232	–	–
PCP–ML	–	15793	–	–
OCMLP	–	–	3393	–
AOC	–	15665	–	–
PRT	–	5175	–	–
PSR	–	–	36415	–
Other	45515	–	164532	262403
Valid	5273477	5135758	5744126	5790576
Invalid	392230	260354	168777	139401
Total	5665707	5396112	5912903	5929977

Spain

Spain returned to democracy only after General Francisco Franco died in November 1975, and the machine he had set up to ensure the continuation of Francoism after him was dismantled by the very leaders he had appointed.

In the autumn of 1976 the Franco-nominated Cortes made way for democratic elections by passing the Ley de Reforma Politica, the political reform law, by which Prime Minister Adolfo Suarez persuaded the Cortes to vote for its own dissolution and re-establishment as a democratically elected Senate and Congreso de Diputados, the Congress of Deputies. Under the 1976 law, which was later passed by referendum, political parties were legalized except those on the extreme left, which included the PCE, the Spanish Communist Party. The PCE had to wait until April 1977, two months before the country's first general election for 41 years, to gain legal status.

There have been two elections in June 1977 and March 1979, the latter being the only constitutional election in Spain since 1936. Before examining the two elections Spain has held since Franco's death, the reasons why Spain was able to move peacefully from Fascism to democracy must be considered.

Throughout the 1960s and early 1970s, the Spanish economic miracle raised productivity at an annual rate between 7% and 9% per annum. Along with the rest of Western Europe, Spain enjoyed a growing prosperity which encouraged foreign investment, strengthened the regime and turned the mobilization of workers away from political motivation towards demands for higher wages and better working conditions.

Several factors following the dramatic economic events in the autumn of 1973 persuaded many on the right that their survival might depend on granting change before it was taken by force: the murder by Basque separatist guerrillas of Premier Carrera Blanca, the fall of Marcello Caetano in Portugal, the defeat of Premier Fanfani in the Italian divorce referendum, the collapse of the Greek Colonels' regime and the good showing and near victory of socialist François Mitterrand in the French Presidential elections of May 1974.

The United States-engineered fall of Salvador Allende in Chile in September 1973 helped convince the left of the need for a broad alliance with centrist and right-wing parties if their socialist deputies were to have any chance of success. This culminated in PCE leader Santiago Carrillo's Pact for Liberty, similar to the Italian communists' proposed historic compromise of power between the parties of both left and right.

In the two elections since Franco's death, in June 1977 and March 1979, the distribution of votes followed a very similar pattern (*Figures 4.22* and *4.23*). More interestingly, the split between left and right was almost exactly the same as the last democratic election, the 1936 provincial election, showing allegiances had survived nearly 40 years of Fascist dictatorship and had been passed down through families and within communities. The election of 15 June 1977 took place with Franco's one-party system only partly dismantled and the PCE legal for only two months prior to the election. It was argued at the time that the result therefore was as expected with Suarez' Union del Centro Democratico (UCD) gaining 165 deputies and a total of 287 parliamentarians,

Political parties			
AP	Popular Alliance (Alianza Popular)	PL	Liberal Party (Partido Liberal)
BEAM	Left Bloc of National Liberation	PNV	Basque Nationalist Party (Partido Nationalista Vasco)
CD	Democratic Coalition	PS	Syndicalist Party
CDC	Democratic Convergence for Catalonia	PSA	Andalusian Socialist Party
CU	Convergence and Union	PSC–PSOE	Socialists of Catalonia
EE	Basque Left (Euskadico Esquerra)	PSD	Social Democratic Party (Partido Social Democrata)
ERC–FN	Catalan Republican Left	PSOE	Spanish Socialist Workers Party (Partido Socialista Obrero Español)
FE–JONS (a)	Spanish Falange JONS (authentic) (Falange Española de las JONS)	PSP	Popular Socialist Party
FN	New Force (Fuerza Nueva)	PSUC	Unified Socialist Party of Catalonia (Partido socialista Unificado Catalan)
FSP	Federation of Socialist Parties	PTE	Spanish Party of Labour
HB	Herri Batasuna	RD	Democratic Reform (Reforma Democratica)
IR	Republican Left (Izquierda Republicana)	RSE	Spanish Social Reform (Reforma Social Española)
LCR	Communist Revolutionary League	UCD	Union of the Democratic Centre (Union del Centro Democratico)
MC–OIC	Communist Movement		
OC–BR	Communist Organization–Red Banner	UCDCC	Union of the Centre and Christian Democrats of Catalonia
ORT	Revolutionary Organization of Workers	UCE	Communist Union of Spain
PAR	Aragonese Regional Party	UFV	Basque Union
PC	Carlist Party (Partido Carlista)	UNE	Spanish National Union (Union Nacional Española)
PCE	Spanish Communist Party (Partido Comunista de España)	UPC	Canary Peoples Union
PCT	Communist Party of Workers	UPE	Spanish Peoples Union (Union del Pueblo Español)
PDC	Democratic Pact for Catalonia		
PDP	Popular Democratic Party	UPN	Union of Navarrese People

both deputies and senators. The UCD was in fact a loose grouping of 15 small parties of the right and centre that united under the leadership of Adolfo Suarez. The Partido Socialisto de Obrero Español, the Socialists (PSOE) came second with 118 deputies, followed by the PCE (Partido Communista España) with 20 and the then Alianza Popular (AP) with 16.

The election pattern was further complicated by regional and autonomist parties. Regional differences in Spain are probably more pronounced than in any other European country and the question of regional autonomy is complicated by economics: the pressure for devolution is greatest in the regions that have a large proportion of the country's industry and commerce, namely Catalonia and the Basque country[1]. These regions now have the Generalitat and the Consejo General Vasco respectively. Other regions granted territorial government are Andalusia, the junta de Andalucia and Valencia, the Consell.

The 1977 elections put the Socialists in the majority in the regional governments, while they were second in the Cortes. One reason for this is the bias of the electoral system which produces over-representation of the rural areas, who traditionally vote for the right. The consequence was that the UCD took 47.1% of the Cortes seats with 34.7% of the nation's vote. In March 1979 the UCD obtained 35.5% of the vote, but 48% of the congressional seats[2]. Following the 1977 elections, the consolidation of democracy

became a matter for the politicians, with party leaders pursuing a policy of compromise. The constitution, passed by referendum in December 1978, was supported by all parties represented in parliament from the para-Francoist to the PCE, with the exception of the Basque Nationalist party (PNV) which abstained.

That parliament should have lasted until 1981, but Suarez opted for an early general election on 1 March 1979, following the breakdown of an agreement with the Socialists (PSOE) in December 1978, formed exactly a year earlier. The collapse of this understanding left Suarez' UCD nine short of an absolute majority in the chamber of deputies.

The parties approached the 1979 election with the belief that the electoral map of Spain had not yet crystallized. Competition focused on the rural areas, on the centrist or moderate vote and on those who had voted for the Workers' Commissions in the trade-union elections of January and March 1978, in which a majority of communists had been returned[3]. While the first two involved straightforward left –right competition, the battle for the third was between left and left. While the workers were prepared to trust the communists with running their trade unions, it seemed they preferred a softer line in socialism to run the country. It is estimated that 60% of those workers who supported the communists in the trade union elections voted PSOE in the general elections[4].

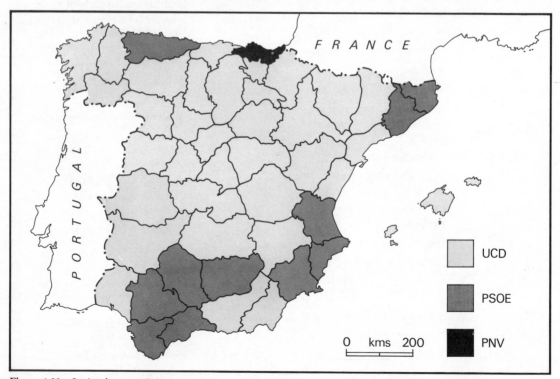

Figure 4.22　*Spain: the general election of 1977*

The 1979 campaign was much more issue-centred than that of 1977, with party propaganda dealing more with unemployment, housing, education, abortion, divorce, public health and investment rather than the broader questions of democracy and dictatorship which had dominated Spain's first post-Franco election. Political rallies were also smaller and the abstention rate higher: although the electorate had grown by 3 457 375 as a result of the voting age being lowered to 18, the number of votes cast was down by 316 839 on 1977. The 1977 abstention rate of 21.6% increased in 1979 to 33.6%. Reasons generally given for the increased abstention were:

(1) Disillusionment with the working of parliament and deals struck between officially opposing parties such as the Pact of Moncloa of 1977.
(2) Persisting problems of inflation and unemployment and terrorism.

The electorate may also have been confused by the choice that confronted it: altogether there were 12 communist parties, four socialist, 18 generally left, 16 centre-right, six right and extreme right plus smaller regional parties[5]. The UCD predictably won: it had an unfair advantage mainly because of the government monopoly of the national news and television networks. Setting aside information slots for party political broadcasts given to each party, from 7–25 February television devoted 2268 seconds to the UCD, eight seconds to the PSOE and 16 to the PCE[6]. At the same time, the findings of the electoral polls carried out by the Centro de Investigaciones Sociologicas were known only to Prime Minister Suarez. The only party to lose was the authoritarian Coalicion Democratica (CD) led by Fraga Iribarne which had competed in the 1977 elections as the Alianza Popular, it took nine seats compared with 16 in 1977.

The PSOE overall vote returned 121 members, a decrease from 124 following the merger with the Popular Socialist Party (PSP). It lost some ground to the autonomists in the Basque country and Catalonia, but pushed forward slightly in the rural areas at the expense of the UCD. Interestingly, the lost PSOE votes were not absorbed by the PCE, which must have been the disappointed party after the election. Its number of deputies increased from 20 to 23: it had claimed in 1977 that it had suffered from late legalization, and a fear campaign against its policies, made all the more poignant after the successes in the trade-union elections of the year before.

The UCD still found itself nine short of an absolute majority in the key Congress of Deputies, having a total of 168 out of 350 seats; it was immediately assured by PSOE leader Felipe Gonzalez that he was prepared to wait four years before another election, and would offer criticism from opposition but would not be a destructive force. Prime Minister Adolfo

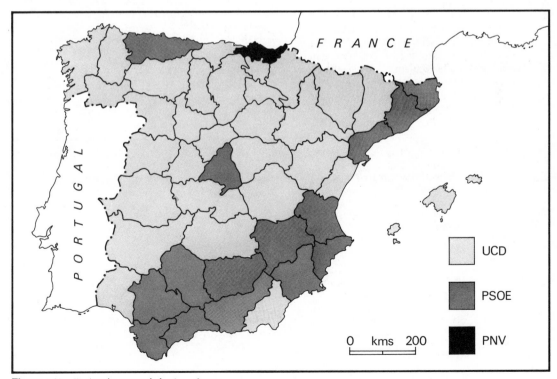

Figure 4.23 *Spain: the general election of 1979*

Suarez said the victory of the UCD would consolidate Spain's West European style of democracy, and his party would carry out a progressive policy over the four years of his new mandate. He must have been reassured by the centre-right victory of the Democratic Alliance in neighbouring Portugal in December 1979 and again in October 1980. The 1979 election result suggested a remarkable crystallization of the party system in Spain, with slight margin for change. It stressed the strength of the UCD: in Southern Europe the self-defined centrist electorate seemed clearly to be leaning to the right-wing and very receptive to Giscard d'Estaing and Suarez-type arguments based on fear. This could be responsible for the creation of Eurocommunism and its appeal in the Mediterranean countries as an attempt to show communism as non-authoritarian.

The gains made by the autonomists in March 1979, from 7% to 10% of the vote showed the importance of their demands if stability is to be maintained. A question mark remains over the future of the troubled northern Basque country, where a radical nationalist coalition that supports the violent military wing of the separatist group ETA (Basque Land and Liberty) won three seats. The coalition called Herri Batasuna, HB (Union of the People) gained a total of 14% of the vote in the three Basque provinces of Guipuzcoa, Vizcaya and Alava, suggesting a large measure of support for ETA's violent campain for an independent Basque state.

Leaders of the PNV, (Partido Nacionalista Vasco) the moderate Basque Nationalist Party, which won seven seats, blamed the UCD and the government for the success of HB; they said the lack of understanding in Madrid for Basque problems, and delays by the government in granting the region an ample autonomy statute alienated many Basques.

Another important fact about the 1979 election is that 4.7% of the vote separated the two major parties, which must serve as a chance for a socialist government in 1983; forces could be mobilized in the political arena either by joining with the Eurocommunists in a common platform as was tried in France in 1978, or by stealing the UCD fear theme, emphasizing differences between the PSOE and the rest of the left and claiming to be the only party to hold off the advance of the left.

Excluding the Basque parties, notably the PNV, the PSOE has 2 796 000 on its left which it could try to attract, while the UCD has 1 445 000 on its right of which more than 65% belong to the Coalicion Democratica (CD), whose philosophy is barely distinguishable from the UCD. But the left must face the institutionalized difficulties in the way of its victory: state-controlled and therefore right-wing media, resources and public administration, pressure of the Catholic church and business. Taking these into account, the left would be able to form a government only following a victory of landslide proportions.

References

1. Sallnow, J. and John, A. (1978). Iberia without Fascism. *Geographical Magazine*, **L** (No. 7), 428
2. *The Economist*, 3 November 1979, All the Spains: A Survey, p. 12
3. Maravall, J. M. (1979). Political Cleavages in Spain and the 1979 General Election. *Government and Opposition*, **14** (No. 3), 299–317
4. Ibid., p. 305
5. *Cambio 16*, (1979). Atlas Electoral, No. 380/18-3-79
6. Maravall, J. M. op. cit., p. 306

Table 4.24 *The Spanish electoral system 1975–1980*

Assembly	Congreso de Diputados Congress of Deputies Cortes (Parliament) is composed of Congress of Deputies (Lower House) and the Senate (Upper House)
Members	Congress of Deputies 350 seats. Senate has 207 elected members and 41 nominated to give total of 248 senators
Dates of elections	15 June 1977 1 March 1979
Method	Proportional representation (PR); d'Hondt system. PR according to population with a minimum of 3 deputies per province
Voting age	1977 over 21, reduced on 10 November 1978 to 18. This applied at the 1979 election
Voter participation *(turnout)*	1977 78.4% 1979 66.4%

Source: Keesings Contemporary Archives; Cambio 16, No. 290, 3-7-77 (1977); Cambio 16, No. 380, 18-3-79 (1979)

Table 4.25 *Number of seats won in Spanish elections 1977–1979*

Party	Number of seats	
	1977	1979
UCD	165	168
PSOE–PSC/PSOE	118[a]	121
PCE–PSUC	20	23
CD (AP)	16	9
CU (CDC)	11	8
PNV	8	7
Socialist Union PSP + FSP	6	–
PSA	–	5
HB	–	3
UN	–	1
ERC–FN	1	1
PAR	–	1
EE	1	1
UPC	–	1
UPN	–	1
UCDCC	1	–
Centre Independents	2	–
Democratic Front of the Left	1	–
Total	350	350

[a] *Increased to 124 following the merger with PSP in 1978*

Table 4.26 *Percentage of votes cast in Spanish elections 1977–1979*

Party	Percentage of votes		
	1977	1979	
UCD	34.7	35.5	
PSOE–PSE/PSOE	28.7	30.8	
PCE–PSUC	9.2	10.9	
CD (AP)	8.2	5.8	
PSP–US	4.3	–	
CU	–	2.7	
PDC	2.9	–	
UN	–	2.1	
PNV	1.7	1.7	
HB	–	1.0	
FDI	1.5	–	
EDC (ERC)	1.4	ERC	0.7
EE	0.5	0.5	
UPC	–	0.3	
PAR	–	0.2	
UPN	–	0.2	
Other	6.9	7.6	
Total	100.0	100.0	

Table 4.27 *Number of votes cast in Spanish elections 1977–1979*

Party	Number of votes		
	1977	1979	
UCD	6 142 460	6 293 878	
PSOE–PSE/PSOE	5 211 038	5 475 389	
PCE–PSUC	1 673 765	1 938 904	
CD (AP)	1 480 657	1 097 653	
PSP–US	783 593	–	
CU	–	482 279	
PDC	517 131	–	
PSA	–	325 842	
PNV	307 611	296 597	
PTE	–	192 440	
HB	–	172 110	
EDC (ERC)	246 584	ERC	123 266
PSOE (h)	131 454	136 000	
EE	n.a.	85 677	
UPC	–	59 342	
PAR	–	38 042	
UPN	–	28 248	
Other	520 676	833 177	
Invalid		326 544	
Total Valid		17 958 404	
Total	17 014 969	18 284 948	

Denmark

> ### Political parties
>
> CD   Centre Democratic Party
>
> DKP Danish Communist Party
>
> KAP Communist Workers Party
>
> KF   Conservatives
>
> R   Retsforbund: Single Tax Party/Justice Party
>
> RV   Radical Liberal Party (Radikale Venstre)
>
> SD   Social Democratic Party
>
> SF   Socialist People's Party
>
> V   Liberal Democratic Party (Venstre)
>
> Left Socialists
>
> Progress Party
>
> Christian People's Party
>
> Liberal Centre
>
> Pensioners Party

Between 1968 and 1979, Denmark has undergone no less than six national elections, at approximately two-year intervals. This is despite the four-year term of office provided for the Folketing (assembly of parliament) under the Danish constitution. The Folketing has 175 members from metropolitan Denmark and two each from the Faeroe Islands and Greenland. Of these, 135 members are elected in multi-member constituencies and the remainder of 40 are top-up seats designed to give proportional representation to parties that have obtained at least 2% of votes cast[1]. In summary, the centre-right has been in power from January 1968 to September 1971, and again from December 1973 to January 1975; for both periods minority governments ruled the country. For the intervening periods the Social Democrats were in power, usually in minority administrations[2].

The Social Democrats suffered a crushing defeat in the January 1968 elections after being in power for 14 years. The three opposition parties, the Conservatives, Liberal Democrats (Venstre) and Radical Liberals (Radikale Venstre) fought the election separately, but shortly before the end of the campaign they stated that, given sufficient seats, they would resolve their differencies and form a coalition government.

In January 1968 the Prime Minister, Jens Otto Krag, was defeated on anti-inflationary legislation; the premiership was taken over by Hilmar Baunsgaard, leader of the Radical Liberals, at the head of a three-party centre-right coalition of the Radical Liberals, Conservatives and Liberal Democrats. This coalition remained in power until September 1971 when the country's economic situation, plus Denmark's application for EEC membership, forced another election. In the 1971 election the Radical Liberals maintained their position with 27 seats but the Liberal Democrats (Venstre) and the Conservatives had losses of four and six seats respectively. The Social Democrats increased their representation from 62 to 70, a gain of eight seats and the Socialist People's Party gained six seats, due largely to its opposition of Danish entry into the EEC. The result in 1971 showed the centre-right coalition to have 88 metropolitan seats, while the Social Democrats and Socialist People's Party held a total of 87.

A delay in the formation of an administration was necessary until the Faeroe Islands voted on 5 October, when one of the two deputies elected was a Social Democrat. Baunsgaard resigned and Krag again became Premier.

Although the opposition had a one-seat majority in the Folketing, the Social Democrats continued in power as a minority government until December 1973. The leadership of the Social Democrats and the office of premier was taken over in October 1972 by Anker Jørgensen.

At the 1973 election the economy was again an issue and the Social Democrats fared badly, dropping to a quarter of the votes, their lowest ever percentage,

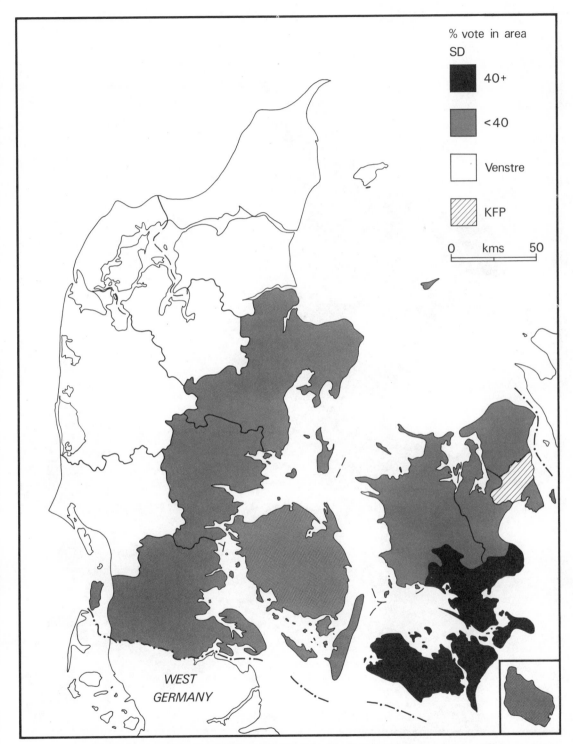

Figure 5.1 *Denmark: the general election of 1968; inset is Bornholm. The 1968 election was contested on different constituency boundaries. The present boundaries, used for all subsequent elections, are shown in Figure 5.2*

110

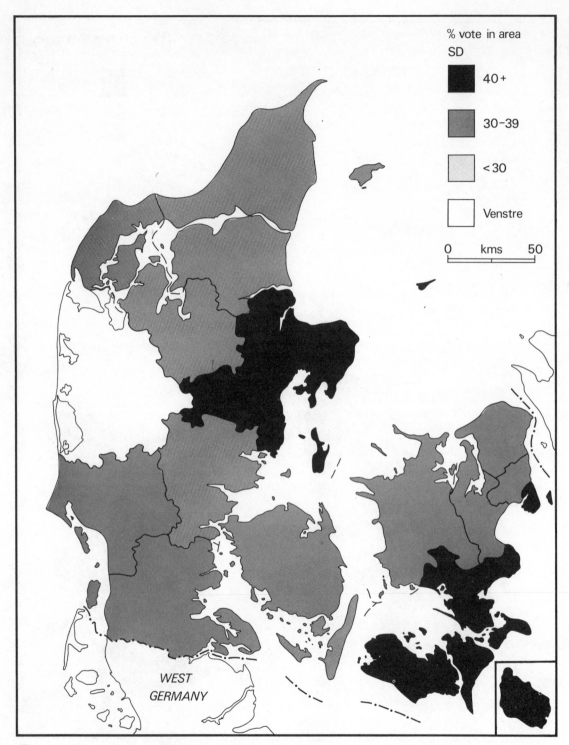

Figure 5.2 *Denmark: the general election of 1971. Inset is Bornholm*

and falling from 70 to 46 seats in the Folketing. Their electoral support diminished markedly throughout the country (*Figure 5.3*). This election has been described as a shock to Danish politics that 'has not completely ceased to reverberate through the system'[3].

The 1973 election resulted in the return of a centre-right coalition, with Liberal Democrats' leader Poul Hartling as Prime Minister. The Liberal Democrats had the smallest parliamentary base (22 seats) of any Danish government for 54 years; constant negotiations were necessary with other parties to secure a majority for the measures the Liberal Democrats wished to push through the Folketing. On occasions it was forced to indulge in concensus politics and modify or withdraw proposals when opposition occurred.

The 1973 election had significant successes for two parties formed since the previous election. The Progress Party won 28 seats and the Centre Democrats 14. The Centre Democratic Party was formed in November 1973 by Erhard Jakobsen, a former Social Democrat deputy on the right-wing of that party. He believed the Social Democrats had become too leftist and aimed to create a middle party that believed in the mixed economy, and was not allied to political ideologies or blocs. The Progress Party, led by Mogens Glistrup, a lawyer and tax expert, was established in January 1973. Its policies included the gradual abolition of income tax; originally the party proposed to replace the defence organizations of Denmark with a telephone answering service repeating 'We surrender' in Russian, but later modified its opinion by endorsing Danish membership of NATO.

The next elections were held in January 1975 and saw the return of a Social Democratic minority government, again headed by Anker Jørgensen. This administration emerged after several rounds of negotiations. Originally Jørgensen attempted to form a five-party coalition of Social Democrats, Radical Liberals, Conservatives, Christian People's Party and Centre Democrats. Then the outgoing Prime Minister Poul Hartling tried unsuccessfully to form a four-party coalition of Liberal Democrats, Conservatives, Christian People's Party and the Centre Democrats.

In January 1975 the Liberal Democrats almost doubled their representation in the Folketing from 22 to 42 seats; hence Premier Hartling's attempt to form another coalition, but the other non-Socialist parties had lost seats.

Eventually a minority Social Democrat government under Jørgensen was formed in February 1975, which remained in power until February 1977. This administration had to negotiate with other parties for support in the Folketing; for example, the 1976 incomes policy was passed with the support of the Radical Liberals, Christian People's Party, Centre Democrats and Conservatives, and set a policy of 6% a year limit on wage rises for two years beginning March 1977.

In December 1976 a wages and prices freeze was introduced, but the government failed to agree with other parties on a series of economic, housing and defence measures. Jørgensen announced the dissolution of the Folketing and new elections took place in February 1977. The results of the 1977 election was a success for Anker Jørgensen and the Social Democrats. In fact, the gain of 11 seats to give a tally of 65 constituted a revival for the party after its poor showing in 1973. The Liberal Democrats were reduced by half from 42 to 21, but the Centre Democrats renewed their advance to take 11 seats, an increase of seven over 1975. The Single-Tax Party (Retsforbund) achieved a return to the Folketing with two representatives after losing its seats in 1975.

In March 1978 the ruling Social Democrats made the biggest party gains in the municipal and county council elections. Female representation increased by nearly 70%, following a drive by many political parties to boost women's responsibility for local government. Social Democrats gained 38% of the total vote, 5% more than at the last local government elections in 1974.

The most significant event in Danish politics in 1978 was Anker Jørgensen's success in forming the first coalition between his own Social Democratic Party and the Liberal Democrats (Venstre). While the Social Democrats have always drawn support from the urban vote, the Liberal Democrats are backed by affluent farmers. The coalition was announced on 30 August 1978 and had 88 supporters of the 179 member Folketing. During the following month a referendum was passed lowering the voting age from 20 to 18.

The Social Democrat–Liberal Democrat coalition lasted until September 1979 but fell into disarray over a disagreement on how to implement a prices and incomes policy. The October 1979 election results show a gain of four seats for the Social Democrats to give them a total of 69 members in the Folketing. The Liberal Democrats, Conservatives, Centre Democrats and Christian Democrats had formed a loose 'four-leaf clover' to challenge Jørgensen and the Social Democrats. They emerged with 55 seats and Mr Jørgensen noted 'The four-leaf clover has withered – the bloc is broken'.

The Conservatives gained seven seats to make a total of 22, mainly at the expense of the far-right

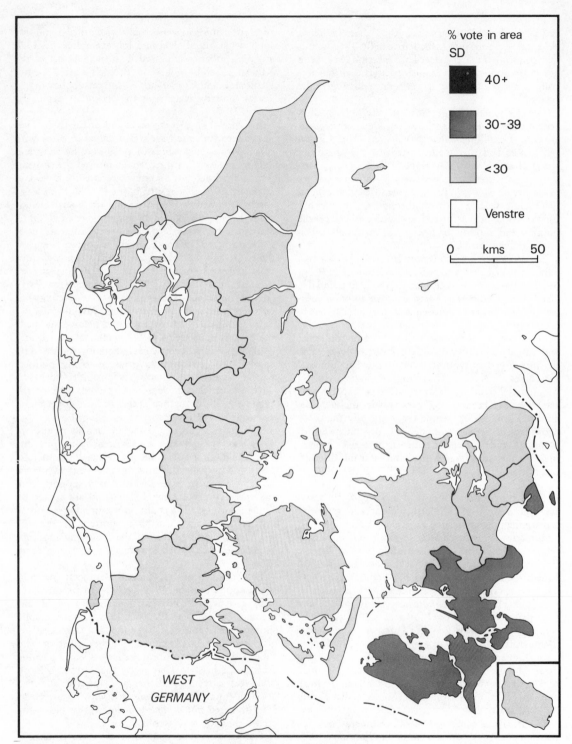

Figure 5.3 *Denmark: the general election of 1973. Inset is Bornholm*

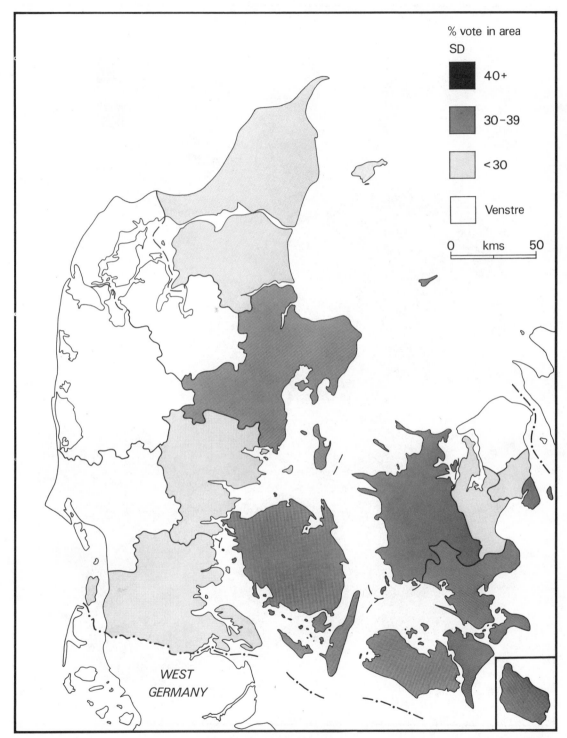

Figure 5.4 *Denmark: the general election of 1975. Inset is Bornholm*

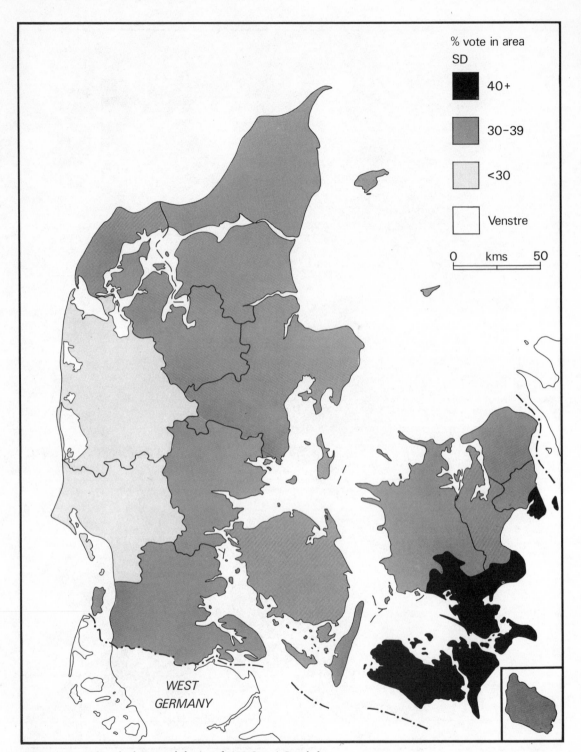

Figure 5.5 *Denmark: the general election of 1977. Inset is Bornholm*

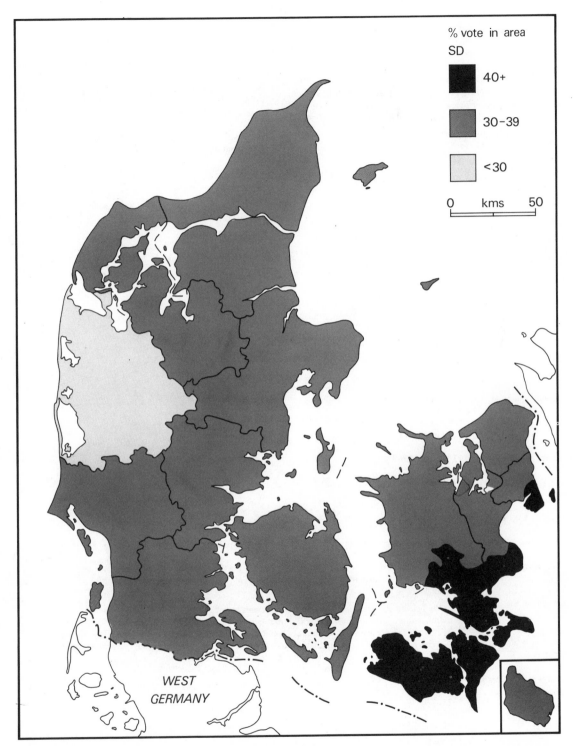

Figure 5.6 *Denmark: the general election of 1979. Inset is Bornholm*

Progress Party, which dropped six seats to 20. The Communist Party, opposed to Denmark's NATO and EEC membership, lost all its seven seats to disappear from the Folketing.

With their revived support, the Social Democrats under Jørgensen have formed a further minority administration. However, on past performance it would appear likely that another election will be forced on the none-too-willing Danish electorate in eighteen months time.

References

1. Fitzmaurice, J. (1979). In *Denmark: Political Parties in the European Community*, p. 29 (ed. by S. Henig). Allen & Unwin/Policy Studies Institute
2. For an assessment of four Nordic countries *see* Boore, O. (1980). Electoral Instability in Four Nordic Countries 1950–1977. *Comparative Political Studies*, **13** (No. 2) 141–171
3. Fitzmaurice, J. op. cit., p. 44. This subject is also discussed in a wider context in Borre, O. op. cit.

Table 5.1 *The Danish electoral system 1968–1979*

Assembly	Folketing

Members	179 seats
	175 mainland Denmark
	  2 Faroe Islands
	  2 Greenland

Dates of elections	23 January 1968 21 September 1971 4 December 1973 9 January 1975 15 February 1977 23 October 1979
Method	Proportional representation (PR); Saint-Laguë system. Initial divisor of 1.4, then 3, 5, 7, 9 and so on
Voting age	21, reduced to 20 on 21 September 1971, and to 18 on 19 September 1978. (The Folketing had approved a reduction from 21 to 18 on 6 June 1969, but this was rejected by a referendum on 24 June 1969.)
	The 1968 election was contested on old boundaries (*see Figure 5.1*). With post 1968 boundaries, 179 members comprise the Folketing; 135 members elected by PR in 17 multi-member districts with 2–15 seats. There are 40 additional seats to ensure PR, plus 2 each for the Faroe Islands and Greenland. Term of legislature is 4 years. There is a 2% minimum clause, i.e. parties must obtain 2% of the national vote for representation in the Folketing
Voter participation (turnout)	1968 89.3% 1971 87.2% 1973 88.7% 1975 88.2% 1977 88.7% 1979 85.6%

Source: Statistisk Arbog 1980; *Statistical Yearbook of Denmark, Copenhagen, 1980 pp. 346–353. Statistisk Arbog 1979;* *Statistical Yearbook of Denmark, Copenhagen, 1979 pp. 350–357.*

Table 5.2 *Number of seats won in Danish elections 1968–1979*

Party	Number of seats					
	1968	1971	1973	1975	1977	1979
SD	62	70	46	53	65	68
SF	11	17	11	9	7	11
KF	37	31	16	10	15	22
V	34	30	22	42	21	22
RV	27	27	20	13	6	10
CD	–	–	14	4	11	6
R	0	0	5	0	6	5
Christian People's Party	–	0	7	9	6	5
DKP	0	0	6	7	7	0
Progress Party	–	–	28	24	26	20
Left Socialists	4	0	0	4	5	6
Liberal Centre	0	–	–	–	–	–
Pensioners Party	–	–	–	–	–	0
KAP	–	–	–	–	–	0
Total	175	175	175	175	175	175

Table 5.3 *Number of votes cast in Danish elections 1968–1979*

Party	Number of votes					
	1968	1971	1973	1975	1977	1979
SD	974833	1074777	783145	913155	1150355	1213456
SF	174553	262756	183522	150963	120357	187284
KF	581051	481335	279391	168164	263262	395653
V	530167	450904	374283	711298	371728	396484
RV	427304	413620	343117	216553	113330	172365
CD	–	–	236784	66316	200347	102132
R	21124	50231	87904	54095	102149	83238
Christian People's Party	–	57072	123573	162734	106082	82133
DKP	29706	39564	110715	127837	114022	58901
Progress Party	–	–	485289	414219	453792	349243
Left Socialists	57184	45979	44843	63579	83667	116147
Liberal Centre	37407	–	–	–	–	–
Independents Party	14360	–	–	–	–	–
Schleswig Party	6831	6743	–	–	–	–
Pensioners Party	–	–	–	–	26889	–
KAP	–	–	–	–	–	13070
Other	127	919	637	539	317	996
Total	2854647	2883900	3053203	3049452	3106297	3171002

Table 5.4 *Percentage of votes cast in Danish elections 1968–1979*

Party	Percentage of votes					
	1968	1971	1973	1975	1977	1979
SD	34.2	37.3	25.6	29.9	37.0	38.3
SF	6.1	9.1	6.0	5.0	3.9	5.9
KF	20.4	16.7	9.2	5.5	8.5	12.5
V	18.6	15.6	12.3	23.3	12.0	12.5
RV	15.0	14.4	11.2	7.1	3.6	5.4
CD	–	–	7.8	2.2	6.4	3.2
R	0.7	1.7	2.9	1.8	3.3	2.6
Christian People's Party	–	2.0	4.0	5.3	3.4	2.6
DKP	1.0	1.4	3.6	4.2	3.7	1.9
Progress Party	–	–	15.9	13.6	14.6	11.0
Left Socialists	2.0	1.6	1.5	2.1	2.7	3.7
Liberal Centre	1.3	–	–	–	–	–
Independents Party	0.5	–	–	–	–	–
Schleswig Party	0.2	0.2	–	–	–	–
Pensioners Party	–	–	–	–	0.9	–
KAP	–	–	–	–	–	0.4
Total	100.0	100.0	100.0	100.0	100.0	100.0

Finland

Political parties

KP   Centre Party

KK   National Coalition Party (Conservatives)

LKP   Liberal People's Party

SFP   Swedish People's Party

SKDL   Finnish People's Democratic League (communist dominated)

SKL   Finnish Christion Union

SKYP   Party of National Unity

SMP   Finnish Rural Party

SPKP   Finnish Constitutional People's Party

SSDP   Finnish Social Democratic Party

Finland's political and electoral geography is influences by a factor that does not apply in the same measure to any other country in this study. It is the special relationship Finland has developed with its large neighbour, the USSR. Immediately prior to the 1979 election for the Finnish assembly, the Eduskunta, a European newspaper pointed out that 'Few electorates in Europe are made as conscious of the exigencies of international relations as are the Finns'[1]. This relationship stems from the 1948 Treaty of Friendship, Cooperation and Mutual Assistance, and is viewed by all Finnish political parties as a guarantee of the country's essentially independent status. The government and parliamentary system of Finland function in a similar way to all other countries of Western Europe.

Coalition government has been the norm in Finland during the 1960s and 1970s. The general election of 1970 brought a swing to the right. However, after four months of negotiations, the members of five parties agreed to form a coalition government of Social Democrats (SSDP), Centre Party (KP), Democratic League (SKDL), Swedish People's Party (SFP) and Liberal People's Party (LKP). The National Coalition (Kokoomus–Conservatives, KK) had increased their seats in the 200-set unicameral Eduskunta from 26 to 37 but were not included in the government. They have not participated in any administration since 1966. In 1970 the government was dubbed 'the Government of the losers'[2].

The support for the Conservatives can be attributed to economic factors: 'The main reason for the swing to the right was the dissatisfaction with the policies of austerity pursued by the outgoing government'[3].

The electoral maps in *Figures 5.7* to *5.10* show that Conservative support is not as marked as the 1979 election when they again increased their support, but

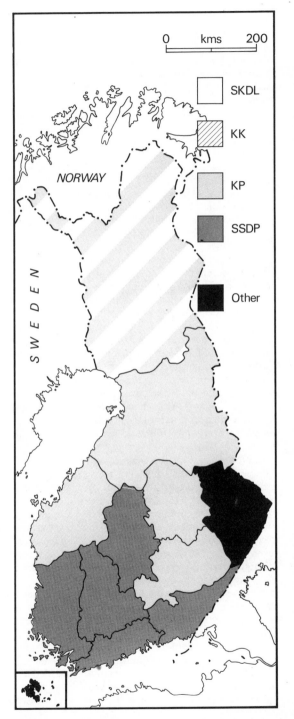

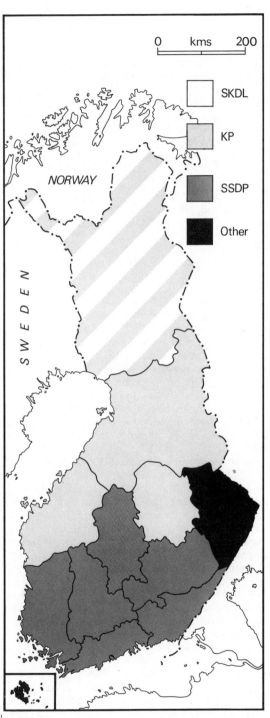

Figure 5.7   *Finland: the general election of 1970. Inset is Åland*

Figure 5.8   *Finland: the general election of 1972. Inset is Åland*

1970 and 1979 are the two dates when Conservatives dominate some of the electoral districts. Despite swings to the right there is no alternative to an SSDP-dominated coalition in Finland. Coalition for the Social Democrats, in the light of Conservative advances, is possible with the SKDL which is communist-dominated as the SKP contests elections through the SKDL. Continued participation by the communists is often deemed essential for the formation of a coalition government in Finland, and this participation tends to be regarded by the USSR as the best guarantee of Finnish neutrality. SKDL support is concentrated in the rural areas such as Lapland.

The 1970 government commanded a large majority with 142 of the 200 seats but was regarded as a weak coalition and lasted barely 18 months with new elections in January 1972. The coalition was led by Ahti Karjalainen, and had started as a five-party coalition, but in March 1971 the 36 members of the communist-dominated SKDL had refused to vote for a government bill involving price control relaxation. They subsequently left the government, but the four parties still in coalition commanded 108 of the 200 seats. The government resigned in October 1971 when the SSDP and the KP failed to agree on the question of agricultural subsidies. The 1972 results showed a slight swing to the SSDP (*Figure 5.8*) and negotiations followed between the four-party coalition and the SKDL. In February, President Urho Kekkonen asked Rafael Paasio, chairman of the SSDP, to form a majority government, but the SKDL withdrew from negotiations and Passio formed a SSDP minority government. This comprised the SSDP, KP, SFP and LKP. The four-party coalition remained in power until June 1975; Kalevi Sorsa was Premiér for most of the period, having taken over in September 1972. By the 1975 election, legislation had been passed to lower the voting age to 18 and include all Finns who had once lived in Finland. In 1975 amid the world-wide trade recession the main issue was the economy, with the four parties attempting to deny responsibility for the country's trade deficit, foreign debts and high rate of inflation. The period since the last election had seen the formation of the Party of National Unity (SKYP) under Mr Kainulainen when 12 deputies broke away from the Rural Party (SMP) over the proposed extension of President Kekkonen's term of office. At the dissolution of the Eduskunta, there were 13 SKYP deputies, but only one managed to retain his seat in September 1975.

The 1975 elections did not produce any marked shift to the left or the right: SSDP lost two seats while SKDL gained three, and KP increased its total by four.

A five-party coalition took office on 30 November 1975 under the premiership of Martti Miettunen, comprising the SSDP, SKDL, KP, SFP and LKP. It lasted less than a year and resigned on 17 September

1976 after failing to reach agreement on the 1977 budget due to a proposed increase in turnover tax from 11% to 13% and the question of agricultural subsidies. It was replaced by a three-party centrist minority coalition with Miettunen remaining as Prime Minister. The coalition of KP, LKP and SFP excluded the SSDP and SKDL but had one independent as Minister of Finance.

The minority government continued until May 1977 when a former Premier Kalevi Sorsa formed a five-party majority coalition. He had been Prime Minister from September 1972 to June 1975. The five parties (SSDP, SKDL, KP, SFP and LKP) had a massive majority with 152 of the 200 seats. The second Sorsa administration was the 60th Finnish government in the 60 years since the state became independent. The Swedish People's Party withdrew from the coalition in March 1978, but this did not greatly reduce its majority.

There was internal tension among the four remaining parties, notably a fundamental clash of views between the SSDP and the KP on the major issue of farm supports. These subsidies provide much of the dynamism of the agrarian-based KP, but arouse little enthusiasm among the industrial-oriented Social Democrats. These supports and controls make Finland almost self sufficient in temperate staple foodstuffs but at considerable cost to the taxpayer. Another raging issue in 1978 was the policy of regional aid for industrial development, which channels funds towards the outlying areas from which the KP wins many of its votes. Premier Kalevi Sorsa suggested every region should have some regional aid.

In November 1978 the coalition of SSDP, SKDL, KP and LKP had a total of 143 seats, although this was often reduced by the refusal of a dozen hardline communists to back government policies. By November 1978 opinion polls were predicting a swing to the right, indicating the National Coalition (that is the Conservative KK) would pick up between seven and ten parliamentary seats, to become the country's second largest party after the SSDP. They also suggested the communist-dominated SKDL might lose five or six seats. However, a coalition with the Conservatives would mean abandoning a stance considered axiomatic in Finnish politics: that a parliamentary split between socialist and non-socialist factions must be avoided at all costs.

The involvement of the Finnish Communist Party, through the SKDL, helps to maintain the guarded air of neutrality which is regarded as essential in maintaining the good relations with their large Soviet neighbour.

The SKP chairman, Aarne Saarinen, who visited the USSR in 1978, has spoken of the need for a discussion on ways in which socialism could be introduced and similarity on issues with other West

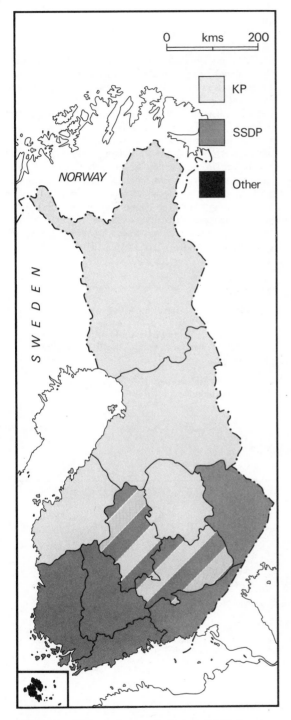

Figure 5.9 *Finland: the general election of 1975. Inset is Åland*

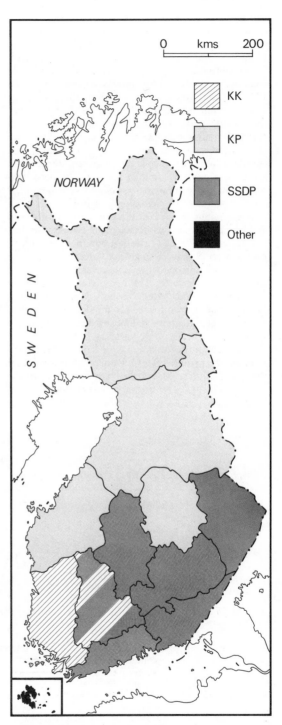

Figure 5.10 *Finland: the general election of 1979. Inset is Åland*

European communist parties. On Eurocommunism he stated: 'If Eurocommunism incorporated negative criticism of the socialist countries, the policies of the Finnish Communist Party are not in line with Eurocommunism.' The SSDP rejected the idea of coalition with the Conservatives before the March 1979 election, and saw themselves as the nucleus of any government coalition. Any chance the Conservatives might have had of being brought into an enlarged coalition appear to have been damaged by clear hints from its superpower neighbour, the USSR, that a KK presence in the government would not be welcome. A commentary in the Soviet Communist Party newspaper, *Pravda*, in February 1979 said conservative participation in the Helsinki government might put at risk the present good political and economic relations between the two countries.

In March 1979 the centre-left coalition held on to power with a reduced majority, after two days of elections saw the opposing Conservatives make large gains (*see Figure 5.10*). The KK increased their total from 35 to 47, SSDP took 52 seats, while the SKDL saw its number drop from 40 to 35. The gains by KK were expected to have a limiting influence on the government's coalition policies.

Post-election negotiations ended on 26 May 1979 with the formation of a four-party coalition under the premiership of Mauno Koivisto, governor of the Bank of Finland. The title of a 'losers' coalition has been applied to the Koivisto coalition[4] in a similar manner to the government formed after the 1970 election, as the parties concerned lost seats in 1979.

The Social Democrats (SSDP), communist-dominated Democratic League (SKDL), Centre Party (KP) and Swedish People's Party (SFP) made up the coalition. Before the Koivisto coalition emerged, President Kekkonen had asked the then KK leader Harri Holkeri to investigate the possibilities of forming a government which would command majority support in the Eduskunta. This move was a recognition of the substantial gains made by KK in the 1979 election. However, not surprisingly, the SSDP and SKDL refused to participate in such a government; the centre-left coalition with 133 seats continues in power, while the Conservatives remain in opposition. Foreign minister Paavo Vayrynen, who succeeded Johannes Virolainen as chairman of the KP in June 1980 has stated that he hopes the government coalition can be broadened after the next elections due in 1983.

References

1. Brady, J. (1979). Finns Vote with Eye on Foreign Policy. *International Herald Tribune*, March 17–18, Paris
2. Schöpflin, G. (December 1970). Finland's move to the Right and Finland after the 1970 election. *The World Today*, pp. 142–144
3. Ibid.
4. *The Times* 27th February 1980, Finland: A Special Report, London

Table 5.5 *The Finnish electoral system 1970–1979*

Assembly	Eduskunta (Diet)
Members	200 seats
Dates of elections	15–16 March 1970 2–3 January 1972 21–22 September 1975 18–19 March 1979
Method	Proportional representation (PR); d'Hondt system. Multi-member constituencies, 15 electoral districts
Voting age	21, reduced to 20 in 1971, to 18 in 1972. Since elections in January 1972, legislation introduced to enfranchise all Finns over age 18 who had once lived in Finland. This measure added 239 000 young voters to electorate as well as 184 000 Finns working in Sweden
Voter participation (turnout)	1970 82.2% 1972 81.4% 1975 73.8% 1979 75.3%

Source: Statistical Yearbook of Finland 1978, pp. 362–365, Helsinki 1979; Statistical Yearbook of Finland 1979, pp. 376–381, Helsinki 1980

Table 5.6 *Number of seats won in Finnish elections 1970–1979*

Party	Number of seats			
	1970	1972	1975	1979
SSDP	52	55	54	52
KK	37	34	35	47
KP	36	35	39	36
SKDL	36	37	40	35
SFP	12	10	10	9
SKL	1	4	9	9
SMP	18	18	2	7
LKP	8	7	9	4
SKYP	–	–	1	0
SPKP	–	–	1	0
Other	0	0	0	1

Table 5.7 *Percentage of votes cast in Finnish elections 1970–1979*

Party	Percentage of votes			
	1970	1972	1975	1979
SSDP	23.4	25.8	24.9	23.9
KK	18.0	17.6	18.4	21.7
KP	17.1	16.4	17.6	17.3
SKDL	16.6	17.0	18.9	17.9
SFP	5.7	5.4	4.6	4.2
SKL	1.1	2.5	3.3	4.8
SMP	10.5	9.2	3.6	4.6
LKP	5.9	5.1	4.3	3.7
SKYP	–	–	1.7	0.3
SPKP	–	–	1.6	1.2
Other	1.7	1.0	1.1	0.4

Table 5.8 *Number of votes cast in Finnish elections 1979–1979*

Party	Number of votes			
	1970	1972	1975	1979
SSDP	594185	664724	683590	691512
KK	457582	453434	505145	626764
KP	434150	423039	484772	500478
SKDL	420556	438757	519483	518045
SFP	135465	130407	128211	122418
SKL	28547	65228	90599	138244
SMP	265939	236206	98815	132457
LKP	150823	132955	119534	106560
SKYP	–	–	45402	9316
SPKP	–	–	43344	34958
Coalition of Åland	8971	7672	9482	9286
Other	39564	25527	21441	4408
Invalid	8728	9111	11405	11620
Total valid	2535782	2577949	2749818	2894446
Total	2544510	2587060	2761223	2906066

Iceland

Iceland, a tiny barren land of 103 000 km² midway between the Old and New Worlds, is unique in two aspects of its political geography. It is the only unarmed country in the Western world and, with the exception of Finland, which has a special and close relationship with its enormous neighbour, the Soviet Union, it is the only Western country, and more significantly NATO member to have had communists in government in the period under study.

Political parties

Independence Party

Liberal and Leftist Union

People's Alliance (Communists)

Progressive Party (Agrarians)

Social Democrats

Five political parties function in Iceland although at the time of writing only four of them are represented in the Althing, the Icelandic parliament. The Independence Party is led by Geir Hallgrimsson; it has been traditionally the country's largest party and able to command up to 45% of the vote, but it has been wracked by dissention since 1979 and may be in danger of splitting. Conservative in outlook, it is a strong supporter of NATO and US bases on the island.

The Progressive Party was established in 1916 and is one of Iceland's oldest parties; currently it is led by Steingrimur Hermannsson. Radical on social questions, but on other issues it is a centrist middle-class party representing the countryside and is economically backed by the farmer-dominated cooperative movement. It supports NATO membership but opposes continued US bases at Keflavik.

The People's Alliance was originally an electoral union between the communists and radical socialists, but it altered its constitution in 1968 to form a single political party and is led by Ludvik Josefsson. Although frequently referred to as the country's Communist Party, it describes itself as a socialist alliance of the left reflecting a Marxist viewpoint[1]. It broke ties with the Soviet Union and other Warsaw Pact countries that took part in the invasion of Czechoslovakia in 1968. Its policies to some extent anticipated the development of the Eurocommunist parties, and it has links only with communist parties espousing the pluralistic ideals of Eurocommunism. It seeks withdrawal from NATO and the dismantling of US bases on the island.

The Social Democratic Party is led by Sighvatou Bjorgvinsson, and is socialist in orientation. Until the election of 1978, when its share of the vote drew level with that of the People's Alliance, it had been very much the junior partner in the labour movement. It supports continued NATO membership.

The Union of Liberals and Leftists was established shortly before the general election of 1971 by two rebel members of the People's Alliance. It won a commendable 9% in that election, and was supported by workers and intellectuals. It had hoped to become the nucleus of a non-Marxist socialist alignment, but was torn by internal splits. It is not represented in the current parliament.

Isolated as it is on the edge of the inhabitable world, Iceland was spared the upheavals sweeping Western Europe in the late 1960s and continued its centre-right administration until 1971, when it caught the European mood and voted in a government of the left. The leftist coalition, comprising the Progressive Party, the People's Alliance and the Liberals, took over on 14 July 1971 and announced its foreign policy would take a stronger, more neutral line than the previous government. It would stay in NATO, but would continue to review the situation and the defence treaty allowing US troops to be stationed on the island at the Keflavik base would be 'revised or annulled'. It also announced there would be no further talks on joining the European Economic Community[2].

Iceland's previous coalition of the conservative Independence Party and the Social Democrats, in power throughout the 1960s, was well known in Europe, and initial talks on linking up with the EEC had had positive results. It had cooperated with NATO and the United States without much friction. But the old government of 1971, facing spiralling inflation and increasing threats to its crucial fishing industry, lost by 28 seats to the opposition's 32 in the scheduled 1971 elections.

The Progressive Party, with 17 seats, the People's Alliance, with ten and the Union of Liberals and Leftists with five, took power under the premiership of progressive leader Olafur Johannesson. Communist leader Ludvik Josefsson took over the fisheries and trade ministry and declared a 50-mile fishing limit around the island. This caused considerable dismay in Europe, especially Britain, as Iceland was at the same time building up its own fishing fleet[3], and pushed the Nordic island further away from the continent politically, although Iceland sought to justify the stand on grounds of its dependence on the fishing industry. At the time it accounted for 20% of the country's national income, while between 80% and 90% of all its exports were fish-based.

By 1974 the rest of Europe was beginning to consider for the first time the possibility of communists and radical leftists coming into or sharing power; Iceland went against the trend by voting back into government the conservative Independence Party in the general election of 30 June 1974. The Independence Party of Geir Hallgrimsson took 42.7% of the poll and gained 25 seats, while the Progressives, leaders in the 1971 to 1974 coalition, came a poor second with 24.9%, but retained all their 17 seats. The People's Alliance again increased their share of the poll to 18.3% and pushed up its representation by one to 11 seats. The third member of the left coalition, the Liberals, split by internal squabbles, slumped from 8.9% to 4.5% and dropped from five to two seats.

After the usual inter-party haggling, Geir Hallgrimsson took over a centre-right coalition comprising his Independence Party and the Progressive Party, but he was facing four years of unprecedented inflation, industrial unrest and the world recession was about to impose itself.

The centre-right coalition faced the electoral reckoning on 25 June 1978 after having been in power for four years. Against the background of worker conflict and inflation approaching 50%, the ruling parties suffered an 18% loss of support, the greatest swing against the government since 1908[5]. Despite

125

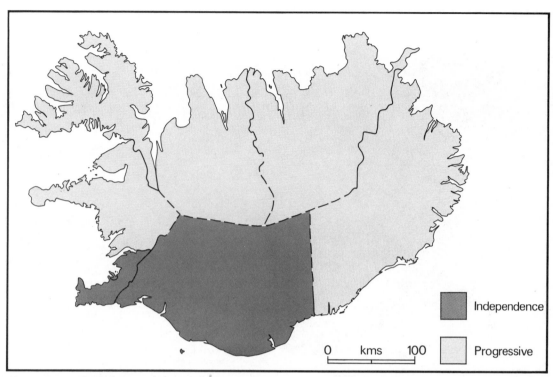

Figure 5.11 *Iceland: the general election of 1971*

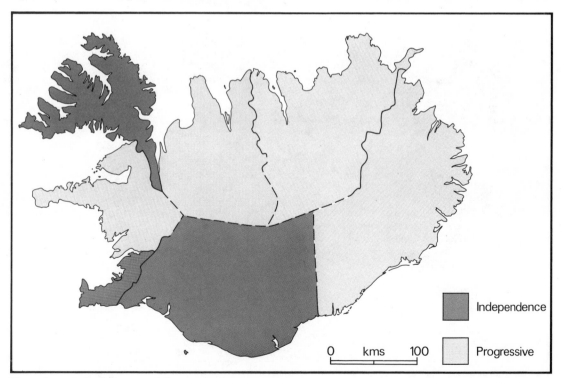

Figure 5.12 *Iceland: the general election of 1974*

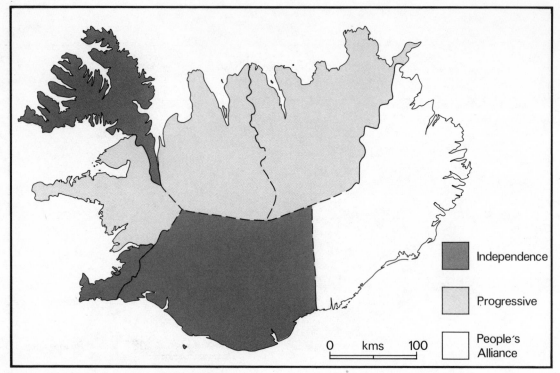

Figure 5.13 *Iceland: the general election of 1978*

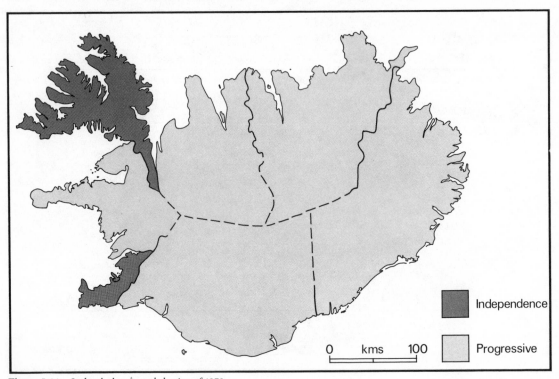

Figure 5.14 *Iceland: the general election of 1979*

the heavy losses in which the Progressive Party dropped a third of its seats to become the smallest party in the Althing, the two coalition parties of 1974 to 1978 retained a narrow majority, but the results had to be taken as a massive vote of no-confidence in the coalition. After two months of crisis, during which President Kristjan Eldjarn asked each party in turn, including the communist-orientated People's Alliance, to form a government, Progressive leader and former Premier Olafur Johansson emerged as Prime Minister of a coalition with the Social Democrats and the People's Alliance, which together held 40 of the Althing's 60 seats.

The strong anti-government swing had benefitted all the parties of the left. But while the People's Alliance had increased its share of the vote again to win 14 seats, the most remarkable resurgence was in the Social Democratic Party, led by Benedikt Groendal, which almost tripled its representation from five to 14 seats. The disparate views of the coalition on foreign policy, especially regarding NATO and the US bases on the island, proved to be the unmaking of communist leader Ludvik Josefsson. Foreign press coverage of this election had been particularly high because of the predicted progress of the left, while the People's Alliance wanted a complete withdrawal from NATO and US bases dismantled, the Progressive Party opposed the bases but did not share the wish to leave NATO, and the Social Democrats remained strong supporters of NATO. On the economic front, the government looked shaky. Inflation, brought down to around 30% in the mid-1970s, had taken a sharp upward turn, not helped by Iceland's trade unions having won automatic wage indexation. The government immediately devalued the Icelandic krona by 15%, the fourth devaluation since 1974. The final bad augury also lay with the People's Alliance. Having promised it would not enter a government prepared to devalue the krona, it further damaged its creditability by agreeing not to push its anti-NATO demands.

In fact, the government collapsed little more than a year later, in the summer of 1979, when the Social Democrats withdrew from the coalition following disputes over the economy. Inflation, running at 35% a year when the coalition took office, had by then reached 85%.

In October 1979, the Social Democrats took over an interim government charged with the task of calling elections for 2 and 3 December, the first winter elections in the country's history, and for the first time Iceland looked to be heading the way of all Western Europe with forecasts of a massive right-wing swing.

The election proved inconclusive, instead of producing a move to the right. In the final days of the campaign, it became clear that the electorate feared the measures Independence leader Hallgrimsson proposed in his pledge to all-out war on inflation.

The Independence Party remained the largest in the 60-seat Althing, gaining one seat to give it 21; the Progressive Party gained the most from the election, increasing its representation from 12 to 17, while the Social Democrats, who had forced the election, dropped from 14 to 11 seats. The People's Alliance went down from 14 to 11 seats, and this was the first time in a decade that the communist-orientated party had decreased its number of seats. Inter-party negotiations followed the 1979 election for a period of two months, during which Steingrimur Hermannsson, leader of the Progressive Party, Geir Hallgrimsson, leader of the Independence Party, Svavar Gestsson of the People's Alliance Party and Benedikt Groendal, former Prime Minister and leader of the Social Democratic Party all made attempts to form a cabinet. None were successful.

It was not until February 1980 that a government was formed, with the rebel Independence deputy leader Gunner Thoroddsen deserting his colleagues to forge a coalition with the People's Alliance, the Progressive Party and two members of his own party. The communists were given the important finance and energy industries and health and social security ministries. The Progressives took the foreign, education, fisheries and communications, trade and commerce portfolios, leaving the premiership, agriculture and justice to the Independents. As a gesture to the divergent interests of coalition members, Mr Thoroddsen's programme made no mention of Icelandic participation in NATO, but by no means can this be taken to mean Iceland may withdraw from the North Atlantic alliance, but more simply a gesture to the communists.

Whether the government will survive its full term is another matter. No left-wing administration in Iceland has survived four years, caught as it is between the country's powerful trade unions who will not give up their hard-won inflation-protected living standards, the country's rampaging inflation and the problems of a more or less seasonal economy based on the fishing industry.

References

1. Madeloy, J. (January 1979). European Elections – Iceland. *West European Politics*, p. 145
2. Sparring, A. (September 1972). Iceland, Europe and NATO. *The World Today*, p. 393
3. Ibid., p. 396

Table 5.9 *The Icelandic electoral system 1971–1979*

Assembly	Althing (Parliament)
Members	60 seats
Dates of elections	13 June 1971 30 June 1974 25 June 1978 2–3 December 1979
Method	Proportional representation (PR); d'Hondt system; 8 constituencies, list system of candidates
Voting age	21
Voter participation *(turnout)*	1971 90.4% 1974 91.4% 1978 90.3% 1979 89.3%

Source: Statistical Yearbook of Iceland 1978; Keesings Contemporary Archives; Elections to Althing, 1979, Elections to Althing 1978; Statistical Bureau of Iceland, Reykjavik, 1979; Statistical Bureau of Iceland, Reykjavik 1980

Table 5.10 *Number of seats won in Icelandic elections 1971–1979*

Party	Number of seats			
	1971	1974	1978	1979
Independence Party	22	25	20	21
People's Alliance	10	11	14	11
Social Democrats	6	5	14	10
Progressive Party	17	17	12	17
Liberal and Leftist Union	5	2	0	0
Other	0	0	0	1
Total	60	60	60	60

Table 5.11 *Percentage of votes cast in Icelandic elections 1971–1979*

Party	Percentage of votes			
	1971	1974	1978	1979
Independence Party	36.2	42.8	32.7	35.4
People's Alliance	17.1	18.3	22.9	19.7
Social Democrats	10.4	9.1	22.0	17.5
Progressive Party	25.2	24.9	16.9	24.9
Liberal and Leftist Union	8.9	4.6	3.3	–
Other	2.2	0.3	2.2	2.5

Table 5.12 *Number of votes cast in Icelandic election 1971–1979*

Party	Number of votes			
	1971	1974	1978	1979
Independence Party	38170	48674	39982	43838
People's Alliance	18055	20924	27952	24401
Social Democrats	11020	10345	26912	21580
Progressive Party	26645	28381	20656	30861
Liberal and Leftist Union	9395	5244	4073	–
Other	2109	448	6810	6249
Total	105394	114106	126385	126929
Valid votes			122207	123751

Norway

The case of Norway and its electoral geography is one of a regular four-year period between elections. In the period 1968 to 1979, national elections have taken place in Norway in September 1969, September 1973 and September 1977, presenting a model of Scandinavian regularity.

Unlike many chambers of elected representatives, the Norwegian parliament, the Storting, cannot be dissolved during its four-year term of office. While other countries would hold a national or federal election after the fall or collapse of a government, the

Norwegian system relies on inter-party consultations, political manoeuvering among the already elected members until a new administration can emerge. This was the case, for example, twice during the 1969 to 1973 session of the Storting. In March 1971, a Labour Party administration replaced a centre-right coalition and in October 1972 a minority coalition replaced the Socialists. From 1945 to 1969 the Norwegian Labour Party, Det Norske Arbeiderparti, took 40% or more of the votes with approximately half the seats in the Storting. However, this proportion decreased to 35.3% in the 1973 election, although it improved to 42% four years later.

The September 1969 election resulted in the return of a four-party anti-socialist coalition with a narrow majority – the closest postwar election in Norway's political history. The centre-right took 76 of the 150 seats in the Storting, giving them a majority of two compared to 12 in the 1965–1969 Storting. In 1969 the largest losers were the Liberals who sustained a loss of five seats, while the Conservatives lost two seats. The Centre Party gained two seats and their leader Per Borten became Prime Minister.

Of the four parties in the coalition, the Centre Party, which represented mainly agrarian interests, was anti-Common Market and against the then proposed Norwegian membership of the EEC; the Conservatives, Liberals and Christian People's Party were in general favourable to Norway's entry to the EEC. The Labour Party, then led by Trygve Bratteli, was broadly in favour of EEC membership if the terms were considered to be to Norway's advantage.

Political parties

Anders Lange's Party: *see* Progressive Party

Centre Party (Agrarian)

Christian People's Party

Communist Party (NKP)

Conservative Party

Labour Information Committee (AIK)

Labour Party

Liberal Party

New People's Party
Progressive Party (formerly Anders Lange's Party for a Strong Reduction in Taxation and Public Intervention)

Socialist Election Alliance (comprising the Socialist People's Party, Norwegian Communist Party and Labour Information Committee)

Socialist Left Party

Per Borten resigned as Premier on 2 March 1971 following the publication by the Norwegian newspaper *Dagbladet* of a leak of confidential state papers to an unauthorized person concerning the country's proposed membership of the EEC. The result was the formation of a minority Labour Party government led by Trygve Bratteli. However, the Labour Party had numerous internal divisions over the question of EEC membership.

The anti-EEC campaign in Norway resulted in the 'no' votes exceeding the 'yes' in the country's EEC referendum, proportions being 53.5% against and 46.5% for membership (*see* EEC referenda statistics, p. 140). The success of the 'no' option was widely rumoured to have caused dismay for the anti-EEC campaigners who had organized it more as a protest.

The effect of the 'no' vote in the EEC referendum was to cause the resignation of the Labour government. Premier Bratteli had announced on 23 August 1972 that he would resign if the vote went against membership. Following the referendum on 24–25 September 1972 the government duly resigned on 7 October and on 12 October Lars Korvald, leader of the small Christian People's Party, with only 14 seats in the Storting, announced he had succeeded in forming a minority coalition government. This comprised his own party, the Centre (Agrarian) Party, and a faction of the Liberal Party opposed to full membership of the EEC. The effect of the EEC referendum, and in particular the fact that it was negative, had a profound effect on Norwegian politics. This was notably true as the other Scandinavian country to apply for membership, Denmark, came out with a resounding 'yes' vote in its referendum with 63% of votes in favour. This helped to contribute to Norway's sense of isolation and threw its politics into a void for the following year. Korvald's minority coalition was represented by only 39 of 150 members in the Storting. This government continued until the September 1973 elections.

The Labour Party reached a working compromise among its members concerning the EEC referendum, who resolved that the outcome of the referendum and the trade agreement subsequently negotiated with the EEC should not be contested in the period of office of the next Storting. However, the internal divisions among Labour members contributed to the lowest percentage poll for 40 years in the September 1973 election.

In September 1973 the most notable electoral advance was that of the left-wing Socialist Election Alliance, which comprised the Socialist People's Party, the Norwegian Communist Party (NKP) and the Labour Information Committee (AIK). This grouping and policies that were anti-EEC and anti-NATO and picked up support from the anti-Common Market feelings among the electorate. The AIK had campaigned within the Labour Party for a 'no' vote

130

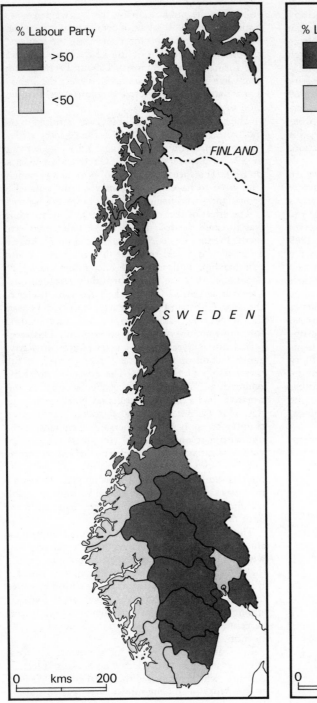

Figure 5.15 *Norway: the general election of 1969*

Figure 5.16 *Norway: the general election of 1973*

in the 1972 referendum. In 1969 the Socialist People's Party and the NKP had contested the election separately, polled 3.5% and 1.0% of the vote respectively, and failed to take any seats in the Storting.

The Socialist Election Alliance was much more successful in 1973 as it gained 16 seats. This included the election of Reidar Larsen, leader of the Communist Party, and the first communist to be elected to the Storting since 1961. The election results indicated the success of the Alliance in capturing votes from the Labour Party, especially in the northern areas of Norway where there had been a substantial 'no' vote in the 1972 referendum. The Liberal Party suffered a severe electoral setback as its number of seats declined from 13 in 1969 to two in 1973. It had already been reduced from 13 to four by the creation of the New People's Party, also called the New Liberal Party (Det Nye Folkepartiet) in the previous government. This party was formed by the pro-EEC elements of the Liberal Party, following a split in the party on the EEC referendum and the subsequent decision of the anti-EEC members, totalling nine of the 13 Liberals, to join the minority coalition led by Lars Korvald in October 1972.

The parties of Korvald's minority coalition, the Christian People's Party, the Centre Party and the New People's Party had 43 seats in the new Storting, compared to 39 in the previous administration. However, there was a socialist majority in the Storting and Labour had remained the largest party, despite its reduced percentage poll. Consequently Labour formed a minority administration under Trygve Bratteli which took office on 16 October 1963.

Membership of the Storting had been increased from 150 to 155; Labour did not have a majority of the seats, but with the left-wing Socialist Election Alliance, the two parties had obtained 78 of the 155 seats.

Bratelli continued as Prime Minister until 9 January 1976 when he resigned and Odvar Nordli took over as leader of the Labour Party and Premier at the head of a new minority Labour government. He announced there would be no change in domestic or foreign policies. After the regular interval of four years the most recent elections to the Storting took place in September 1977. On this occasion the Labour Party improved its showing and increased its percentage poll from 35.3% to 42.3% and its seats in the chamber from 62 to 76. The Socialist Left, which campaigned separately from the NKP, gained only two seats, but in alliance with the Labour Party this was sufficient to provide the two parties with an aggregate majority of one seat over the four non-socialist parties in the 155-member assembly. In September 1977, the minority Labour government with Odvar Nordli as Premier continued in office. The Socialist Left and the NKP did not continue the

Figure 5.17 *Norway: the general election of 1977*

Socialist Election Alliance of 1973 and the NKP failed to secure any representation in the new Storting.

Notable points from the 1977 election were the failure of the Progressive Party, formerly known as the Anders Lange Party, and the New People's Party to retain any of their seats. The Progressive Party was formed by Anders Lange, a dog-kennel owner nationally known for the political comments in the dog-breeding magazine which he edited. The full title of his party was Anders Lange's Party for a Strong Reduction in Taxation and Public Intervention.

The loss of the one seat held by the NKP, as well as the seats of the Progressive and New People's Parties may suggest that Norwegian politics are developing along the lines of a two-party system with the socialist and non-socialist factions. This prediction has been mooted for the past 15 years[1], but has failed to fully materialize.

However, it seems fair to say that the political scene in Norway is still largely dominated by the Labour Party, which has the allegiance of about 40% of the electorate. Norway employs the electoral system of proportional representation under the Saint–Laguë method. This was introduced in 1953 and uses 1, 4, 3, 5, 7 and so on as divisions instead of 1, 2, 3, 4 and so on in the d'Hondt system. This means the Saint–Laguë system is more proportional[2].

While the Norwegian parliament or Storting is elected as a single unit, one quarter of its members are then elected by the whole house to serve as members of the Upper house, the Lagging; the remainder form the Lower house, the Odelsting[3].

References

1. Steed, M. and Abadan, N. (April, 1966). Four Elections of 1965, *Government and Opposition*, 1 (No. 3), 297–344 and note p. 306
2. Ibid., footnote p. 301
3. Mackie, T. T. and Rose, R. (1974). *International Almanac of Electoral History*, p. 305, Macmillan, London and Basingstoke

Table 5.13 *The Norwegian electoral system 1969–1977*

Assembly	Storting – composed of the Lagging (Upper House) with one quarter of the members and the Odelsting (Lower House) with the remainder
Members	150 seats in 1969, increased to 155 in 1973; there is a fixed term of four years with next election in 1981
Dates of elections	7–8 September 1969 9–10 September 1973 11–12 September 1977
Method	Proportional representation (PR); Saint–Laguë system with initial divisor of 1.4, also called modified Sainte–Laguë, divisor 1.4, 3, 5, 7, etc. also known as Balanced Method
Voting age	21
Voter participation (turnout)	1969 83.8% 1973 80.2% 1977 82.9%

Source: Statistical Yearbook of Norway 1977, pp. 375–376; Keesings Contemporary Archives; Statistical Yearbook of Norway 1980, pp. 372–375

Table 5.14 *Number of seats won in Norwegian elections 1979–1977*

Party	Number of seats		
	1969	1973	1977
Labour Party	74	62	76
Conservatives	29	29	41
Christian Democratic People's Party	14	20	22
Centre Party	20	21	12
Socialist Left Party	–	16[a] }	2
NKP	0	}	0
Liberal Party	13	2	2
Progressive Party (Anders Lange's Party)	–	4	0
New Liberal Party }	–	1	0
New People's Party }			
Other	0	0	0
Total	150	155	155
Of which			
Women	14	24	37

[a] *Socialist Electoral Alliance of Socialist Left and Communists in 1973*

Table 5.15 *Percentage of votes won in Norwegian elections 1969–1977*

Party	Percentage of votes		
	1969	1973	1977
Labour Party	46.5	35.3	42.3
Conservatives	19.6	17.4	24.8
Christian People's Party	9.4	12.3	12.4
Centre Party	10.5	11.0	8.6
Socialist Left Party	3.5	11.2[a] }	4.2
NKP	1.0	}	0.4
Liberal Party	9.4	3.5	3.2
Progressive Party (Anders Lange's Party)	–	5.0	1.9
New People's Party	–	3.4	1.4
Other	0.1	0.9	0.8

[a] *Socialist Electoral Alliance of Socialist Left and Communists in 1973*

Table 5.16 *Number of votes cast in Norwegian elections 1969–1977*

Party	Number of votes		
	1969	1973	1977
Labour Party	1 004 348	759 499	972 434
Conservatives	406 209	370 370	569 839
Christian People's Party	169 303	255 456	285 569
Centre Party	194 128	146 312	197 298
Socialist Left Party	73 284	241 851[a] }	96 248
NKP	21 517	}	8 448
Liberal Party	202 553	49 668	74 669
Progressive Party (Anders Lange Party)	–	107 784	43 351
New People's Party	–	73 854	33 029
Joint Lists	86 276	128 091	–
Single People's Party	–	5 113	2 740
Freely Elected Representatives	–	1 866	1 149
Democratic Party	560	2 125	1 322
Red Electoral Alliance	–	9 360	14 515
Other	534	855	499
Invalid	3 884	3 530	3 386
Total valid	2 158 712	2 152 204	2 301 110
Total	2 162 596	2 155 734	2 304 496

[a] *Socialist Electoral Alliance of Socialist Left and Communist in 1973*

Sweden

Political parties	
C	Centre Party
FP	People's Party (Liberals)
KDS	Christian Democrat Party
KFML	Communist League Marxist-Leninist
M	Moderate Party (Conservatives)
S / SAP	Social Democratic Party
SKP	Swedish Communist Party (pro-Chinese)
VPK	Communist Left

Sweden has undergone major electoral changes during the period 1968 to 1979. National elections have taken place on five occasions during the period: in 1968, 1970, 1973, 1976 and 1979 – in the case of the four most recent elections these have taken place at regular three yearly intervals.

It is questionable as to how useful a three-year term of office can be. One opinion from a British newspaper suggested: 'Sweden is doing itself no good by going to the polls every three years'[1], following the most recent election.

In 1968 the Swedish parliament or Riksdag was divided into two chambers, with the lower chamber having 233 members. This was replaced on 20 September 1970 by a single-chamber Riksdag with 350 members, which came into existence on 1 January 1971. In the single-chamber Riksdag, 310 members are elected in 28 multi-member constituencies. The remaining 40 seats are distributed on allocation to the parties that are under-represented in the Riksdag with the aim of absolute proportionality. In this way seat allocation should reflect the nationwide distribution of votes as closely as possible. This system was further modified following the 1973 election when the number of 'adjustment' seats as they are known was reduced from 40 to 39 to avoid the problem of two groups obtaining 175 seats in the assembly, as had occurred in 1973.

The major theme of Swedish politics and electoral geography in the 12 years under study is the change from the ruling Social Democrats (Arleetarepartiet –Socialdemokraterna) which had ruled Sweden virtually uninterrupted for 44 years from 1932 to 1976, but which found itself out of office following the September 1976 elections. *Figures 5.18* to *5.22* show the extent of Social Democrat support, which has

remained strongest in the centre and north of the country. The formation of the unicameral Riksdag, which became effective in January 1971, must rank as one of the major changes in European political systems in the 1970s.

In 1966 the Social Democrats suffered a marked set back in the local elections. It was therefore somewhat surprising that they achieved their largest majority since 1940, taking 50% of the vote and gaining 125 of the 233 seats in the lower house of the Riksdag. This result was remarkable in the light of defeats for socialist parties in Norway and Denmark and the general decline of the socialist movement. The Social Democrats decided to abandon their former agricultural programme, which through nationalization had threatened the existence of small farmers. The high voter turnout at around 90% appears to have worked in the Social Democrats' favour.

In the 1968 election, the only centre-right party to win was the Centre Party, which had a strong agricultural bias and only after changing its name from the Farmers Party did it make an impression and acquire electoral support in the cities.

In the 1970 national election 350 seats were contested for a single-chamber Riksdag. As in the Federal Republic of Germany, a barrier clause was instated which prevents a party having representation in parliament if it does not win 4% of the total vote. (In Federal Germany the barrier is set at 5%, while in Denmark it is 2%.) There was an additional proviso that any party which gained at least 12% of the vote in a particular constituency could still be allowed to compete for seats in that constituency[2].

Olof Palme became leader of the Social Democrats and Prime Minister in October 1969. In the 1970 elections the Social Democrats suffered an electoral setback and lost 4.8% of their votes. After September 1970, Palme and the Social Democrats with 163 seats had to rely on support from the Communist Left (VPK) with 17 seats for the government's majority.

Three opposition centre-right parties, including the leader of the Centre Party Thorbjorn Fälldin, argued the need for change after nearly 40 years of Social Democrat rule.

The results for 1973 elections were the closest possible in a democratic system with an exact number of seats for both opposing factions[3]. The Social Democrats with the VPK obtained 175 seats and the Centre (Agrarian) Party, Moderates (Conservatives) and Folkepartiet (Liberal Party) gained 175 seats. The result was the continuation in office of a minority Social Democrat administration headed by Palme, although the party's share of the poll was lowered to 43.6%, its lowest since 1945. The Communist Left added two seats to the 17 previously held; the Centre Party advanced notably with an increased representation of 19 seats to give it a total of 90 in the new Riksdag.

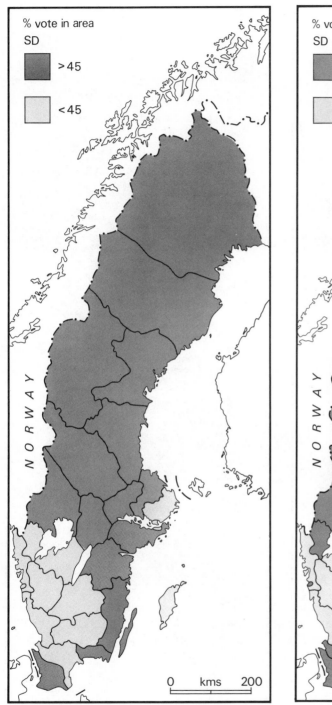

Figure 5.18 *Sweden: the general election of 1968*

Figure 5.19 *Sweden: the general election of 1970*

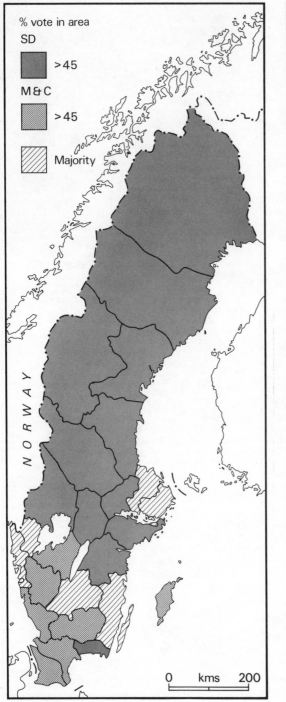

Figure 5.20   *Sweden: the general election of 1973*

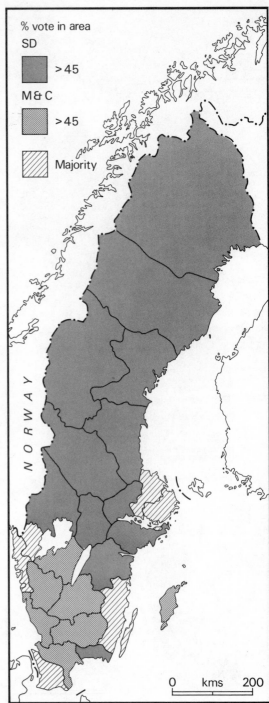

Figure 5.21   *Sweden: the general election of 1976*

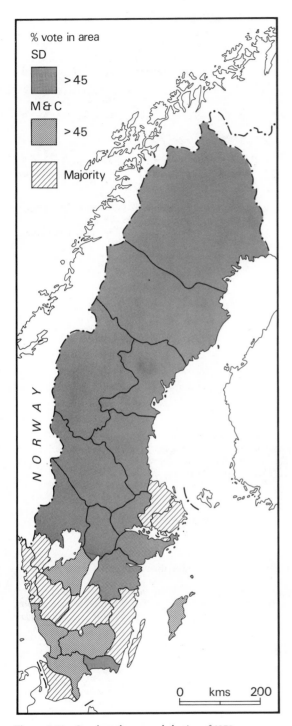

% vote in area

SD

> 45

M & C

> 45

Majority

NORWAY

0   kms   200

Figure 5.22   *Sweden: the general election of 1979*

Following the 1973 elections, the number of adjustment seats was reduced from 40 to 39 under a new constitution from 1 January 1975. This had the aim of avoiding the possibility of opposing sides of the chamber having the same number of seats.

The elections that took place in September 1976 were significant for Sweden and the development of social democracy in Northern Europe. It is apparent that social democracy has been declining in Northern Europe during the second half of the 1970s; this contrasts with the continued support it enjoys in Central Europe, especially in the Federal Republic of Germany and Austria. In 1976 a shift to the right of the political spectrum caused the end of 44 years of social democratic government in Sweden.

There were four issues in the 1976 election campaign[4]:

(1) The performance of the Swedish economy, especially compared with Western Europe, as inflation and unemployment were low and living standards continued to increase.
(2) The Social Democrats used the slogan: 'Don't vote away your social security – vote Social Democratic', which emphasized the high level of social security provision.
(3) The issue of economic democracy was exemplified by a trade-union plan which argued that businesses with 50 people or more should pay 20% of the profits to a central fund controlled jointly by employees' representatives and trade-union branch funds.
(4) The issue of atomic energy divided the parties. The Social Democrats, Liberals and Moderates (Conservatives) argued for a programme of atomic power stations to help Sweden's energy-supply problems; the Centre Party and Communist (VPK) opposed. This issue confused the united centre-right parties attempt to present a unified platform.

However, in 1976 the Centre, Liberal and Moderate Parties gained 180 seats in total, compared to the Social Democrats and VPK total of 169.

The new government in October 1976 was a centre-right coalition headed by Thorbjorn Fälldin, leader of the Centre Party. This coalition continued in power until the most recent election held in September 1979, although the premiership was taken over by Ola Ullsten, leader of the Liberal Party in 1978.

The 1979 election was very close and eventually resulted in a single-seat victory for the centre-right coalition. Prior to the counting of the postal votes, only 2000 votes separated the two power blocs in Swedish politics. the non-socialist block of Centre, Moderate and Liberal Parties won 2040 votes more than the socialists in the election, but electoral boundaries gave former Premier Olof Palme's Social

Democratic Party and the VPK a one-seat lead. Palme hoped to form a minority Social Democrat government with communist support. The Moderate Party gained 18 more Riksdag seats to give it a total of 73 members, while the Centre Party, most popular in the 1976 election, dropped 22 seats to 64.

The final count gave the coalition of Centre, Moderate and Liberal Parties a total of 175 seats, which meant a single-seat victory for the coalition over the Social Democrats and communists. The counting of 40 000 postal votes swung the balance against the socialist bloc, which had a total of 174 seats.

Thorbjorn Fälldin returned to the office of Prime Minister at the head of a three-party coalition. Although Olof Palme had victory snatched from him, the Social Democrats increased their percentage poll and gained two more seats. Therefore Palme must consider his chances of winning the next election are quite good.

It must remain debatable whether it is to Sweden's advantage to hold elections every three years, especially with the two power blocs so closely matched in the Riksdag.

References

1. *Financial Times*, 18 September 1979, London
2. Mackie, T. T. and Rose, R. (1974). *International Almanac of Electoral History*, p. 341, Macmillan, London and Basingstoke
3. Archer, T. C. (November 1973). Elections in Norway and Sweden. *World Today*, pp. 455–458
4. Archer, T. C. (November 1976). Sweden: Shift to the Right. *World Today*, pp. 396–398

Table 5.17 *The Swedish electoral system 1968–1979*

Assembly	Riksdag
Members	349. In 1968, 233 members in the Second Chamber (Andra Kammaren). This became a unicameral legislature on 1 January 1971 with 350 members. In 1976 this total was reduced to 349 following a tie in 1973 election, with both left and centre-right having 175 members
Dates of elections	15 September 1968 20 September 1970 16 September 1973 19 September 1976 16 September 1979
Method	Proportional representation (PR); Saint–Laguë system with initial divisor of 1.4
Remarks	310 permanent seats are divided among 28 constituencies in relation to the number of votes in each. The remaining 39 seats are allocated to the parties in proportion to totals of unused votes in a 'pool'. The whole country is regarded as a single constituency for these 'adjustment seats'; the aim is to give absolute proportionality
Voting age	In 1968, was 21, reduced to 20 in 1969, and to 19 in 1970
Voter participation (turnout)	1968 89.3% 1970 88.3% 1973 90.8% 1976 91.8% 1979 90.7%

Source: Statistisk Arsbok 1979, Statistical Handbook of Sweden 1979, pp. 413–414; Statistisk Arsbok 1980, Statistical Handbook of Sweden 1980, pp. 420–422

Table 5.18 *Number of seats won in Swedish elections 1968–1979*

Party	Number of seats				
	1968[a]	1970[b]	1973	1976	1979
S	125	163(14)[c]	156(10)	152(13)	154(12)
VPK	3	17(10)	19(9)	17(9)	20(9)
C	39	71(4)	90(10)	86(7)	64(4)
M	32	41(5)	51(4)	55(5)	73(8)
FP	34	58(7)	34(7)	39(5)	38(6)
Total	233	350(40)	350(40)	349(39)	349(39)

[a] In 1968, members were elected to the lower chamber or Andra Kammaren of the Riksdag

[b] This replaced by single-chamber Riksdag in 1970

[c] All seats shown in brackets are adjustment seats

Table 5.19 *Percentage of votes cast in Swedish elections 1968–1979*

Party	Percentage of votes				
	1968	1970	1973	1976	1979
S	50.1	45.3	43.6	42.7	43.2
VPK	3.0	4.8	5.3	4.8	5.6
C	16.1	19.9	25.1	24.1	18.1
M	13.9	11.5	14.3	15.6	20.3
FP	15.0	16.2	9.4	11.1	10.6
KDS	1.5	1.8	1.8	1.4	1.4
Other	0.3	0.5	0.5	0.4	0.8

Table 5.20 *Number of votes cast in Swedish elections 1968–1979*

Party	Number of votes				
	1968	1970	1973	1976	1979
S	2420277	2256269	2247727	2324603	2356234
VPK	145172	236659	274929	258432	305420
C	779749	991208	1295246	1309669	984589
M	670509	573812	737584	847672	1108406
FP	724736	806667	486028	601556	577063
KDS	72377	88770	90388	73844	75993
Other	16559	22711	28244	21972	40933
Total	4829379	4976196	5160146	5437748	5448638

Results of referendums in Denmark, Ireland, Norway and the United Kingdom on accession to the European Communities

Table A1 *EEC referendum results in Denmark*

Date	3 October 1972	
Votes	Yes 1958115	63.3%
	No 1135691	36.7%
	Total 3093806	
	11907 blank votes 7409 spoiled or non-valid papers	
Participation (turnout)	90.1%	
Total electorate	3453763	

Table A3 *EEC referendum results in Ireland*

Date	10 May 1972. Referendum on constitutional change, approval of amendment to constitution	
Votes	Yes 1041880	83%
	No 211888	17%
Participation (turnout)	71.0%	

Table A2 *EEC referendum results in Norway*

Date	24–25 September 1972	
Votes	No 1099389	53.5%
	Yes 956043	46.5%
	Total 2055432	
Participation (turnout)	77.6%	
Total electorate	2647000	

Table A4 *EEC referendum results in the United Kingdom*

Date	5 June 1975. First referendum in British constitutional history	
Votes	Yes 17378581	67.2%
	No 8470073	32.8%
	Total 25848654	
	848654 non-valid papers	
Participation (turnout)	64.5%	
Total electorate	40086677	

Breakdown of votes

	Electorate	Votes	Turnout
England	33339959	21722222	64.6%
Wales	2015766	1345545	66.7%
Scotland	3698462	2286676	61.7%
Northern Ireland	1032490	498751	47.4%
Total	40086677	25853194	64.5%

Electoral systems of Europe

Four major types of electoral system are in use by the 18 European countries who have formed the subject of this study. This appendix is adapted from the one included in Mackie T. T. and Rose R. (1974), *The International Almanac of Electoral History,* pp. 431 –434, Macmillan, London, which can be consulted for further details and examples.

The four electoral systems are : plurality, relative majority, list systems of proportional representation (PR) and the single transferable vote (STV).

Plurality

This is the system where the winner is the candidate who has the highest number of votes, even when this total is less than half of all votes cast. The successful candidate has simply to poll more votes than any other single opponent. The system is commonly known as the 'first-past-the-post' or 'the winner takes all'. It has been suggested that this system is acceptable in relatively stable political environments, where consensus prevails. The voting system tends to favour large parties and to ensure their continuation in power, as they are most likely to have a national network of supporters. Smaller parties need to be regionally concentrated with their votes in certain districts to achieve electoral success under the plurality system.

The United Kingdom uses the plurality system and its two major political parties resist electoral reform as the system is to their advantage, and to the disadvantage of the Liberal Party.

Plurality is used to elect half of the members of the Bundestag, the assembly of the Federal Republic of Germany.

It was formerly employed by several European countries but most changed over to some form of PR between 1900 and 1920.

Relative majority

This system is designed to ensure that the elected representative secures 50% of the vote in the constituency. Both plurality and relative majority operate in single-member constituencies.

If the candidate polls more than 50% of the ballot, that is has more votes than all his or her opponents, he is declared elected under relative majority. If no candidate obtains half the total votes, another ballot is required. This can take the form of the alternate preference vote where the voters rank the candidates and the weakest candidate is eliminated until one name secures a majority: an alternative is to use simple plurality on the second round of the ballot.

This system is used in elections to the French National Assembly: two-round voting occurs on consecutive Sundays and on the first round a candidate must secure more than 50% of votes cast, plus 12.5% of the registered vote in the constituency. If no candidate meets these requirements, the second ballot is on the plurality system.

Neither of the two above systems, plurality and relative majority, distribute seats in a country's assembly in proportion to the share of the popular vote given to political parties at the ballot. Both systems tend to give electoral advantage to stronger parties, awarding them a disproportionate share of seats, while at the same time providing a considerable limitation on smaller parties and those who wish to enter the political arena. A small party (for example, the Scottish National Party in the United Kingdom) can only make progress and avoid the inequity of the electoral system if it has a regionally concentrated electoral support.

Proportional representation

Three types of proportional representation list systems are used in Europe. They are: d'Hondt, Saint –Laguë, Hagenbach–Bischoff. PR presents the voter with a list system, so that he or she has to select from a party-compiled list of candidates, rather than individual names as under the plurality and relative majority systems. Calculations after the ballot are carried out on the basis of party affiliation, so that seats won by a party are allocated to candidates in the order in which they appear on the ballot list.

The d'Hondt system is named after its Belgian inventor, Victor d'Hondt, and is usually referred to as a system of highest average formula. Total votes for each party are used, not those for candidates. The largest average means that the number of votes gained by each party is divided by the number of seats held, plus one. Under the d'Hondt system the first seat is awarded to the party with the highest number of votes, since no seats have been allocated. The important feature of this type of PR system is the initial divisor. Under the d'Hondt system, the initial divisor is 1. When a party wins a seat, the formula denominator is increased by one, and so the party's chance of winning the next seat are reduced, as its total national vote is halved. The available seats are awarded to parties one at a time in each round to the party with the greatest average in that round. The divisors under d'Hondt are 1, 2, 3, 4, 5 and so on.

The Saint–Laguë system operates on the highest average like d'Hondt, but utilizes different divisors. These are an initial divisor of 1.4, then 3, 5, 7, 9 and so on. Like d'Hondt, the available seats are gained by parties with the highest average in each round, and electors are presented with a list of party candidates. The Saint–Laguë formula increases the electoral cost of the initial seat and of additional seats and thus reduces the gain for larger parties and tends to be more generous to medium and small parties.

Both the d'Hondt and Saint–Laguë systems usually operate with a minimum percentage clause, which means that to obtain representation in the assembly, a political party must poll a certain minimum percentage of the national vote. This can be as little as 2%, which is threshold in Denmark. In order to achieve proportional allocation of assembly seats, some countries utilize a system of additional or adjustment seats which are distributed in relation to the national vote.

The Hagenbach–Bischoff system of PR requires the calculation of a quota, which is obtained when the total ballot is divided by the number of assembly seats plus one. The votes cast for each party are divided by this quota and seats distributed accordingly. Any outstanding seats are allocated by dividing

votes cast for a party by assembly seats already gained plus one, two and so on. The highest average total in each calculation secures the unallocated seats.

Another type of proportional representation list system is that known as the largest-remainder formula. This establishes a vote quota for each seat in an electoral district by dividing the total vote in the constituency by the number of competing political parties. Seats are awarded for as many times as the party obtains the full quota. When seats are not all allocated under the full quota, they are distributed to the party with the largest remainder of votes, hence the title of this system. The remainder consists of the total after the quota has been subtracted. Seats are awarded in order to parties until all are taken.

This system in a modified form, known as the Imperiali formula, is used in Italy. Under the Imperiali formula a quota is established by dividing the total ballot by the number of parties plus two. This variation tends to increase the representation of smaller parties in the assembly, but slightly distorts the proportional ideal of allocating seats as closely as possible in relation to votes cast.

Single transferable vote

This system allows the elector to rank candidates in order of preference. When the votes are counted, any candidate who receives the necessary quota of first-preference votes is declared elected. This quota, usually known as the Droop quota, is outlined in Mackie and Rose (1974). It consists of the votes cast divided by the number of available seats plus one, this calculation has the figure one added to it. In the calculations, votes given to candidate already elected and in excess of the quota are transferred to other candidates in accordance with the preferences marked on the ballot paper. Under the STV system a voter does not have to vote for a party list as he can rank candidates irrespective of their party affiliation.

This system is used in Ireland, where it operates in three-, four- or five-member constituencies.

Index

Index of political parties

Parties are listed alphabetically, with acronym if appropriate. Each country has a list of major parties at the beginning of its political commentary.

AD	Democratic Alliance	Portugal
—	Anders Lange's Party (Progressive Party)	Norway
AIK	Labour Information Committee	Norway
—	Alliance of Progressive and Left-Wing Forces	Greece
AOC	Alliance of Workers and Farm Labourers	Portugal
AP	Popular Alliance	Spain
AR	Anti-Revolutionary Party	Netherlands
AUD	Action Association of Independent Germans	Germany
AVP	Action Association Fourth Party	Germany
BEAM	Left Bloc of National Liberation	Spain
BP	Citizens Party	Germany
BP	Farmers Party	Netherlands
BSP–PSB	Belgian Socialist Party	Belgium
C	Centre Party	Sweden
C	Conservative Party	UK
CBV	Christian Bavarian People's Party	Germany
CD	Centre Democratic Party	Denmark
CD	Democratic Centre Party	France
CD	Democratic Coalition	Spain
CDA	Christian Democratic Appeal (comprising AR, CHU, KVP)	Netherlands
CDC	Democratic Convergence for Catalonia	Spain
CDP	Centre for Democracy and Progress	France
CDS	Central Social Democratic Party	France
CDS	Social Democratic Centre	Portugal
CDU	Christian Democratic Union	Germany
—	Centre Party (Agrarian)	Norway
CERES	Centre for Study of Research and Education of Socialists (Left wing of PS)	France
—	Christian People's Party	Denmark
—	Christian People's Party	Norway
CHU	Christian Historical Union	Netherlands
CIR	Convention of Republican Institutions	France
—	Communist Party	Norway
—	Conservative Party	Norway
CPGB	Communist Party of Great Britain	UK
CPN	Communist Party of the Netherlands	Netherlands
CSA	Christian Social Workers Movement	Austria
CSU	Christian Social Union (Bavaria)	Germany
CSV	Christian Social Party; also Christian Socialists	Luxembourg
CU	Convergence and Union	Spain
CVP	Christian Democratic People's Party	Switzerland
CVP–PSC	Christian People's Party	Belgium
DC	Christian Democratic Party	Italy
—	Democratic Labour Party	Ireland